Low Intensity Democracy

Low Intensity Democracy

Political Power in the New World Order

Edited by Barry Gills,
Joel Rocamora and Richard Wilson

Pluto  Press
London • Boulder, Colorado

First published 1993 by Pluto Press
345 Archway Road, London N6 5AA
and 5500 Central Avenue
Boulder, CO 80301, USA

The extract from the lyrics of 'Get Up! StandUp!' by Bob Marley and
Peter Tosh is reproduced by kind permission of Blue Mountain
Music Ltd, Media House, 334–336 King Street,
London W6 0RA

British Library Cataloguing in Publication Data
A catalogue record for this book is available from the British Library

ISBN 0 7453 0535 0 cased
ISBN 0 7453 0536 9 paperback

Library of Congress Cataloging in Publication Data
Low intensity democracy : political power in the new world order /
  [edited by] Barry Gills, Joel Rocamora, and Richard Wilson.
    260p. 22cm.
    Includes bibliographical references and index.
    ISBN 0-7453-0535-0 (cased). – ISBN 0-7453-0536-9 (pbk.)
    1. Democracy. 2. Democracy–Developing countries. 3. Developing
  countries–Politics and government. I. Gills, Barry, 1956– .
  II. Rocamora, Joel. III. Wilson, Richard.
  JC423.L69   1993
  321.8'091724–dc20   93-25787
                                                                    CIP

Designed and produced for Pluto Press by
Chase Production Services, Chipping Norton
Typeset from author's disks by
Stanford DTP Services, Milton Keynes
Printed in the EC by T.J. Press, Padstow

Contents

Acknowledgements

The editors would like to thank the Fellows of the Transnational Institute for their many contributions to this project. In particular, we would like to thank Xabier Gorostiaga for giving us the inspiration on the title of this book, and Dan Smith and Susan George for editorial comments and their patient support. Our deepest debt of gratitude goes to Wim van der Schot of the TNI staff in Amsterdam, without whose help the final stage of copy-editing might not have been possible. Thanks are due also to Laurian Zwart of the Amsterdam staff of TNI for general administrative support throughout the project. Special thanks are also due to Patrick Costello. At Pluto Press we would like to thank Roger Van Zwanenberg for all his many efforts on our behalf, and Rick Bouwman, Diana Russell and Anne Beech for their direct involvement in preparing the final manuscript.

Contributors

Samir Amin is Director of the Africa Office, Third World Forum, Dakar, Senegal. He is the author of numerous works, including *Accumulation on a World Scale* (1974), *Imperialism and Unequal Development* (1977), *Eurocentrism* (1989) and *Maldevelopment* (1990).

Roger Burbach is currently working on *The New World Disorder* to be published in early 1994. He has written extensively on Latin America and US policy issues, and more recently on Russia and Eastern Europe. He is director of the Centre for the Study of the Americas, based in Berkeley, California.

Noam Chomsky is Institute Professor in the department of Linguistics and Philosophy at the Massachusetts Institute of Technology, Boston. He is a member of the American Academy of Arts and Sciences and of the National Academy of Science. Among his recent works are *Manufacturing Consent* (1988, with E.S. Herman), *Necessary Illusions* (1989) and *Deterring Democracy* (1991).

Andre Gunder Frank is Professor of Development Economics and Social Sciences at the University of Amsterdam. His hundreds of publications in over 20 languages have covered a very broad range of interests and include *Crisis in the World Economy* (1980), *Transforming the Revolution: Social Movements and the World-system* (1990) and *Underdevelopment of Development: an autobiographical essay* (1991).

Barry Gills is a Fellow of the Transnational Institute, Amsterdam, and Lecturer in Politics at the University of Newcastle upon Tyne. He is a founding editor of the *Review of International Political Economy* and serves on the editorial board of *Third World Quarterly*. His recent works include *The World System: 500 or 5,000 years?* (1993), edited with Andre Gunder Frank, and *The Crisis of Socialism in the Third World* (forthcoming) with Shahid Quadir.

Joel Rocamora is a Filipino political scientist currently working and writing in the Philippines. He is a Fellow and a former Associate

Director of the Transnational Institute, Amsterdam. He has published extensively on Philippine and Indonesian politics, including *Nationalism in Search of Ideology – The Indonesian Nationalist Party* (1975) and *Rural Development Strategies in the Philippines* (1976). He holds a PhD from Cornell University in politics and Asian studies.

Miguel Teubal teaches at the Centre for Advanced Studies at the University of Buenos Aires, Argentina. He has published article on Latin American debt and other development issues in Argentine and international journals. He is currently working on a book on the political economy of democracy in Argentina. He has a PhD in agricultural economics from the University of California at Berkeley.

Richard Wilson is Lecturer in Sociology at the University of Essex. He has written about the cultural effects of state counterinsurgency on Mayan peoples of Guatemala in *Critique of Anthropology* (1991), and has a forthcoming book entitled *Mountains of the Maya-Q'eqchi': Identity, Religion and War in Guatemala* (University of Oklahoma Press). He is a Director of the Central America Human Rights Committee in London.

Part One

Global Analyses

1. Low Intensity Democracy

BARRY GILLS, JOEL ROCAMORA AND RICHARD WILSON

By evoking the American counterinsurgency catch-phrase 'Low Intensity Conflict', it is our intention to show that perhaps more than at any other time in the recent past, it is now that the struggle to define 'democracy' has become a major ideological battle. 'Democracy' has replaced 'development' as the buzzword for the 1990s. Democracy seems to be sweeping the globe, driving before it both communist party dictatorships and rightist military regimes on every continent. Yet the paradox of this new wave of democratisation is that its 'success' is built upon the failure of 'development' both in the Third World and the former Second World.

Some have tried to explain this wave of political change as the historical triumph of an idea/ideal, heralding the dawn of a grand new age of global democracy (cf. Fukuyama 1992). Alternatively, there are grounds to be sceptical of both the purported causes, and the ends, of this putative democratic New World Order. Whereas some regard formal democracy as sufficient in itself, if the content of this new democracy is critically examined it may be found to be seriously flawed on many counts.

This book constitutes a critique of the democratic claims of the large majority of new civilian elected democracies in the Third World. Although they may have formally instituted some of the trappings of Western liberal democracies (for example, periodic elections), in a real sense these new democracies have preserved ossified political and economic structures from an authoritarian past. Not only have they not come close to operating a political structure modelled on actual Western liberal democracies, this is not part of a long-term agenda for the future. In short, these transitions do not even represent a movement towards present forms of bourgeois democracy. We are not judging the new Third World democracies against some unrealised ideal of Western pluralism, but in relation to real, flawed liberal political forms. In the West, full participatory democracy is profoundly limited, though not to the same extent as it is in the Third World, by domestic inequality and the exigencies and strictures of global capital.

3

This book began as a project involving a series of case studies of transitions from authoritarian to democratic regimes in the Third World. In these studies, the contributors discovered that the institutions of formal democracy that have recently re-emerged in many countries of the Third World have failed to broaden popular political participation in a very meaningful way. They found little evidence to support the widespread assumption that formal electoral democratisation alone would bring about a lasting progressive breakthrough in these societies or that it is capable of solving their fundamental social and especially economic problems. What should more accurately be called 'elite democracies' in effect coexist with tacit military dictatorships. Social reform agendas that could have established the basis for broader popular participation and greater social justice have been abandoned. Human rights violations continue virtually unabated. The new regimes are more readily manipulated by external forces such as the International Monetary Fund (IMF) or via bilateral political and economic pressures, particularly from the United States. Economic policies often mandate austerity for the majority without, in most cases, bringing about significant economic growth. Progressive movements find it virtually impossible to implement an agenda for reform when powerful domestic and international groups opposing such change, not least the military, remain in place.

The case studies undertaken in this project – Argentina, Guatemala, the Philippines and South Korea – all share the common characteristic of a history of significant US influence in their affairs. These countries have different resource bases, different histories and different types of social development. But there are also important similarities, indicating that there are common structural sources of political developments cutting across national borders. This realisation reinforces the conclusion that state-centric analysis is not sufficient to understand these similarities. Rather, an analysis of political economy on a world scale is necessary to determine the main lines of development. This book is an attempt to contribute to an alternative critical interpretation of the current drive towards democracy, viewed as an integral aspect of the economic and ideological restructuring accompanying a new stage of globalisation in the capitalist world economy, and as a consequence of a shift in US foreign policy after the onset of serious economic and hegemonic crises. In this sense the new formal democratisation is the political corollary of economic liberalisation and internationalisation. It may also be viewed, in a number of cases, as the political consequence of a prior period of foreign intervention. Such interventionism could take the form of either a shift in external support away from overt authoritarianism, or Low Intensity Conflict strategy, such as in Central America.

The analysis here goes against much of the mainstream of scholarship on Third World politics, especially in the United States. This mainstream has three intellectual and ideological biases.

- Firstly, 'political democracy' *per se* is a goal worthy of attainment, even at the expense of foregoing alternative paths that would seem to promise more immediate returns in terms of socialisation (social reform)' (O'Donnell and Schmitter 1986, pp. 13–14). However, without *combining* political democracy and social reform, one could argue that democracy itself is undermined in the medium to long term. Formal democracy without social reform increases economic inequality and thereby intensifies unequal distribution of power in society. The first and most important task of democratic regimes is social reform. In the absence of progressive social reform the term 'democracy' is largely devoid of meaningful content. Indeed, it is in danger of becoming a term of political mystification or obfuscation, serving as a euphemism for sophisticated modern forms of neo-authoritarianism. As such, the structures of democratic institutions and the social base of democratic regimes must, from the beginning, assure the pursuit of such reform.
- The second bias is that 'all democracies (in our sense) are to some degree capitalist; production and distribution of goods are determined mainly by competition in the market, rather than by the state, and there is significant private ownership of the means of production.' (Diamond, Linz and Lipset 1989 p. xxi). While Diamond, Linz, and Lipset, *et al.* go to great lengths to show that this was not an *a priori* assumption, the identification of capitalism with democracy is a not very well-hidden ideological bias of certain Western studies of Third World democracy. Today, the particular forms of democracy promoted by the West in the Third World are specifically tailored to serve the interests of global capital in these countries. Here, a political economic orthodoxy of hegemonic power holders is presented as being a matter of natural law, whether economic or developmental, rather than as a specific product of historical conditions, conflict over the pursuit of interests, and class struggle.
- The third bias, found in a much wider range of studies of politics in the Third World, is that *external* factors do not play a significant causal role in Third World political economic development. Intellectually, this bias is ultimately derived from modernisation

theory's Eurocentric linear view of development, whereby the future of the peripheral countries is supposedly represented by the present modernity of the core countries, but change is determined by endogenous factors. On the contrary, external factors, ranging from IMF-World Bank adjustment policies, to foreign support for the military, to direct forms of foreign military, political and economic intervention, are often decisive in determining the outcome of sociopolitical conflicts in the Third World. At a minimum, in a world increasingly dominated by an ubiquitous international capitalist system, national politics in the Third World – or in any other part of the world for that matter – cannot be properly understood in national isolation.

The Struggle for Meaning

Everyone applauds democracy, and those who in practice oppose it applaud most loudly. As a slogan it is very effective, yet democracy is a contested term. Like so many terms employed in modern political discourse, its meaning varies with the context in which it is being used. It is undesirable to oppose 'democracy', but 'actually existing democracy' should and indeed must be criticised. At this moment of world history, 'democracy' is extolled as the best of all possible worlds both by the holders of global power and by 'the people', not least by those struggling for social justice and self-determination in a world of inequality. Those invoking the Goddess of Democracy use the same language but do not convey the same meaning. As Noam Chomsky argues, 'the guardians of world order have sought to establish democracy in one sense of the term, while blocking it in a different sense' (Chapter 4, this volume).

Chomsky argues that now, as in the past, power holders use democracy as justification for their power and as an ideological instrument for keeping the public quiescent and out of decision-making processes.

Samir Amin points to another trend that has accompanied democratisation,

a kind of generalised offensive for the liberation of 'market forces,' aimed at the ideological rehabilitation of the absolute superiority of private property, legitimation of social inequalities and anti-statism of all kinds ... The coincidence of these two trends makes ours an era of intense confusion ... The 'market' – a euphemism for capitalism – is regarded as the central axis of any 'development,' and such development is seen as part of an 'ineluctable worldwide expansion.' The desirability of total openness to the forces governing worldwide evolution and simultaneous adoption of an internal system based on the 'market' are taken to be self-evident. *Democratisation is considered the necessary and natural product of submission to the rationality of the worldwide market.* A simple equation is deduced from this logic: capitalism equals democracy, democracy equals capitalism.' [emphasis added] (Amin, chapter 3, this volume; see also Frank, Chapter 2).

This is a compelling argument which points out a central characteristic, and perhaps even captures the real essence, of the ongoing democratisation process in the Third World.

In the recent past, and for most of this century, the principal dichotomy of meaning was between socialist democracy and capitalist democracy. The two meanings competed for legitimacy. Now one meaning, the capitalist, is emerging as globally hegemonic. The idea that this form of politics is universally valid and as applicable to the periphery as it is to the states of the core of the global political economy is as doubtful now as it was in the past, and for all the same good historical (as opposed to ahistorical) and 'structural' reasons.

The political forms existing in the world are being restructured to reflect and accommodate the present realities of the global political economy. It should now be obvious to everyone that there is only one capitalist world economic system and not two separate contending world systems: one socialist and one capitalist. In the ideal New World Order as conceived by present hegemonic power holders all states will be 'capitalist' and incorporated in the capitalist world economy to a greater or lesser degree. In the ideal New World Order all these states will also be 'democratic'. This 'crusade' for democracy is the new ideological agenda of global capitalism.

However, why should one conclude automatically, without critical reflection, that the present economic reality of the capitalist world system will be any more conducive to genuine democracy in the Third World than in the past? It is also equally possible to conclude that, on the contrary, this new democratic facade will cloak new forms of authoritarianism, repression and conservatism, and legitimise further incorporation and subordination to global capital.

The Origins of Low Intensity Democracy

The case studies reviewed below affirm that the overthrow of these authoritarian regimes was first and foremost the result of popular impetus. Except in a few isolated cases when the trend towards democratisation was well under way, as in Chile in 1988, the US did not actively push against authoritarian regimes and for democracy until the authoritarian regime was already in the midst of domestic crisis, usually brought on by its failure to resolve deep economic and political problems or stem the rapid development of popular anti-dictatorship forces. In most cases, the US response was based on the realisation that authoritarianism could not sustain itself indefinitely and that democratisation was inevitable in the long term. Therefore, it was preferable for the US to gain a guiding influence in the process of democratisation before it developed along lines out of US control, as had occurred in the latter part of the 1970s in the Iranian and Nicaraguan revolutions.

By the early 1980s, the US realised that conditions were favourable for an 'apertura', a democratic opening, in many Third World client states given that years of military rule had greatly reduced the organisational power of the Left, labour and other popular forces. The Carter administration policy on human rights can be viewed as the direct predecessor of the more overt US policy of democratisation that followed under President Reagan. The United States wanted stable viable 'democratic' regimes that could pre-empt more radical change by incorporating broad popular forces in electoral participation, yet guarantee continuity with the anti-communist and anti-reformist traditions of their military predecessors. If the new democratic processes were to get out of hand and allow the Left too much social power, the military would always be available as an alternative to democratic 'ungovernability'. Thus, Low Intensity Democracy was conceived as a halfway house between previous 'unstable' representative democratic systems in the Third World and the moribund and counterproductive military dictatorships of the 1960s and 1970s which had often been established and maintained with US support.

Democracy as defined by the US was in fact a component of Low Intensity Conflict. Democracy was thus used as a form of intervention. Its intent was to pre-empt either progressive reform or revolutionary change. Beyond seeking to demobilise popular forces, it also sought to legitimise the status quo. Authoritarianism was thus discredited and delegitimised. The new 'democratic' regime, which temporarily enjoys increased legitimacy, can in fact undertake economic and social policies of 'adjustment' that impose new hardships on the general population and compromise economic sovereignty. The paradox of Low Intensity Democracy is that a civilianised conservative regime can pursue painful and even repressive social and economic policies with more impunity and with less popular resistance than can an openly authoritarian regime. From the point of view of the US and conservative domestic elites in these countries, this quality must make it an interesting and useful alternative to traditional overt authoritarianism.

In 1982, President Ronald Reagan announced a 'Crusade for democracy' in a speech to the British Parliament in London.

From then on, the US, long a staunch supporter of anti-communist authoritarianism in the Third World, adopted a more positive attitude to facilitating democracy. From the mid-1980s, the US found itself increasingly forced to take sides against political clients in their moments of crisis: Marcos in the Philippines, Chun Doo Hwan in Korea, Duvalier in Haiti, Pinochet in Chile and Stroessner in Paraguay. Paradoxically, Jeanne Kirkpatrick, former US Ambassador to the United Nations, established a doctrine of double standards on authoritarianism which justified US support for capitalist authoritarianism in the context of Cold War rivalry. This doctrine eventually gave way to a pragmatic preference to replace certain client authoritarians with 'democratic' successors. US policy was most successful in its own sphere of interest, that is, its so-called 'backyard' in the Caribbean, Central America and indeed throughout Latin America. By the end of 1989, the dictatorships of Latin America, many originally put in place with US help and afterwards supported by it against their own people, had virtually all been replaced by ' democratic' governments. In Central America, by 1990, there had been an overall consolidation of power by conservative civilian governments: Cristiani and the Nationalist Republican Alliance (ARENA) in El Salvador, Chamorro and the United Nicaraguan Opposition (UNO) in Nicaragua, Callejas in Honduras, Calderon in Costa Rica, and Serrano in Guatemala.

Still, the new sympathy for democracy was only one aspect of a larger policy shift. The Reagan Doctrine exemplified an aggressive foreign policy posture designed to halt any further progress of revolutionary forces anywhere in the world and, beyond that, to roll back revolution wherever feasible through various forms of covert or overt intervention (cf. Halliday 1987). The 'Second' Cold War, during which the US greatly increased military spending (and in the process national debt) was partly aimed at achieving victory in superpower rivalry through Soviet default. The US correctly reasoned that the Achilles heel of the Soviet Union was its economic base. After decades of 'stagnation', the Soviet economy could not stand the strain of increased military competition at home and abroad. It was eventually compelled by circumstances to make deep and thoroughgoing changes, as well as important political concessions to the

United States, particularly on a range of strategic issues and in ongoing Third World conflicts.

Taken together, these strands of policy form a coherent whole. The US was on the defensive throughout the 1970s, as a wave of revolutions swept the Third World and American economic and political leadership came under challenge from rivals and partners alike. Few perhaps realise how threatened the US felt as the international system in the mid-1970s seemed to be on the verge of a radical shift in the relations of power. The New International Economic Order (NIEO) was the Third World's reform programme aimed at improving the terms of trade and achieving the 'democratisation of international relations'. US Secretary of State Henry Kissinger first formulated the US response in an attempt to drive wedges into the Group of 77 (G-77) and the Non-Aligned Movement, the vanguard Third World organisations in the battle for a NIEO. However, the initial thrust of the US counteroffensive was somewhat blunted during the years of the Carter presidency, with its tolerance for sustaining a North–South dialogue and the policy of 'human rights'. In the 1980s, under Reagan's leadership, the US returned to the offensive. Reagan unilaterally pronounced the definitive death of the NIEO at the summit with selected Third World leaders held in Cancùn, Mexico. The global economic reform agenda proposed by the G-77 and the Non-Aligned Movement was defeated and replaced by an agenda of resubordination of the Third World to the First World, relying on austerity measures, debt servicing, privatisation, economic liberalisation and structural adjustment, promoted by the US via the IMF, the World Bank, and the Group of Seven Industrialised Countries.

The US jubilantly greets the new democratic governments and hails them as milestones or triumphs, but its support does not come free. The new regimes must satisfy certain conditions if they expect continued smooth relations with the US. The US applies continuous monitoring and pressure *vis-à-vis* these governments. Low Intensity Democracy regimes may actually be more susceptible to US pressures than their predecessors, particularly where economic policy is concerned.

With 'legitimacy' achieved, US aid may be increased or restored and new opportunities may open with other diplomatic and trade partners. For Central American regimes, democratisation meant rehabilitation in the US Congress and renewal of American aid. For South Korea it smoothed the way to expanded diplomatic and trade relations with the communist states and entry into the UN, but South Korea was also subject to heavy US pressure to open its markets and liberalise controls on financial services.

Low Intensity Democracy complemented the economic policy offensive managed principally by the IMF, one of the key goals of which was to break down political barriers to the further transnationalisation of capital. IMF policies replaced the prospect of debt relief with that of perpetual debt service, despite the fact that many debtors repaid the amount of the principal several times over. In the process, much of the Third World lost an entire decade, and a human generation, to servicing the debt. The social and political results in many parts of the Third World were a toxic cocktail of absolute decline in living standards for the majority, growth in inequality and social instability, and massive transfer of wealth from the poor to the rich both within the countries of the South and between them and the rich in the North (cf. George 1988). The global economic crisis extended to the former Second World. The fall of communist party governments at the end of the 1980s can be understood as a political culmination of some 20 years of gradual economic re-incorporation of these countries into the capitalist world economy (Frank, 1980; Chase-Dunn 1982), and as the political preparation for a final stage of reincorporation.

Thus, when US Secretary of State James Baker defined the post Cold War mission of the US as the 'promotion and consolidation of democracy' in March 1990, he presumably included both the old Third World and the newly Third-Worldised former Second World. According to Roger Burbach (Burbach, Chapter 5, this volume) 'the United States is caught in a fundamental dilemma between its declared support for democracy and its perception of its economic needs and interests abroad.' Whilst the Cold War still raged, Reagan's support of counter-revolutionary movements in the Third World in the name of democracy, such as the Contras in Nicaragua, succeeded in 'wedding the concept of democracy to anti-communist campaigns around the globe'. The US went a step further under President Bush, by moving from a limited policy of acting through proxies, to that of direct US military intervention, though still within the constraints imposed on interventionism by the Vietnam Syndrome. The invasion of Grenada and the air raid on Libya established the momentum for the dramatic invasion of Panama during Christmas 1989. The success of the military campaign against Noriega, in turn, set the stage for Operation Desert Storm in Kuwait and Iraq.

Yet, the 1980s were a decade of economic failure and largely pyrrhic victories for the US in its quest for democracy. The new democracies of Latin America remain extremely fragile and threatened by political upheaval. Burbach argues that 'If there is one lesson that emerges from the 1980s in the countries to the south of the United

States, it is that the much lauded policy of neoliberal economics has not strengthened democratic institutions' (Burbach, Chapter 5, this volume). The IMF's policies of austerity and liberalisation were an ideological ploy that, in the name of economic efficiency, had the real effect of spreading economic disorder and fomenting social and political upheaval, thus sowing the seeds of a future crisis of 'ungovernability'. The coup in Peru in April 1992, the earlier aborted coup in Venezuela in February 1992, and the overthrow of President Aristide in Haiti in 1991 all illustrate the potential for reversal in such a serious crisis environment.

The next item on the neoliberal economic agenda is the 'Initiative for the Americas' announced by President Bush in December 1990. This is what the US calls its plan for a free trade zone, or dollar bloc, that will encompass the whole of the western hemisphere. Critics argue that the implications of the free trade zone for democracy in the hemisphere are largely adverse (cf. Cavanagh *et al.* 1992). Economic bloc formation is antithetical to real democratisation because of the underlying logic of capitalist economics as

US capital unfettered in the hemisphere will seek out the cheapest labour markets, undermining already weak trade unions, and decimate many industries that are now located in the more advanced countries ... The Initiative will concentrate economic power even more throughout the hemisphere, lead to the intensified exploitation of workers, and undermine rather than sustain whatever democratic institutions may exist. (Burbach, Chapter 5, this volume.)

Like the other global manifestations of US neoliberal economic policy, the free trade zone/dollar bloc is conceived to promote US economic interests and not to build democracy or alleviate poverty and economic deprivation.

Economic and political reform and restructuring of bank debt in several Latin American countries in the later part of the 1980s and early 1990s has produced very mixed results. It is true that capital has begun to flow back to some major Latin American countries since 1990, much of it returning flight capital attracted back home by high domestic interest rates resulting from tight monetary policies, widespread implementation of privatisation plans and austerity budgets. Trade liberalisation has further undermined the basis of the old national protected import-substitution industries. This has been accompanied by liberalisation of controls on capital movement. The upshot of these measures has been stimulation to capital to return

on the one hand, and a move towards continental free trade arrangements on the other. Thus, these free trade arrangements presage the
transcending of the limitations of national markets on economic
growth in favour of continental markets. This trend seems to favour
far-reaching corporate restructuring in order to exploit these new
market conditions. All this amounts to what the *Financial Times*
refers to as 'an investment bankers' paradise' (*Financial Times*, 6
April 1992), which is already being expressed in heightened investor
expectation of higher economic growth, and thus higher profits,
following the economic reforms. President Bush's administration interpreted these reforms as welcome prerequisites for fulfilling the
ambitious goals of the hemispheric free trade zone. As of spring
1992, the US had signed framework agreements with 31 governments
in the hemisphere, envisaged as possibly the first stage on the road
to the hemispheric free trade zone after consolidation of agreements
with Canada and Mexico. However, the real signs of economic
recovery in Latin America are weak. Despite the trend since 1987 for
an increase in foreign direct investment and portfolio investment
in the region, and the initiatives of James Baker to reduce the debt
burden and renew capital flows, the debt service burden (the ratio
of debt service payments to exports) has begun to increase again, from
26 per cent in 1990 to 30 per cent in 1991. Average per capita output
in Latin America remains at the level of the late 1970s, reflecting over
a decade of steady economic decline. Modest economic growth of
an average of 2.7 per cent in 1991 has indeed been stimulated, but
is hardly sufficient to warrant great enthusiasm given population
growth rates and the long term economic decline mentioned above.

The Inter-American Development Bank recognised in its 1992
annual report that Latin America continued to suffer 'severe social
problems' stemming from high levels of unemployment, depressed
incomes and poor provision of social services. The region suffers from
decline in demand from a recession-ridden industrial world, continuing
decline in commodity prices on the world markets and still worsening
terms of trade. Hardly the preconditions for stable democracy.

Africa too is in the midst of a wave of popular unrest that may lead
to democratisation. The demise of one-party states of all ideological
persuasions and the dismantling of large public sectors is firmly on
the agenda. The attraction of multiparty systems has emerged as a
potential continental trend as a series of dictatorships have been either
toppled or forced to share power with opponents. When the Berlin
Wall came down in late 1989, some 30 out of 45 sub-Saharan African
states were under either one-party rule or military government.
Though initially it looked as though perhaps most of these regimes

would be toppled, by mid-1992 the momentum of the democratisation wave seemed to be lessening. In West Africa, for instance, in
two years of constant popular unrest only four authoritarian regimes
were removed from power, and in only one of these, Kerekou in Benin,
did rulers lose power through elections.

Africa's economic crisis, carried over from the 'lost decade' in the
1980s, is probably the most acute in the Third World. Africa, more
visibly and sharply than elsewhere, suffered an absolute decline in
living standards. Despite the checkered instances of 'success' in privatisation, liberalisation and stabilisation under IMF auspices; despite
the five-year special UN economic recovery programme for Africa;
in August 1991, the then UN Secretary-General Perez de Cuellar
sparked off a new debate on the failure of African development. His
report predicted Africa would descend yet further into an 'unrelenting crisis of tragic proportions' due primarily to adverse *external*
circumstances – unless drastic measures were taken to relieve the
pressure of debt and provide new capital for investment. The report
chronicled a worsening crisis: collapsing real wages, acute deterioration of social services, rapidly rising unemployment, falling foreign
exchange earnings due to downward pressure on commodity prices
of African exports, and so on. Most surprisingly, the UN cites the
IMF/World Bank austerity and adjustment policies as key factors accelerating the general deterioration they were supposed to reverse. Yet,
by late 1991 the US had rewarded eight African states that fully
accepted adjustment programmes, writing off several hundred million
dollars of their debts.

Indeed, the past two decades of economic failure under authoritarian regimes in Africa are a direct cause of the present wave of political
rebellion throughout the continent under the slogans of democratisation and multipartyism. Ironically, whereas Western powers were
long complacent about and often supportive of authoritarian regimes
in Africa, they now generally view their removal as a prerequisite for
the success of the economic liberalisation and stabilisation they
promote. Yet, the overthrow of established regimes in Africa (and
elsewhere) is not always followed by stability. For instance, the US
tolerated the overthrow of Samuel Doe in Liberia, leaving that country
in a state of near anarchy. And nowhere has the spectre of anarchy
in the aftermath of the Cold War been more pronounced than in
Somalia. Rather than a transition to democracy and progress, Somalia
after the overthrow of Said Barre has descended into nightmarish chaos.
A number of other African countries must be wary to avoid a similar
descent into chaos and political disintegration in the future.

However, in some cases Western powers are less enthusiastic
actively to promote democratisation and are more keen to preserve

their interests and stability. For instance, though the US cut aid to Mobutu's embattled regime in Zaire and France sent a small military force there in September 1991 and made progress toward democratisation a precondition for further aid, Mobutu successfully delayed the progress of the national political conference. Zaire remains important to the US and the West, both in terms of geopolitics and by virtue of its natural resources. It is doubtful that the US or other Western powers would like to take the risk of Zaire descending into a crisis of ungovernability or disintegration after the overthrow of Mobutu. By contrast, in nearby Angola the US, then still tacitly backing the National Union for the Total Independence of Angola (UNITA) against the Marxist Popular Movement for the Liberation of Angola (MPLA) regime, continuously pressed for early national elections.

France initially favoured national conferences to be convened to establish new multiparty systems in Francophone countries, and suggested that progress towards democratisation would influence France's aid policies. Such national conferences have now taken place in many of the Francophone countries. France exerted direct pressure on recalcitrant rulers such as President Ratsiraka in Madagascar, but was less forthright in places such as Togo or the Ivory Coast, or anywhere else France felt vital interests were at stake. By mid-1992 France reconsidered the policy of active promotion of national conferences as the preferred avenue to multipartyism, in favour of a policy openly preferring the virtue of stability. France's about-face was a reaction to the instability already created by previous national conferences, including increased tribal conflict and military unrest, leading to the prospect of ungovernability. The remaining repressive regimes in former French colonies in West and Central Africa were thereby given a signal that repression of the democratic opposition might be seen as preferable to the risk of instability.

An initially reluctant Britain publicly chided Kenya's President Daniel Arap Moi, stressing that he should 'respect popular aspirations for democratic participation'. In November 1991, Western donors suspended US$800 million in aid to Kenya, which resulted in Kenya announcing multiparty elections. However, President Moi set no date for these elections and continued harassment of the opposition, especially the main party, the Forum for the Restoration of Democracy (FORD). In Nigeria, the military government of President Baban Gida arrested leaders of the new Campaign for Democracy in mid-1992, followed by another crackdown on the opposition in October 1992 and refused to accept the outcome of elections in mid-1993.

The trend in Africa seemed by mid-1992 to be back towards repression of the democratic opposition. The outcome of the democratisation process in Africa is very much in doubt and it is far too soon to predict whether multipartyism may be eventually consolidated or whether political conflict and instability will increase. Partly as a consequence of this political situation, the prospects for sustained economic recovery in Africa are equally uncertain and perhaps even more bleak.

The democratisation of Pacific Asia is in a different category since its economic base is quite distinctive from the Latin American and African cases. With the exception of the Philippines, recent democratisation in East Asia has come on the heels of rapid economic growth. This is certainly the case in South Korea and Taiwan, which have both gradually retreated from open authoritarian rule on the strength of sustained economic growth over the past three decades. The case of Thailand, however illustrates how fragile formal democracy remains in South-East Asia. Reversal from 'democracy' to military coup and then back to 'democracy' still characterises politics in Thailand, where the real power remains the military elite, aided by corrupt politicians. In Indonesia, only the most transparent of formal democracies has been tolerated by the ruling elite, as illustrated in the national elections of mid-1992. The military remains the real power. In the Philippines, formal democracy has produced a new quasi-military regime in the shape of the presidency of General Fidel Ramos, a former Marcos loyalist who previously headed the Philippine Constabulary. Thus, the progress of democratisation seems far from advanced in East Asia, and continues to embody deep compromises with the military establishment throughout the region along with a commitment by elites to preserve the status quo. Foremost in that status quo is the commitment to economic growth and to protecting the vested interests of powerful domestic and foreign economic elites. Another distinctive feature of the region is the fact that communist party regimes have not succumbed, and thus there is no post-communist democratisation along the lines of Eastern Europe and the former USSR. Economics is in command, however, in the communist as well as in the capitalist states of Asia, and so democratisation and multipartyism are firmly ruled out in such countries as China, North Korea and Vietnam.

Democracy, Global Capitalism and the New World Order

Where some see a sharp turn in events in the dawning of the so-called 'New World Order,' others sees continuity. President Bush's attempt to deploy this concept seems to have met with little success. The reality of the Old World Order remains, now largely devoid of the old rhetorical framework of Cold War ideological rivalry. In the Old/New World Order, under the auspices of American hegemonic power, the Third World is subordinated in the international division of labour as a source of raw materials and cheaper manufactured commodities, and as a market. The elites in the Third World – the oligarchies, the business community and the military who serve US and foreign interests (as well as their own) – are relied upon to control their local populations (Chomsky, Chapter 4, this volume). Repression is often acceptable to the United States just as 'stability' is preferred by Western bankers. In the past, both the global hegemonic power holders and the international financial elite agreed that a repressive anti-communist regime in the Third World was normally preferable to reformist governments that were 'soft on (domestic) communism.' In reality, the primary threat to US interests was not communism, but rather any nationalistic regime responsive to popular demands for immediate improvement in standards of living and which therefore interfered with US efforts to encourage private investment and repatriation of profits. Thus Arbenz in Guatemala in 1954, Mossadeq in Iran in 1953, Sukarno in Indonesia in 1965 and Allende in Chile in 1973, to name only a few, all fell under the CIA's ambit to destroy nationalistic regimes and replace them by compliant authoritarian regimes.

Yet, the US eventually embarked upon a 'crusade for democracy'. Especially in Central America, this was accompanied by state-sponsored campaigns of murder, torture and general barbarism. In most cases this war was waged from 'within' by the military and paramilitary death squads. The main exception was Nicaragua, where the US waged a war of terror across borders to destabilise democracy in the name of anti-communism. In reality, the US viewed Nicaragua's form of democracy as a threat to the region, while it heaped fulsome praise on the elite conservative 'democracies' that it promoted in the rest of Central America. Now Nicaragua is descending further into a crisis of ungovernability, while the US seems largely uninterested. At best, the US tolerated, and at worst directly promoted the most grotesque abuses of human rights in recent history throughout Central America. Probably no other region on earth has suffered as much economic and social damage in the past decade as Central America during this decade of pacification and so-called 'democratisation'. The extreme concentration of wealth and widespread abject poverty that characterises the region remains, as does the institutionalised power of the military behind the new democratic facades. By 1991 the region was in the happy state wherein all five Central American presidents revealed in the Declaration of Antigua that they were 'committed to free-market economics' and have abandoned land reform or welfare policy for the poor in favour of a trickle-down approach that does not threaten the basic economic power structure.

In reality, the so-called 'New' World Order began to emerge some 20 years ago as the bipolar configuration of global power (the US and USSR) gave way to the emerging tripolar configuration (the US, Germany, Japan) and the world economy entered a period of crisis. With the recent fall of communism in Europe the '70 Years' Crisis' may be over (Cumings 1991) but this does not mean that US interventionism will now cease. During the Cold War the US and other capitalist powers used the threat of communism as a pretext for intervention in pursuit of their own interests. Now that Soviet power has collapsed, the deterrent to US intervention has disappeared. The existence of Soviet power was a restraining factor upon the uses of US military power in some if not all past instances. It is generally acknowledged that Operation Desert Storm in 1991 could not have occurred under the old Cold War relations of power. Nevertheless, although there is now only one superpower in military terms, multinational interventionism dominates the public debate concerning the future of Western security strategy. There is much discussion of 'turning NATO' to out-of-area operations undertaken by multinational rapid deployment forces. This American-inspired proposal is also being discussed by European powers seeking a new foreign and defence policy role for the European Community, perhaps via the Western European Union. The Gulf War caused a near constitutional crisis in both Germany and Japan over the question of foreign intervention. Its aftermath may witness an increase in Japanese and German participation in multinational interventionism. Japan has already passed legislation allowing its troops to serve in UN peacekeeping operations, and there has been serious debate over Germany's role in the civil war in the former Yugoslavia after 1992.

The policies of the IMF and the free trade agenda reflected in the Uruguay Round of the General Agreement on Tariffs and Trade (GATT) will have the effect of restricting Third World governments 'to a police function to control their working classes and superfluous populations, while transnational corporations gain free access to their resources and monopolise new technology and global investment and production' (Chomsky, Chapter 4, this volume). The bloated military budgets of Third World states are typically held inviolate from the cuts that ravage social expenditure under IMF structural adjustment programmes. While economic sovereignty is stripped away from the states of the Third World, the state itself, and particularly the apparatus of repression, is left intact as a means of indirect rule by the North over the South. Where such indirect means of control prove insufficient to maintain the necessary 'order' either the new multinational or US unilateral intervention will be employed.

Economic sovereignty in the emerging world order is even more compromised than previously. In a world dominated by international capitalism, the most important decisions – those on the economy – are beyond the control of national power holders (Frank, Chapter 2, this volume). Under these conditions, democracy is impossible. Andre Gunder Frank argues that recent history illustrates the policy irrelevance of political ideology given the all-pervading realities of the world economy. For example, throughout the 1970s and 1980s many communist governments followed the same export/import led growth strategies and debt service policies as other authoritarian governments in the Third World and their 'democratic' successor governments. Rather than a sharp break in policy in the 'socialist' East, there is real continuity. The new democracies merely accelerate a process already over two decades in the making. This process can be explained by reference to the exigencies of competition in the world economy. None of the communist states was able to break away from or overcome the constraints of competition in the world economy through 'socialist national development' policies. Instead, the legacy was both an absolute decline in standards of living and a relative decline *vis-à-vis* Western capitalist states and the East Asian newly industrialising countries (NICs).

It is not wise nor necessary to conflate the democratisation processes of the post-communist regimes of Europe with those of the Third World, nor of these with the First World. These three zones of the global political economy still retain distinctive characteristics that caution against too much generalisation. Nevertheless, in a single global economic system their domestic political and economic processes become ever more interrelated. There is a 'crisis of democracy' in the world today as much as there is an opportunity for democracy. All states, in all three zones of the world economy, face increasing economic competition at the international level, and are beset by mounting social tensions with which they are less and less able to deal effectively, using the traditional national policy tools at their disposal.

Rather than advance in the GATT towards a fully liberal world economy, the more realistic prospect is continued growth of managed trade and growing tension in the GATT liberal trading regime between the emergent economic blocs. Politically this may mean the reconstruction of spheres of influence by each of the core powers in their respective regions. For the periphery, this holds out the threatening prospect of new forms of incorporation and subordination to the core. Roughly speaking, this redivision of the world into blocs would entail appending Latin America and the Middle East to the US sphere; Africa, the Mediterranean and Eastern Europe to the German/EC sphere; and Pacific Asia to Japan's sphere. Areas that do not quite 'fit' into this neat scheme are Central Asia, South Asia and the emerging powerhouse known as 'Greater China', which includes Taiwan, Singapore, South China and the Chinese diaspora communities in South-East Asia. This is a portrait of a world divided into regional hegemonic spheres; quite distinctive in character from the previous Pax Americana.

Perhaps nowhere else at present is this particular crisis/opportunity problematic more poignant than in Eastern Europe and the former Soviet Union. Post-communist Eastern Europe is now faced with the real prospect of becoming a 'victim' of the imperative to achieve efficiency and competitiveness in the international division of labour within the capitalist world market. Poland, which led the way in the revolutionary wave that swept the region in 1989, has already been economically Latin Americanised and politically paralysed in a crisis of ungovernability. Poland, like most of the other East European states, now has no political or economic alternative to IMF austerity. The current 'privatisation craze' in Eastern Europe (and in the former USSR as well, particularly Russia), can be viewed as ideologically driven rather than economically rational. The net effect will almost certainly be an increase in real poverty and inequality, and an inevitable increase in social tension (Frank, Chapter 2, this volume). Politically, the panacea sought by virtually all the Eastern European regimes is membership of the EC, by which they hope both to get a better deal economically and to safeguard their sovereignty. This road is obviously attractive, but the question is how many will get it, and how soon? The delay of a decade, which seems likely, means that in the short term conditions may worsen and instability increase.

Will such an outcome be conducive to democracy? Burbach regards the revolutions of Eastern Europe as 'aborted revolutions' and maintains that 'in Eastern Europe the Bush administration did little to strengthen or build authentic democratic institutions' (Burbach, Chapter 5, this volume). Despite all the public assurance that the West will not intervene in the internal affairs of these states, the West may be accused of supporting conservative political forces in the region, and pushing those who support neoliberal economic policies. Beyond the immediate transition period, the severity of the economic, social, political and ideological crisis in Eastern Europe and the former

Soviet Union raises the spectre of neo-authoritarianism amid resurgent nationalism and regionalism. As in much of the Third World, which these countries are now joining, the current democratisation of Eastern Europe and the former USSR may prove in the end to be a phase rather than the ultimate destination of history. That is, *democracy may be a transitional regime* between one form of authoritarianism (communism) and another form of authoritarianism (Low Intensity Capitalism).

The Political Pattern of Low Intensity Democracies

All four case studies (Argentina, Guatemala, the Philippines and South Korea) demonstrate that democracy as understood in the West is basically incompatible with societies characterised by extreme concentration of wealth in the hands of a tiny elite. In all four cases, the new democracy is compromised by, if not subservient to, the established power structure. Consequently, the status quo is protected while progressive reform is obstructed. Democratisation remains confined to the level of formal electoral participation. This cosmetic democratisation brings some limited change in civil and human rights and widens the legal space in which popular mobilisation for change can take place. But repression and abuse of human rights continue, usually against the familiar targets of labour, students, the Left and human rights activists.

Low Intensity Democracy is a fragile political system. Its fragility stems from two sources. On the one hand, the new democratic order widens the space for popular mobilisation and therefore raises the possibility of increased social instability as radical demands threatening the establishment are articulated. On the other hand, the military hovers over the scene as a grey eminence, always suspicious of the lessening of social control and the consequent threat to established interests. The military wields a silent veto over the extent of change permissible under Low Intensity Democracy. The conservative leaders of the democracies must constantly look over their shoulders to the barracks and the officers' club. Thus, the new democratic order is threatened with destabilisation from both the Left and the Right. It is therefore logical that these conservative regimes typically present themselves as moderates or centrists.

Their leanings are, however, distinctively to the Right and to ruling coalitions with the military. The civilian conservative government is usually a willing accomplice to the military. Together, they and the business elite form a hegemonic bloc. The difference between the previous dictatorships and the new 'democratic' regime lies in the relationship between these three fractions of the elite. Whereas in the past the military may have been overtly in control of the ruling coalition, under democratic regimes conservative politicians take the lead, closely backed by the business community (including agribusiness) with the electoral support of the middle class(es). This change in the configuration of intra-elite power is also one of the causes of democratisation, as the business elite asserts increasing autonomy from the state.

In the Philippines, the military actually gained more power as a direct consequence of the democratic transition. In South Korea, 'civilianised' military governments have been the norm since the military *coup d'état* of 1961. The Noh Tae Woo government stood in this tradition, being presided over by a former general. In Guatemala the military remained in control throughout the 'democratic' period, and counterinsurgency and the suppression of the Left continue. Richard Wilson argues that there is a cycle of Low Intensity Conflict and war which operates independently of any regime type in Guatemala (Wilson, Chapter 6, this volume). The military remains the power behind the throne and retains full autonomy in dealing with the insurgency in the countryside. Indeed, so anxious are the conservative politicians in Guatemala to be the 'willing accomplice' of the military, that the military was allowed to proclaim its own amnesty and view 'democracy' as the 'final stage of counterinsurgency'. The civilian government defines its economic and social policies so as not to provoke either a military coup or a confrontation with the oligarchy. The ruling conservatives continued the repressive anti-labour policies of their military predecessors, while death squads declared 'open season' on trade unionists and student leaders.

A further distinction between these four cases is the extent to which the elite ruling coalition incorporates popular strata. In some, labour in particular continues to be excluded, as in South Korea and Guatemala, while in others, for example Argentina, labour is part of the ruling coalition. Miguel Teubal argues that the shift from the middle-class Radical Party government to the working-class Justicialista (Peronist) Party government in 1989 did not bring a change in policy parallel to the putative shift in class base of the ruling party (Teubal, Chapter 7, this volume). Instead, President Menem 'fell into line' with the establishment and followed a 'responsible economic policy' geared to maintaining 'stability'. Menem's promises of reform, made in the heat of electoral contest, evaporated in an abrupt *volte face* that included a blanket pardon or *indulto* for the military. Menem turned his back on the popular sectors in favour of the economic and financial elite and foreign capital. He imposed harsh austerity measures and pushed liberalisation, while dropping progressive reforms. The IMF rewarded Menem with a new loan of US$1 billion, citing the 'success' of his privatisation and austerity measures. Menem reciprocated by showing his eagerness to join the New World Order. He abruptly took Argentina out of the Non-Aligned Movement, declaring that Argentina now belongs to a 'single world ... a new juridical, political, social and economic order', led by the US. Few leaders have shown such unbridled enthusiasm. Despite certain exceptions, Latin America and East Asia have distinctive populist traditions. Whereas labour has at various times and in various countries been part of the ruling coalition in Latin America over a period of decades, the export-oriented national security states of East Asia, like South Korea and Taiwan, have permanently excluded labour from participation in power (Deyo 1989; Ogle 1990; Bello and Rosenfeld 1990). These separate historical experiences continue to differentiate the two regions under Low Intensity Democracy. In South Korea, labour continues to be excluded from full participation in the political system. In Latin American cases, democratisation had a much less dramatic impact on the potential political role of labour.

The onset of formal representative government changes the conditions under which labour and other popular movements must operate. The pattern emerging from the four cases can be summed up under the headings 'mobilisation and realignment'. Mobilisation consists of strengthening and broadening organisational work, outside the electoral arena. The growth of new popular organisations is facilitated by the political opening and the wider legal space available, despite continuing use of repression by the authorities. This may take the form of newly democratic and independent trade unions that break free of corporatist frameworks, as in South Korea, or extend into new social areas such as the environment and peace, 'citizens' rights' and women's issues. The growth and strengthening of these popular organisations are an indication of the emergence of a nascent democratic culture, but one which is in all cases peripheral to the centre of power.

As social movements grow and the opportunity presented by electoral competition widens, the progressive movement undergoes a period of realignment. Under authoritarianism the 'opposition' is often composed of a broad coalition of forces, in which the middle class(es) is usually allied with the working class, the urban poor and the peasantry. When formal democracy is achieved, the alliance between the middle class and other popular sectors usually comes under considerable strain. The middle class is satisfied by limited formal democracy and demobilises, realigning its political support to centrist and conservative political parties and politicians. This realignment reinforces the position of the ruling coalition and the pursuit of conservative economic and social policies that preserve the distribution of economic power. A 'dictatorship' over the working class and other popular sectors continues under the form of democracy with the implicit blessing of the complacent middle class(es). This 'dictatorship' usually takes the form of a strengthened presidential office at the expense of greater power to the popularly elected parliamentary representatives. Real power and government authority continue to reside in the President and the administration, implemented through the bureaucracy and ultimately reinforced by the military and the police. This is because the legislature would be the locus of any attempt at reform.

The onset of formal democracy always challenges progressive social movements to choose whether or not to form political parties and participate in mainstream electoral contests. A political party is an entirely different political animal from a social movement. This dilemma inevitably leads to intense political debate and usually to splits. New coalitions are formed as realignment proceeds. Two broad wings emerge: one oriented to electoral competition, the other extra-parliamentary, usually allied either tacitly or openly to an underground movement. The strategy and tactics of these two wings of the popular movement differ considerably. These differences, augmenting the continuing ideological differences within and between the two wings, contribute to a fragmentation of forces. However, a counter-vailing trend emerges to form national and broad popular coalitions by both wings. Low Intensity Democracy can therefore be characterised as a new stage in the long war of position between the elite and popular forces preparing the ground for a new form of political competition between them; one in which the social power of popular movements will increasingly challenge the status quo dominated by the conservative ruling coalition. However, the real social power of the progressive movements still remains limited and circumscribed by the continued repressive power of the state. Risking open confrontation with the state and the elite from such a position of weakness is dangerous whatever the temptations to do so.

For the underground and insurgent movements, the effect of realignment may be profound. Armed struggle may come to be viewed primarily as a means of improving one's position in political negotiations with the government, rather than as a strategy to achieve state power. In this strategic shift, the armed struggle becomes a means of forcing constitutional concessions from the elite that will widen the juridical space for the Left and thus break the mould of political culture, allowing the Left's political parties to compete on more equal terms with the conservatives. This is essentially what happened in El Salvador in 1992, when Farabundo Martí National Liberation Front (FMLN) leader Joaquin Villalobos led the insurgents into Copaz, a national commission responsible for monitoring the peace accords between the government and the FMLN. This is not a strategy of capitulation. On the contrary, it reflects the heightened politicisation of class conflict under the new conditions. For example, when the M-19 guerrillas in Colombia laid down their arms in early 1990 they immediately became the country's most popular political party in constituent assembly elections later in the year. In El Salvador, the FMLN hopes to emulate this achievement in time for the presidential elections of 1994. A negotiated political settlement to armed conflict poses dilemmas not only to revolutionary armed groups but also to ruling governments. In El Salvador, the Cristiani government had to overcome the opposition of the military in order to advance the peace process. A similar process is under way in Guatemala and, at a much earlier stage, in the Philippines, where newly inaugurated President Fidel Ramos promised fresh negotiations with the insurgents and a possible amnesty.

The realignment process also includes the Right, which seeks to exploit the democratic form and forge an electoral advantage that will keep conservatives in power. The Right always operates through political parties, since social movements are essentially antithetical to its aims. From the Right's point of view the ideal Low Intensity Democracy creates dominant conservative parties that retain power and thereby provide 'stability', that is, preservation of the economic status quo. The conservatives, however, are sometimes bedevilled by competition among themselves for the electoral spoils of power. Nevertheless, their access to political funds from business and their close ties to the state and the economic elite give them a built-in electoral advantage over their financially and politically marginal progressive rivals. This hegemonic position of conservatives usually elicits a paradoxical outcome of 'democracy' – widespread voter apathy and alienation. As people realise that the electoral road is limited in what it can provide under the circumstances of continued conservative domination of society, they drop out of the electoral arena. Initially immense enthusiasm for the prospect of electoral participation soon becomes equally immense disillusion with the system. Political parties do not lead to genuine popular participation. On the contrary they usually encourage clientelism and operate as elite-run electoral machines.

Even so, the general legacy of political culture after decades of authoritarianism is a peculiar one. So much so that any electoral succession is itself considered as a great achievement of the new regimes – far preferable to the *coup d'état*. When one elected civilian succeeds another, it is hailed as nothing less than a historic triumph for democracy. When Menem succeeded Alfonsín in Argentina in 1989, it was the first such peaceful transition in decades. When Serrano succeeded Cerezo in Guatemala in 1991, this too was a first. In South Korea, when former General Noh Tae Woo succeeded former General Chun Doo Hwan in the office of President in 1988, this was hailed by the establishment as a historic first 'peaceful transfer of power'. This achievement of electoral succession is often presented as proof of the new 'maturity' of the political culture, rather than conservatism by another name.

The typical political pattern in these four cases is an early 'liberal' phase of the democracy, in which reform is promised and the level of repression decreases. Scores are settled with the old regime and the popular movements are encouraged to demobilise as the professional politicians take the initiative in 'normal' political culture. In the second, 'repressive' phase, promises of real reform prove hollow and the regime imposes a conservative economic policy which protects the interests of the established elites, both domestic and foreign. Not only are socioeconomic reforms abandoned, but externally imposed structural adjustment policies intensify exploitation of the lower classes and widen the gap between the rich and the poor. The level of overt repression against popular movements and labour increases, and these forces are excluded from influence in government. New compromises are struck with the military and the Right, explicitly exonerating them from past misconduct and reassuring them of their role.

Low Intensity Democracy is designed to promote stability. However, it is usually accompanied by neoliberal economic policies designed to restore economic growth. This usually accentuates economic hardship for the less privileged and deepens the short-term structural effects of economic crisis as the economy opens further to the competitive winds of the world market and global capital. The pains of economic adjustment are supposed to be temporary, preparing the society to proceed to a higher stage of development. The temporary economic suffering of the majority is further supposed to be balanced by the benefits of a freer democratic political culture. But unfortunately for them, the poor and dispossessed cannot eat votes! In such circumstances, Low Intensity Democracy may 'work' in the short term, primarily as a strategy to reduce political tension, but is fragile in the long term, due to its inability to redress fundamental political and economic problems.

In this volume, Rocamora (Chapter 8) describes how in the Philippines the failure of the democratic experiment can be attributed either to President Corazon Aquino's inability to break out of the confines of the existing power structures or to her own upper-class background. Her emergence as the figurehead of the anti-dictatorship movement signified a shift from Centre-Left to Centre-Right, assuring continuity with the policies of the Marcos era. Despite punitive measures against the Marcos-era 'crony capitalists', her regime revived the power of the traditional oligarchy, which dominates electoral politics at both local and national levels. In the initial, liberal, phase of her government, Aquino placed leading liberals and reformists in the cabinet, alongside conservatives in key positions, considered land reform and repeal of repressive labour laws, and sought negotiations with the insurgent New People's Army. In the following repressive phase, Aquino abandoned the liberals in the cabinet, dropped land reform and labour legislation, unleashed a wave of police, military and vigilante terror, and reversed course on negotiations with the National Democratic Front. Thereafter, her regime became hostage to the restive military (Rocamora, Chapter 8, this volume). National elections in spring 1992 demonstrated that though the power of the oligarchic families had been considerably revived it was still not sufficient to prevent the victory of General Fidel Ramos on a mere 23.5 per cent of the vote. Ramos, though a former Marcos man and more conservative and openly pro-American than Mrs Aquino, won legitimacy by having repeatedly 'saved' democracy and the Aquino presidency from military rebels and by timely posing as a 'democrat' supported by Mrs Aquino.

According to Gills' analysis (Chapter 9, this volume) of South Korea, economic growth was the indispensable prerequisite for 'democratisation' there. The transition from authoritarian rule to formal electoral democracy was accepted by the elite as being instrumental in upgrading the national economy to a skill- and capital-intensive structure capable of sustaining high levels of growth in an increasingly competitive international environment. Throughout the 1970s and 1980s, state-led economic development nurtured a powerful set of business groups, the *chaebol*, which dominate the Korean economy. Democratisation was part of the adjustment of power relations between fractions of the elite: the military lost its exclusive dominant position in the ruling coalition and was forced to share power with big business and conservative politicians. General Noh Tae Woo successfully posed as a 'democrat' and announced the 'era of the common man', winning the presidency against a split opposition. This realignment in the ruling coalition did not, however, extend to incorporation of popular sectors, especially labour, which continued to be excluded from power. Predictably, most of the middle class offered its political allegiance to the new conservative parties. After the initial liberal phase, during which the regime promised greater freedom and improved living standards, the regime returned to repression, particularly against the Left, students and labour, and abandoned meaningful reform, including measures aimed at reducing the immense power of the *chaebol* in the economy. A realignment among conservatives produced a new ruling party, the Democratic Liberals, marginalising the remaining mainstream opposition and confounding the purposes of electoral competition in the quest for permanent hegemony (Gills, Chapter 9, this volume).

Despite what may seem to be major changes, precious little real change occurs under a regime of Low Intensity Democracy. The maxim of the 'enlightened' elite is that 'the more things change, the more they stay the same.' Low Intensity Democracy's effectiveness is its ability to implement limited and carefully selected agendas of change. It purports to open a hot pressure cooker without getting scalded. When steam is let off slowly and carefully it cools the whole thing down a bit and makes it manageable. Though on the surface the situation looks manageable, it is unlikely to remain so for very long.* The economic and political conditions of Third World societies often generate more 'steam' than can be let off manageably. Samir Amin's comment about Africans applies to people in Asia and Latin America as well: 'Africans will not accept a meaningless pluralism, a semi-fabricated democracy to stabilise the unbearable' (*Guardian*, 8 July 1991).

Participatory Progressive Democracy

Progressive democracy is the only answer to 'Low Intensity Democracy.' Democracy in most of the Third World is impossible under conditions currently imposed by international capitalism, with its extreme wealth and extreme poverty, its terror, repression, material and spiritual deprivation. The fight against these conditions defines the tasks of progressive democrats the world over.

---

* If the lid is let off too quickly, the whole thing can blow up in one's face.

If democracy is not working anywhere, much less in the Third World, then we can rightly assert that there is a crisis of political power in the New World Order. What alternative is there to actually existing models of democracy? We would point towards several domestic requirements for a thriving democracy, including real reform of social inequality which abrogates the political and economic power of business and military elites. There will also need to be a reorganising of the political system itself and the judiciary to make them more independent and representative of the whole of society's interests.

Democracy requires more than mere maintenance of formal 'liberties'. The only way to advance democracy in the Third World, or anywhere else, is to increase the democratic content of formal democratic institutions through profound social reform. Without substantial reform and redistribution of economic assets, representative institutions – no matter how 'democratic' in form – will simply mirror the undemocratic power relations of society. Democracy requires a change in the balance of forces in society. Concentration of economic power in the hands of a small elite is a structural obstacle to democracy. It must be dismantled if democracy is to emerge.

The military should be significantly reduced in size and political influence and fully subordinated to civilian authority. This will require genuine adherence to the promotion of human rights, an end to terrorism and the dismantling of the state's repressive apparatus. Anti-labour laws and other laws restricting self-organisation of popular sectors should be repealed. Most important, structures of government must be changed by strengthening representative organs at the expense of the executive organs; devolving power from the centre to the localities and regions; and establishing an independent judiciary to guarantee human and civil rights. All political parties should be guaranteed equal electoral participation, including those of the Left. These reforms would strengthen, not weaken, the state. Strong governments are required to implement social reform and to negotiate effectively with powerful foreign governments, multinationals and international institutions like the IMF.

Most Third World governments today are weak because they lack the support of their own people. Civil society and popular organisations must grow in autonomy in order to build strong government and to articulate the interests of the majority – most importantly, workers, the peasantry, women and other oppressed sectors of society. Strong governments are possible only if they reflect the views and serve the interests of the majority. The weakness of Third World governments also lies in their connection with international capitalism and, more specifically, the intervention of governments of advanced capitalist countries, especially the United States. International capitalism prevents the consolidation of Third World bourgeois ruling classes and fractionalises these classes. Government financial resources are limited by debt service payments and chronic balance of payments crises. Militaries built on foreign military assistance and training undermine government authority and often become the instruments of foreign intervention.

This leads us to the third requirement of democracy in the Third World, the achievement of genuine independence. The operation of the world economy in the present era subjects all to the same logic. But the 'free market' left to its own devices will never be the historical agency of genuine democratisation, and indeed it systematically undermines democracy by subjecting everyone to the 'objective laws of economics'. If the market is inherently undemocratic, then how can we expect the market 'naturally' to create a democratic world? The question of democracy in the Third World, and in the former communist countries now (re)joining the Third World, cannot therefore be separated either in theory or in practice from the question of democracy in the global system as a whole. The dilemma is that everyone, whether they like it or not, is caught within this global system. The question facing progressives throughout the world is whether any kind of 'delinking', in Samir Amin's terms, is possible. The other question, again using Amin's terms, is whether a 'polycentric' world is possible (Amin 1990).

Unfortunately, there is very little that Third World peoples can do about the ongoing transformation of international capitalism, or about whether warring trading blocs lie in store for the early twenty-first century. The global requirements for democracy are daunting. Democracy at the national level can only begin to become possible if the institutions of global capital can be made accountable. This would entail reining in the undemocratic free market proposed by GATT talks, opposing the North American Free Trade Agreement (NAFTA) and its anti-labour ethic, and contesting elements of the Maastricht treaty which project an unrepresentative bankers' version of Europe. Sooner or later, Third World attempts at democracy will have to organise a concerted defiance of IMF austerity plans and the agenda of World Bank programmes. There must also be a united opposition to the way in which the UN has been recently used as a vehicle for the North's foreign policy, such as during the Gulf (Oil) War. In short, there must be a new global participatory politics aimed at the hitherto unaccountable governing institutions of the international system.

In most Third World countries, popular organisations and other progressive forces do not, at this point, have the critical mass necessary for decisive internal reform. But this should not mean capitulation to adjustment in the form of intensified immiseration. If adjustment is inevitable under prevailing conditions, then every effort must be made to turn it around to more progressive ends. For example, progressive forces can call for slashing the military budget to reduce the public deficit rather than savaging health and education budgets, and fight to replace corrupt elitist regimes with truly popular governments dedicated to participatory democracy, while simultaneously building local democracy in the workplace, the communities and the regions.

The conditions in the real world call for a reformulation of revolutionary theory and practice. In the coming period it will be more necessary than ever to combine the organisational form of the political party with those of popular self-organisation and self-help. Political struggle through the Party with the sole or primary aim of achieving state power should no longer be the central focus. On the one hand, it remains essential not to default on state power to the forces of exploitation and oppression. Therefore, a 'defensive' political action by progressive political parties is always needed. On the other hand, it is imperative to go beyond struggles within the framework of bourgeois representative democracy by combining this level of struggle with workers and popular direct democracy.

On the domestic level the concepts of struggle that will guide progressive movements for participatory democracy will resemble well-known notions from the past, such as dual power, within a historical context of protracted war of position between social blocs. The paradigm of the Spanish anarchists earlier in the twentieth century should now be re-examined as an alternative model of revolutionary social transformation. From this perspective, democracy must be painstakingly built up and constantly defended through concrete popular organisations embedded in the workplace and the community, and *then* reinforced and extended by gaining at least a share of state power through electoral competition. This has in fact always been the bedrock of real democratic gains. We agree with Samir Amin (Chapter 3, this volume) that a national and popular response 'is even more essential now than in the past'. However, it is equally imperative that this domestic level of struggle be directly linked to larger regional and global terrains of struggle. The reality of the global economy, as Frank argues in this volume, largely 'precludes the exercise of real national sovereignty and the implementation of truly democratic decisions'. The struggle for democracy must therefore go directly to the local level and simultaneously transcend the traditional and dangerous limitations imposed at the national level. This is the great challenge of the future.

As Samir Amin points out in this volume, the ideology of Western liberal democracy sees the democratic transformation of society as 'largely the product of evolution; hence the functional role of the revolutionary process in history can be played down'. We disagree with this interpretation of history. With Amin, we affirm the 'crucial function of revolutions, moments of qualitative transformation and crystallisation of potentialities inconceivable without revolutions'. The wave of democratisation of the late 1980s and early 1990s was precisely a wave of popular 'revolutions' against corrupt and repressive regimes. However, in their wake, profound socioeconomic reform may seem to be less likely now than for most of recent international history. Even so, it is more objectively necessary than ever before. What has changed most are the conditions within which progressive movements operate.

If we have criticised the results of popular uprisings against business and military elites, it is not out of a disrespect for the global struggles of peoples against authoritarian governments. In most/all cases, these have been authentic, well-organised and intelligent expressions of popular will against various sorts of tyranny. If democracy is going to come from anywhere, it is from popular struggles. These include revolutionary movements such as those of the FMLN in El Salvador, the Guatemalan opposition's 30-year war, the Sandinistas in Nicaragua and the National Democratic Front in the Philippines. Apart from the overt and publicised uprisings, there are also the everyday and often silent forms of struggle of women's and human rights groups, indigenous peoples' organisations, and environmental movements around the world. The struggles of the labour movement are still central to all progress towards democratisation everywhere (Reuschemeyer, Stephens and Stephens 1992).

As in every crisis, the present situation has elements of both despair and hope, of destruction and reconstruction. As Gramsci said, 'The old order is dead, but the new order cannot yet be born.' The collapse of old authoritarianisms is truly a welcome historic event, and the democratic hopes and aspirations of the masses of people who made these revolutions should be recognised and fully embraced. Yet the danger exists that the enormous revolutionary energy of the past few years will be dissipated and the potential for genuine progressive transformation greatly reduced. We can expect the US, the West and the conservative elites of the Third World and the new post-communist governments to continue to seek to abort these popular revolutions in the name of economic rationality and stability. The challenge, therefore, is to keep the momentum going in the right direction and to fight against the tendency for conservative elites to hijack popular revolutions in order to preserve their own interests.

There is a concrete reason for this book's analysis of the limits of change, the parameters of societies' transformations enforced by unrelenting domestic elites and the perennial iron cage of global capital. We make our critical theories in the hope that this reflection may serve to enhance strategies for the future, to avoid repetition of the past, and in order to break out of the transient and unstable Low Intensity Democracies towards that which all people deserve: authentic participatory democracy.

As the 1990s dawn the global system is descending deeper into an economic and political crisis, indeed a global crisis of democracy. This prognosis has nothing to do with 'pessimism' versus 'optimism', but rather with reality versus illusion. Instead of a bright New World Order of global democracy, we see the very real and dangerous prospect of a dark period of deepening economic chaos, deprivation and neo-authoritarianism in much of the world. The Gulf War supposedly heralded the rosy dawn of the New World Order, but it was precisely democracy – in both Kuwait and Iraq – that was quickly sacrificed by the US and its allies on the high altar of economic and strategic self-interest.

If such is the nature of the new 'democratic' world order, it is inevitable that there will be new forms of national-popular resistance, though not all of them may be 'democratic', as everyone struggles to compete and survive. The coming age will certainly be one of increased hardship and conflict. But out of this crucible may yet emerge new hope for progressive social movements and democracy. The best slogan for the 1990s may be found in the words of the Jamaican reggae poet Bob Marley:

Get Up! Stand Up!
Stand Up for your rights.
Get Up! Stand Up!
Don't give up the Fight.

References
Amin, Samir 1990. *Delinking: Towards a Polycentric World*. London, Zed Books.
Bello, Walden and Rosenfeld, Stephanie 1990. *Dragons in Distress*. San Francisco, Institute for Food and Development Policy.
Cavanagh, John, Gershman, John, Baker, Karen and Helmke, Gretchen 1992. *Trading Freedom: How Free Trade Affects our Lives, Work and*

ronment. Institute for Food and Development Policy, San
:isco.

Chase Dunn, C.K. (ed.) 1982. *Socialist States in the World Economy*.
London, Heinemann.

Cumings, Bruce 1991. 'The End of the 70 Years' Crisis: Trilateralism
and the New World Order', *World Policy Journal*, vol. VIII, no. 2
(spring), pp. 195–222.

Deyo, Frederick 1989. *Beneath the Miracle: Labour Subordination in the
New East Asian Industrialism*. Berkeley, University of California
Press.

Diamond, Larry, Linz, Juan and Lipset, Seymore Martin 1989.
Democracy in Developing Countries: Asia. London, Admantine Press,
preface, p. xxi. There are three other volumes in this series, on Africa,
Latin America and a synthesis volume called *Persistence, Failure and
Renewal*.

Frank, A.G. 1980. *Crisis: In the World Economy*. London, Heinemann.

Fukuyama, Francis 1992. *The End of History and the Last Man*. London,
Hamish Hamilton.

George, Susan 1988. *A Fate Worse than Debt*. Harmondsworth, Penguin
Books.

Halliday, Fred 1987. *Beyond Irangate: The Reagan Doctrine and the
Third World*. Amsterdam, Transnational Institute.

O'Donnell, Guillermo and Schmitter, Phillipe 1986. *Transitions from
Authoritarian Rule*, vol. 5, *Tentative Conclusions about Uncertain
Democracies*. Baltimore, Maryland, and London, Johns Hopkins
University Press, pp. 13–14.

Ogle, George 1990. *South Korea: Dissent within the Economic Miracle*.
London, Zed Books.

Reuschemeyer, D., Stephens, E. and Stephens, J. 1992. *Democracy and
Capitalist Development*. Cambridge, Polity Press.

2. Marketing Democracy in an Undemocratic Market

ANDRE GUNDER FRANK

'Democracy' is in and 'development' is out as buzzwords for the Third World. The very 'development' idea and the word itself are in apparently terminal crisis. The new idea to replace it is 'democracy'. When Gandhi was asked what he thought of 'Western civilisation,' he answered 'it would be a good idea'. We can say as much of development and democracy as well. However, for the Third World, 'democracy' is likely to become no more real in the future than 'development,' or Western civilisation for that matter, did in the past. Instead like the latter, 'democracy' may well become a flag – or the figleaf – for continued exploitation and oppression of the South by the North.

In Abraham Lincoln's words, there can be little real and meaningful democratic government by the people, of the people and for the people in any *part* of the 'Third World' South as long as their economic possibilities are limited and their policy options are controlled by their participation in the *whole* world economy, which is run from the North. Of course, there is no present claim or forseeable hope of making decisions for the whole world economy on a democratic basis. As long as this lack of democracy remains for the world economy as a whole, political democracy in any 'sovereign' part thereof can be of limited scope at best.

An Introduction to 'Development' as a Precursor to 'Democracy'

'Development' ideology has been the flag and figleaf of political economic reality and policy for the third world since the end of the Second World War. Yet, economic underdevelopment persists and has partly even been aggravated in most of the Third World South in the face of almost all manner of ideological solutions and political efforts to overcome it. This story is not new and requires little elaboration here. However, there are some new ironic twists of late, which merit note in the present context. In this regard, I may be permitted to repeat some reflections in my recent and partly auto-biographical and autocritical essay 'The Underdevelopment of Development' (Frank 1991).

Real world system development has never been guided by, or responsive to, any global or local 'development' thinking or policy. In this world economy, sectors, regions and peoples *temporarily and cyclically* assume leading and hegemonic central (core) positions of social and technological 'development.' They then have to cede their pride of place to new ones who replace them. Usually this happens after a long interregnum of crisis in the system. During this time of crisis, there is intense competition for leadership and hegemony. The central core has moved around the globe in a pre-dominantly westerly direction. At the subsystem levels of countries, regions or sectors, all 'development' has occurred through and thanks to their (temporarily) more privileged position in the international division of labour and power. The recently prevalent notions of 'national development' are the result of a myopic optical illusion. These notions and the illusion are derived from a self-interested selective tunnel vision. It lacks an objective global assessment of real world development. This development ideology was based on and is now doomed by this self-illusory perception. It is less and less sustainable in the face of hard reality. We now need to replace this development theory, as well as micro-supply and-macro-demand-side economic theories, by another more rounded, dynamic and all-encompassing supply-and-demand-side economics which analyses and guides *world* economic and technological development.

The most widespread political ideology and development theory for the last decade or two has been that 'national development' is best pursued through the 'magic of the market' by letting 'free enterprise' promote 'export-led growth'. The stellar models are South Korea and Taiwan. These two have indeed done well in the world market recently. Unfortunately for the ideological model, however, their success was not the result so much of free enterprise as of state intervention. Moreover, their states' ability to do well was in turn based on three earlier *political* factors: prewar Japanese colonialism, postwar US-imposed land reform and massive Cold War subsidies.

Beyond the peculiarities of these cases, the thesis that all or even many other countries could copy their 'success' is a fallacy. The world market could not absorb the exports of a China-sized Hong Kong. The need for better economic analysis, however, does not mean that there is or can be a model of or for development which would be applicable around the world.

Unfortunately for the ideological peddlers of this political model and for the many countries of Latin America, Africa and South-East Asia who pursued essentially the same export-led growth strategy (apart from the city states Hong Kong and Singapore), it failed miserably elsewhere. Moreover, the possibility of continued success by Korea and Taiwan is now increasingly questioned (for example, Bello and Rosenfeld 1990), not to mention the political and social costs of these dictatorships while they lasted. The reasons, of course, are the exigencies of competition in the changing world market, particularly during the world economic recession existing since 1990.

In this increasingly technological competition for the world market, it is not yet clear who has made the grade to survive. To put it differently, in this world economic game of musical chairs, it is not yet clear who will still have a seat when the music stops the next time, as it well may in this recession. Perhaps Korea and Taiwan have, but more than likely not: their success in carving out a world market share will be temporary at best.

However, it is clear that outside Japan much of the remainder of Asia, Africa and Latin America, as well as most of Eastern Europe and the republics of the former Soviet Union have not made the grade. Resource saving industrial development and the development of a service/information society deprives them of their 'traditional' world markets for raw materials and reduces their comparative advantage as low labour cost producer exporters. At the same time, technological upgrading to remain competitive in the world market has failed in most of this 'Third' and 'Second' World, but of course also in many sectors and populations in the industrially developed 'First' World and particularly in the United States.

What *is* a realistic prospect, therefore, is the growing threat to countries, regions and peoples that they will be marginalised. That is, they may be involuntarily delinked from the world process of evolution or development. However, they are then delinked on terms which are not of their own choosing. The most obvious case in point is much of sub-Saharan Africa. There is a decreasing world market in the international division of labour for Africa's natural and human resources. Having been squeezed dry like a lemon in the course of world capitalist 'development,' much of Africa may now be abandoned to its fate. However, the same fate increasingly also threatens other regions and peoples elsewhere; in the South (for instance Bangladesh, the Brazilian north-east, Central America); in the ex-industrial rustbelt, the south Bronx, and other regions and peoples in the West; and in whole interior regions and peoples in the formerly 'socialist' East, for example on both sides of the Sino–Russian border.

Events in 1989–92 accelerated and aggravated the marginalisation of millions of people in Eastern Europe and what was the Soviet Union. Discarding the already squeezed-out lemon of Central Asia was the political position, for instance, represented by the Russian President Boris Yeltsin. The Southern inhabitants' wrath at having so long been exploited in the past and demanding that this cease in the future is understandable. So is the appeal to (or discovery of) 'traditional' ethnic and national identity and inter-ethnic strife in response to aggravated economic deprivation, such as 30 per cent unemployment in parts of Central Asia when it was part of the Soviet Union. However, political 'independence' and inter-ethnic strife in Central Asia or Central Africa now can afford the people of those areas little economic benefit in the future. On the contrary, the erection of politically motivated ethnic and other barriers to economic interchange, and even exploitation, threatens to convert them separately and altogether (back) into backwaters of history. (However, the 'Centrality of Central Asia' was a fact of history for millennia before the world's present North–South arrangement took shape in the sixteenth century, as I argue in Frank [1992b].) Many of these regions are more likely to be Latin Americanised, and some even Africanised and Lebanonised, instead of achieving the West Europeanisation to which they aspire.

People in all these and other places may now be sacrificed on the altar of growth-oriented development policy. They fall victim to efficient competitive participation in the international division of labour in the world capitalist market and to contemporary social evolution. However, the West may well receive many more migrants from the few who can, among the many who wish, to escape this marginal existence in Central America and Africa. North America, Western Europe and Japan will be the magnets. Many people prefer to survive exploited by the division of labour in the North than to suffer death by war and starvation or marginalised life without hope in the South.

The incorporation of various parts of the Third and formerly 'Second' Worlds into possible American, West European and Japanese-led economic blocs may seem to contradict this process of marginalisation. Nonetheless, for the majority of the people involved, such 'incorporation' does not contradict but actually reinforces marginalisation. The reason is that their regions and resources, and their own labour and buying power, are incorporated into these regional political economic blocs in formation only to bolster the fortunes of the economic powers and the competitive capacity at the top of these blocs. Therefore, incorporation into these blocs only occurs in so far as there is anything to exploit at the bottom. Where and when people's labour or purchasing power cannot contribute to this end, they remain or are marginalised just the same. Indeed, the competitive pressures both within and among these economic blocs only exacerbate the process of marginalisation within the blocs from top to bottom. That is why, for instance, masses of Canadians have already complained about the Canadian–American free trade pact. Spokespersons for labour in Canada, the United States and Mexico warn that the extension of this zone to Mexico will increase either the exploitation or the exclusion of labour or both, in all three countries. Moreover, if a country is incorporated into a political economic bloc, it is also more exposed to having to toe the political line of the bloc's dominant power. That would deprive the dependent country of a measure of the political benign neglect, or the 'Sinatra Doctrine' of being able to 'do it my way,' which it might otherwise enjoy in a wider world of economic marginalisation.

In other words, a *dual economy and society* may now indeed be in the process of formation on a global scale at this stage of social evolution *in the world system*. However, this new dualism is different from the old dualism I rejected in my earlier writings (Frank 1967 and others). The similarity between the two 'dualisms' is only apparent. According to the old dualism, sectors or regions were supposedly separate. That is, they supposedly existed without past or present exploitation between them *before* 'modernisation' would join them happily ever after. Moreover, this separate dual existence was seen within countries. I denied all these propositions. In the new dualism, the separation comes *after* the contact and often after exploitation. The lemon is discarded after it has been squeezed dry. Thus, this new dualism is the *result* of the process of social and tech-nological evolution, which others call 'development'. Moreover, this new dualism exists between those who do and those who cannot participate in a worldwide division of labour. To some extent, the ins and outs of this world division of labour are in part technologi-cally determined. Thus, this new dualism may partake of the old technological dualism.

Ironically, the same present-day political and ideological changes in Eastern Europe through which its people aspire to join the First World in Western Europe now threaten instead also to place Eastern Europe economically in the Third World – again, for that is where it was before. Poland has already been Latin Americanised. Romania's dependent agricultural (and, only temporarily, oil) export economy will be lucky and thankful if it can even recuperate the position (now challenged by Bulgaria), which developed agribusiness for export during the 'socialist' regime.

The same problem obtains a *fortiori* in the republics of the former Soviet Union. A few parts of Russia and the Ukraine were Westernised by Peter the Great and industrialised by him, Witte and Stalin. But most of the former Soviet Union is at best still a Third World economy, like Brazil, India and China, which also have industrial capacities, especially in military hardware. The Transcaucasian and Central Asian regions, whether they remain in the Commonwealth of Independent States or not, are not even likely to be Latin Americanised, but rather economically more Africanised or, God forbid, politically Lebanonised. The same sad fate befell what was Yugoslavia.

Bitter experience has shown that 'Second World, socialist national development' in China, the former Soviet Union and Eastern Europe was unable to break out from or overcome the constraints of competition in the world economy. These countries of the Second World, like those of the Third World, are handicapped by their position in the world economic international division of labour, quite irrespective of being blessed by political democracy or cursed by its absence or failure. They are constrained by their lack of foreign exchange, or in one word by their lack of dollars. The events of 1989 and 1990 eliminated all remaining ideological legitimacy and credibility in these 'Second' World 'socialist' countries. However, while many observers limit their attention to the bankruptcy of the 'socialist' component of this ideology in Europe and Asia or Africa, reality has undercut its 'nationalist' component equally or even more so. Other *national* development strategies in Africa, Latin America and Asia were essentially similar and often failed equally or even more so. So we observe in our comparative review below of economic policy by Communist parties, military dictatorships and their successor democratic governments.

Thus, the long-term economic irony is that the prospects for 'another' national development by any other political means, whether separately or together, are not good. On the contrary, these prospects are now quite bad for the *under*developing Third World regions of Eastern Europe and the republics of the former Soviet Union. Independent of their national ideology or state policy, the future is bleak and in some cases even worse for most underdeveloping Third World regions.

The Recent Economic Irrelevance of Political Ideology

The 1980s marked the transition in much of the East and the South from the ideology of 'development' to that of 'democracy.'

Yet these same 1980s also should have demonstrated the irrelevance of national political ideologies in an international world economy.

The most important international and national economic and political policies adopted and implemented around the world during the l980s were often contrary to the 'dominant' ideologies. These in turn were largely irrelevant to the necessary political economic responses to world economic conditions beyond anyone's control. In my review of the revolutions in Eastern Europe in l989 (Frank l990a) and in my answer to Francis Fukuyama (Frank l990b), I sought to demonstrate that Fukuyama's ideological thesis that 'in the long run ideology wins out over the material world' was belied by material reality. The latter proved the opposite in recent years – and threatens to do so again in the future:

In the 1970s, the same export/import-led growth strategies were adopted by Communist Party-led governments in the East (Poland, Romania, Hungary) and military dictatorships in the South (Argentina, Brazil, Chile).

In the l980s, the same debt service policies on the IMF model were adopted and implemented by Communist Party-led governments in the East (Poland, Hungary, Romania, Yugoslavia) and by military dictatorships, other authoritarian governments, *and their successor democratic governments* in the South (Argentina, Brazil, Mexico, Philippines).

There were variations on the theme of debt service, but it is difficult to correlate, let alone explain, them by reference to the political colour or ideologies of regimes or governments: The most stellar pupil of the IMF was Nicolae Ceaucescu in Romania, who actually reduced the debt until the lights went out, first for his people and then for himself. In Peru, on the other hand, the newly elected President Alan Garcia defied the IMF and announced he would limit debt service to no more than 10 per cent of export earnings. Actually, they were less than that before he assumed office. Then they rose to more than 10 per cent under his presidency. Real income fell by about half, and the novelist Vargas Llosa sought to succeed to the presidency after moving from the political Centre-Left to the extreme Right. But what does that mean, if anything? The Peruvian people voted *against* Vargas Llosa, elected Fujimori – and got 'Fujishock'. The economic policies of President Fujimori have been exactly the ones his rival offered – and which his voters rejected. Afterwards came cholera – and a *coup détat* by this same President.

Communist General Jaruselski in Poland and the populist Sandinistas in Nicaragua also imposed IMF-style 'adjustment' and 'conditionality' on their people. Both did so *without* the benefit of pressure from the IMF, since Poland was not a member and Nicaragua had no access to it. In Nicaragua, there was *condicionalidad sin fondo*, that is conditionality without the Fund and without any bottom or end to the Sisyphian policy. Hungary had the most reformed economy and the most liberal political policy still led by a communist party in the Warsaw Pact. Yet Hungary paid off the early 1980s principal of its debt three times over – and meanwhile doubled the amount still owed. That is more than is owed by Poland or Brazil or Mexico, who on average paid off the amount of debt owed only once or twice, while at the same time increasing their totals only twice. No matter, the *Solidarnosc* government that replaced General Jaruselski and the Communist Party in Poland benefited from IMF membership and imposed even more severe economic sacrifices on its population than its predecessors had.

So was economic policy any different in the 'socialist' East before the arrival of democracy – or for that matter is it now that democracy has 'finally' arrived in Eastern Europe? Take Poland for instance. Why did the governments of the Communists Gomulka and Gierek, the Communist General Jaruselski and *Solidarnosc's* Prime Minister Mazowiescki *all* implement the same anti-popular policies? Indeed, *Solidarnosc* and the Communists proposed essentially the same weak economic reforms in l981 before General Jaruselski imposed martial law on 13 December. At that time he lacked the political power to impose even the *Solidarnosc*-sponsored reforms, because he was governing with martial law instead of the people's will, as represented by *Solidarnosc*. Where and what was the democratic expression of that when *Solidarnosc* was in power (or rather in government) and was using its popular goodwill to force even more drastic anti-popular economic belt-tightening on the population than the previous government had? The same question might be asked of governments, democratically elected or not, in Hungary and elsewhere. In Hungary's first free elections, all parties agreed to follow the IMF prescriptions after the election.

So are there any 'ideological' lessons to be learned from the comparisons and patterns of these economic policies – or successes and failures? Well yes, some: In the cases of Latin America and South-East Asia, it is still possible to appeal to 'nationalism', 'anti-imperialism' and sometimes even to 'socialism' to voice and mobilise popular opposition to these political economic austerity polices. Nowhere is that now possible in Eastern Europe – since 'socialism is a failure' and the Communist parties are discredited. They engineered the domestic economic crisis in the first place and then implemented the debt service and austerity policies. And of course, they were subservient instruments of Russian imperialism. So nobody could appeal to them or their policies. On the other hand, the West represents the future. Moreover, the Western IMF and its policies were the 'secret weapon' and 'de facto ally' of the opposition groups. They are now in power or making their bid for it thanks primarily to the economic crisis and secondarily to the political crisis, which was engendered by the implementation of these austerity 'adjustment' policies with IMF support. So now there is not only no economic but also no political alternative to further austerity policies, which are tied to IMF and other Western advice and conditions.

The economic crisis has been expanding and deepening in Eastern Europe and the republics formerly in the Soviet Union. The economic crisis and related economic factors contributed materially to the desire and ability of these social (and also ethnic/nationalist) movements to mobilise so many people at this time for such far-reaching political ends. The decade of the 1980s, indeed beginning in the mid-1970s, is now called 'the period of stagnation' in Soviet history; accelerating economic crisis and absolute deterioration of living standards in most of Eastern Europe (as also in Latin America, Africa and some other parts of the world, vide Frank 1988) were its features. Significantly, especially in Eastern Europe, this period also marked an important deterioration and retrocession in its *relative* competitive standing and standards of living compared to Western Europe, and even to the newly industrialising countries (NICs) in East Asia.

Moreover, the course and (mis)management of the economic crisis generated shifts in positions of dominance or privilege and dependency or exploitation among countries, sectors, and different social (including gender) and ethnic groups within the former Soviet Union and Eastern Europe. All of these economic changes and pressures generated or fuelled social discontent, demands and mobilisation, which expressed themselves through enlivened social (and ethnic/nationalist) movements – with a variety of similarities and differences among them. It is well known that economically based resentment is fed by the loss of 'accustomed' absolute standards of living as a whole or in particular items *and* by related relative shifts in economic welfare among population groups. Most economic crises are polarising, further enriching, relatively if not also absolutely, the better off; and further impoverishing, both relatively and absolutely, those who were already worst off, especially women.

Thus, the momentous economic and political changes of *perestroika* and *glasnost* in the former Soviet Union and Eastern Europe and therewith the end of the Cold War did not simply emerge, like Pallas Athene out of Zeus, from the head of Mikhail Gorbachev. He said himself that they were 'inevitable'. As (economic) necessity is the mother of (political) invention, had Gorbachev himself not existed, he would have had to be invented. His pragmatic praxis outpaced and overturned ideological preconceptions, including his own and those of his opponents at home and abroad. The exigencies of the world economy generated all manner of pragmatic praxis and political ironies in the 1980s.

The political irony is that 'actually existing socialism' failed not least because of the unsuccessful implementation of import/export-led growth models and IMF-style austerity policies in the East. 'Actually existing capitalism' pursued the same models and policies in the South and also failed. However, nobody in the West or East says so; and nobody in the South any longer has a plausible 'socialist alternative' to offer. Why was there a 'change of system' in (part of) the East in the face of failure, but none in the South in the face of the same failure? Jeanne Kirkpatrick was wrong when she said that 'totalitarian' countries in the East don't change, while 'authoritarian' ones in the West do. Actually, it is arguable whether in either case there was any 'change of system', or an 'end of history'. The new democratic regimes will be able to resist and counter the exigencies of the world economy even less than their totalitarian predecessors could.

The Privatisation Craze

Another example of ideological confusion is the currently fashionable 'privatisation', which is also identified with 'democracy'. Unfortunately, this ideologically promoted privatisation is no remedy for the ills of Central/Eastern Europe, any more than stabilisation and privatisation policies have been for the ills of Latin America and elsewhere. Indeed, during the present worldwide recession, these privatisation policies can only socialise and aggravate poverty further.

The current privatisation craze is just as economically irrational and politically ideological as was the earlier nationalisation craze. It makes very little difference whether an enterprise is owned privately or publicly; for all have to compete with each other on equal terms in the world market. The only exceptions to this rule are public enterprises that are subsidised by the state budget, and private enterprises that are also subsidised from the state budget and/or are otherwise bailed out 'in the public interest'. Well-known examples in the

United States are Detroit's Chrysler Corporation; Chicago's Continental Bank and Trust Company (at the time the eighth largest US bank); the Ohio, Maryland, California and Texas Savings & Loans; and even New York city. Moreover, in the market, public and private enterprises can both make equally good and bad investments and other management decisions. In the 1970s, (public) British Steel over-invested badly and (private) US Steel underinvested badly. In the 1980s, both firms closed down steel mills over the public objections of labour. So did the private steel industry in Germany under a Christian Democratic government and the public steel industry in France under a Socialist government.

Privatising public enterprises in the East and South now at bargain basement share prices that double in the first week on the national stock exchange is just as fraudulent a practice as nationalising loss-making enterprises and paying for them above market value, or nationalising profitable enterprises with little or no indemnification. This 'now you see it, now you don't' game is all the more egregious in the case of enterprises in the East and the South which are now privatised and bought up with devalued domestic currency purchased (or swapped for debt) by foreign companies or joint ventures with foreign exchange from abroad. In sum, the privatisation debate is a sham; it is far less about productive efficiency than about distributive (in)justice.*

Does Freedom of the Market Equal Democratic Freedom?

At first sight, it is curious how free market 'capitalism' and electoral political 'democracy' are now fashionably identified as though they were inseparable, if not indistinguishable.** On further consideration, however', this new fashion may be little more than a way to

---

* *Editor's note*: In October 1992 the Adam Smith Institute in London published a report on privatisation and reform in post-communist European republics (*Eastern Promise*, Paul Reynolds and Peter Young). This report concludes that initial expectations of privatisation within four to five years were 'wildly optimistic'. It predicts a scenario wherein 'The reform process will become politically and socially unsustainable and will be abandoned ... causing major economic and political destabilisation.' The authors reject privatisation as a panacea and suggest that the example of East Asian exporters be emulated for competing successfully in world markets.

** *Editor's note*: see Chapter 3 in this volume by Samir Amin, 'The Issue of Democracy in the Contemporary Third World'.

sell more 'capitalist' market inequality and disempowerment dressed up as 'democratic' self-determination.

Like money, electoral democracy appears very desirable, especially when one does not have any. Then it is easy to appreciate such things as the coming of elections among multiple parties and a free press to debate political and other options. This is particularly the case in the formerly 'socialist' East, where oppressive Communist Party bureaucracies and foreign domination hamstrung economic development and political expression. The return of electoral democracy is also welcome in those parts of the South, in the Americas and South-East Asia, where military or other authoritarian regimes have run the economy into a hole of debt. The human cost has been, first, tens of thousands of assassinations, disappearances and torture, and then increased hunger, disease, infant mortality and crime. A whole generation suffers from tragically reduced life opportunities. It should not be necessary to point out that all this has been quantitatively and qualitatively worse in the (capitalist) South than in the 'socialist' East. However, the new democracies offer little hope to reverse this human tragedy.

In the face of this material world history, some people may well wish now to associate democracy with the free market and/or capitalism. In the East, most people associate capitalism with promises of a bright future. In the South, however, capitalism is associated with bitter experience past and present. In some countries, the dismal state of the economy again threatens the democratic state. Unfortunately, the Poles, for instance, are already experiencing the same bitter fruits of market democracy (cum debt) as the Argentinians, Brazilians and Filipinos have in recent years.

On the other hand, the 'successes' of the East Asian NICs and Japan have scarcely been associated with much electoral democracy. Japan has had elections, but the Liberal Democratic Party (LDP) has been unalterably dominant almost as long as the Institutional Revolutionary Party (PRI) has in Mexico. Moreover, the LDP and PRI factions do not reflect alternatives of political choice as much as of personal leadership. South Korea, Taiwan and Singapore have prospered under completely authoritarian regimes, which are only now beginning to yield in response to economic success. In Hong Kong, of course, there is still no question of any kind of political democracy being granted by the mainland Chinese. The Hong Kong Chinese, on the contrary, demand democratic self-determination.

In North America, Western Europe and more recently in parts of Southern Europe and Oceania, political social democracy has been much less the cause than the effect of economic success in the capitalist market – and importantly so in the *world* capitalist market. These countries in the West have been able to afford the precious luxury of electoral political democracy only where and when the basis of their economic wealth afforded it to them. It is of course delicate and controversial to point out that without a regime of West/South relations based on 'imperialism' and 'colonialism' in the past and 'unequal exchange' to this day, the West would not have been able to gain and maintain its basic economic wealth, income, social democracy – and therewith also political democracy. Unfortunately for them, the 'socialist' countries in the East were only very moderately able to benefit from such inflows of income from the South. The reasons for this failure have less to do with the inadequacies of socialist planning at home than with their inadequate insertion in the world market abroad. As for the dependent South, it has long suffered economically, socially and politically from the support that it affords to economic development and political democracy in the West.

The Third World is of course the clearest case of the failure of electoral popular democracy to govern the material world or to implement its own economic policy. Where was the democratic governance over the material world or even of economic policy by, of and for the people of Argentina in the elected governments of Mrs Perón, the Junta generals from Videla to Galtieri, and the elected presidents Alfonsín and then Menem? All of them implemented one unpopular economic austerity policy or another. All failed to satisfy both the consumer desires of the people and the producer development of the nation/country/state. After a crisis already a decade and a half long, in 1989 national income declined by another 10 per cent and the people's income declined by 50 per cent. In the 1980s, the share of wages and salaries declined from 50 per cent to 20 per cent of national income. Now the populist Peronist President Menem is imposing even more austere economic policies than his predecessor Alfonsín did.

In Peru, under the democratically elected President Alan García, national income declined by 20 per cent in 1989 and the people of the social democratic APRA's income probably by more than 50 per cent. Is that the 'democratic' governance over the material world by, of and for the people? As noted above, the Peruvians voted against the IMF stabilisation policy offered by the 'dead cert' candidate Vargas Llosa and elected the 'dark horse' Alberto Fujimori instead. Dark horse indeed, for they got the 'Fujishock' of their lives when the new President implemented the very economic policy his rival had threatened and the electorate had rejected.

In Central America, the economic crisis has ravaged the economies of all countries about equally, irrespective of democracy in Costa Rica, more or less veiled military power behind the thrones of the elected presidents in El Salvador and Guatemala, or formerly the 'Marxist socialism' in Sandinista-governed Nicaragua, which implemented *condicionalidad sin fondo* of its own accord, as observed above. Of course, the US-sponsored Contra war had helped shoot up the rate of inflation beyond 30,000 per cent a year anyway.

The Nicaraguans were presented with a choice between continuation of conscription and the war (threatened by Bush against the Sandinistas) and money (offered by Bush to Chamorro). The Nicaraguan people chose money and peace. Yet, the winning side delivered only some of the peace but none of the money it promised. The Panamanian-'elected' and American-installed President Endara went on a Lenten fast/hunger strike in an attempt to get the money he says he was promised for his people. Due to the embargo and then to the invasion, Panamanians now suffer from 50 per cent unemployment. Little wonder – or is it? – that the East Germans, like the Nicaraguans and any normal electorate, also voted with their pocketbooks. But to how much avail? They became a dependent economic colony of the West and got 2 million, going on 3 million, unemployed which they had not bargained for.

Why did all these electorates vote with their pocketbooks? Because they had no better choice. Yet their Hobson's choice and their elected governments completely failed all these and other electorates. Why did and do *all* these governments follow essentially the *same* economic policies in the face of the same material economic circumstances? They all did so, because they *had to*, with the possible exception of the Kohl government in (West) Germany, which may still have had some less costly options it declined to use. That is, these governments all *had to* do not what 'the people' wanted, but what economic circumstances demanded. However, it was not simply the 'national' economy and its wealth or poverty constraints on the exercise of the popular will that were determinant for the policy 'choices' that were and are made. It was and is first and foremost the *dependence within the world economy* which sets out the narrow margins of 'democratic' choice and policy. So is there really a 'democratic end (of evolution) of history'? Or does the electorate only choose the political leaders on each of 100-odd 'sovereign' national houseboats, which float on an ocean of changing economic currents and recurrent storm crises, over which governments have no control whatsoever? Even the steward and/or the passengers who might have rearranged the chairs on the deck of the *Titanic* had more 'democratic' powers of self-determined choice by, of and for the people. However, on the *Titanic* 80 per cent of fourth-class passengers died; 60 per cent of third-class; 40 per cent of second-class; 20 per cent of first-class. The rich and powerful at least have a 'democratic' first choice, both on the *Titanic* and elsewhere. Money talks louder than idea(l)s.

So when Fukuyama says that 'we have to recognise that an important revolution is under way in the world, and in that revolution, ideas count', (Fukuyama 1989), we should exercise a bit more care than he does to recognise just what ideas that may be and why they count. It is an ideological cover-up to claim that what is happening in Germany and elsewhere is done first and foremost in the good ideological name of democracy or even secondarily in the bad ideological name of nationalism. Both ideologies serve to cover up both rank materialist motives and real material forces. In this regard as well, Fukuyama's thesis (Fukuyama 1992) cannot stand up to the evidence – or even to much of his own analysis.

There is little material basis, if any, to expect significant improvements in these economic-political relationships in the world economy in the foreseeable future. On the contrary, material development in the world economy is likely to make matters worse in the short and medium/long term. As long as the debt burden continues and even mounts in the near future, the debt-ridden economies in the South will continue to suffer and the debt will continue to threaten their democracies. Alas, the same is true of the new or aspiring, but still debt-ridden, democracies of Poland, Hungary and elsewhere in Eastern Europe. Any financial arrangement *à la* IMF, or even the commercial terms for the new European Bank for Reconstruction and Development, can inevitably only maintain and aggravate these burdens and dangers. Such policies would extend the same burdens and dangers to other parts of Central and Eastern Europe and perhaps to the Baltic republics.

World economic material and labour-saving long-run development is furthering marginalisation of ever larger parts of the Third World along African lines. However, industrial and agricultural progress and decline in the West are also marginalising growing parts of its population into racial, ethnic and drug- and crime-ridden ghettoes. Now that massive unemployment, increased regional differentiation and social polarisation are also coming to the East, it too is threatened by the same kind of economic, social and political marginalisation. Indeed, in southern parts of the Balkans and the ex-Soviet Union, not to mention western and other parts of China, this marginalisation is already making its mark.

So it is hardly the case that market and democracy, or economic and political freedom, always go together. In fact, the opposite could be argued equally well. In an electoral democracy, it is one man (now, fortunately, one person), one vote. In the market, it is one dollar, one vote. That is, many dollars, many votes; no dollars, no vote. Indeed, those who have or can earn only few or no dollars at home are marginalised not only from voting economically, but tend to be also excluded from voting politically. It is no accident that the most marginalised poor vote the least in elections. In the United States 50 per cent of the poor vote, while the homeless have no residence and therefore not even the right to vote.

Similarly, those who have no or earn only few dollars abroad, but only pesos or zlotys at home, are also marginalised, both economically and politically, in the world system, unless they now have marks or yen. The yearly 'Economic' (actually, political) summits of the Group of Seven (G-7) offer a vivid illustration of this principle. They illustrate it all the more so, since the 'G-5' only admit Canada and Italy into their circle by traditional *noblesse oblige*. Moreover, the charmed circle of real decision makers is limited to the 'G-3' governments or central banks of only the United States, Germany and Japan, with even those of Britain and France on the outside looking in. There is also a wider sort of consultatory circle of 24 OECD (Organization for Economic Co-operation and Development) industrialised countries, with some voice but no vote. In the political economic councils of the world outside the UN General Assembly's talking chamber, the rest of (wo)mankind, however, who live in the 'Third' and 'Second' Worlds in the South and East, have no real voice or vote.

What is worse, the market not only excludes the already dollarless from this political influence at home and abroad. The operation of the market is both domestically and internationally polarising, making the rich richer and the poor poorer – and thus even more marginalised. The Bible tells us that this is not a recent fact of life when it observes that 'to those that hath, shall be given; and from those that hath not, shall be taken;' even the little economic and political power that they have. Of course, the market, like a lottery, does offer the opportunity to some, and the illusion to many, to win a better position in it, mostly through the exercise of some temporary monopoly power, legal or illegal, moral or immoral. *That* opportunity is what makes the market – and the lottery – so attractive to so many, including the losers. The latter, however, also have one other political option to press their case to be heard: they can and do mobilise themselves through social movements to exercise another form of democracy.

Sovereign Democracy in a Global Economy: a Contradiction in Terms

Thus, the operation of the global economy precludes the exercise of real national sovereignty and the implementation of truly democratic decisions by the people, of the people and for the people, especially in Third World countries. The reasons for this impossibility of liberal representative democracy are many, and we can here recall only a few, which are internal and external to the countries concerned.

Even the best of newly democratically elected parliaments can be no more than an ineffective talk shop if its powers are limited by a constitution and/or a judiciary, as well as parts of the executive branch that are holdovers from a previous undemocratic regime. That is the case today in Chile, for instance. General Pinochet deliberately had the constitution written so that it would preclude the exercise of democracy. The judiciary is also a holdover from his dictatorship and continues to rule or threaten to rule all sorts of democratic initiatives to be unconstitutional or otherwise illegal. General Pinochet himself continues as Commander-in-Chief of the army and has publicly declared that the army is independent of and not subject to the control of the democratically elected President, not to mention the Parliament. Just before leaving the presidential office, moreover, General Pinochet also introduced changes into the administration of the economy in general and the Central Bank in particular, which intentionally and effectively preclude both parliamentary and presidential influence over a whole series of vital economic decisions. However, this was only some icing on the cake; for the new democratic government in Chile, just as elsewhere, is in any case obliged to continue pursuing the same economic policies as those initiated by its undemocratic military predecessors.

Indeed, these specifically Chilean arrangements are only particular examples of widespread general limitations to the exercise of democracy by, of and for the people. The most obvious general limitation is that imposed by the generals themselves. All around the Third World, from the Philippines through South and West Asia, throughout Africa, and in Latin America, armed military power continues to stand behind the new democratic throne. Democratically elected governments in Pakistan, Thailand, Haiti and Peru were recently again overthrown by their armies. President Aquino in the Philippines and both Presidents Alfonsín and Menem in Argentina suffered various military coup attempts. Civilian presidents, not to mention the legislatures, in El Salvador and Guatemala are powerless in the face of the effective power of their military forces. In Brazil and elsewhere in Latin America as well as throughout Africa, the options of any civilian government are conditioned and limited by the ever-present threat of governing under a military sword of Damocles. That sword may fall again elsewhere, as it did in Thailand, Pakistan, Haiti and Peru. These military forces and their commanding officers were often trained by, and are still under manifold influence of, Western powers. However, even if they were not, these militaries would still be an arm of the anything but democratic economic elites of their respective countries. They did and continue to pursue economic policies which are in their own and their foreign partners' interests. These policies are certainly not designed or implemented in the interests of the majority of the people or in accordance with the desires they express through their democratic votes. Democratically elected parliaments and almost all democratically elected presidents and their ministers are not in a position to pursue any alternative economic policies.

However, the greatest structural limitation to the exercise of democratic policy by, of and for the people is their participation and place in a world economy over which they have and can have no control. To put it the other way around, effective democracy is limited indeed if it extends only to the formulation and implementation of relatively unimportant domestic political policy, and it is barred from effective intervention in the most important economic policy decisions, which are made outside the range of democracy by, of and for the people. What is worse, the economic policy of others elsewhere not only conditions the economic policy of the government at home, but that foreign economic policy may also intervene directly in the political process and the very nature of the government at home.

We may briefly review only two related examples of American economic policy decisions, which had far-reaching worldwide economic and political consequences. The October 1979 decision by the Chairman of the US Federal Reserve, Paul Volcker, to raise the rate of interest and thereby also to increase the value of the dollar was the single most important cause of the debt crisis and consequently the depression and 'lost decade' of the 1980s in much of the Third World. The same decision also promoted the recession, which began in 1979 and helped elect Ronald Reagan to the presidency. By law, the American electorate and Congress, and even the American President, have no right to intervene in such a decision by the Federal Reserve. Law and political 'sovereignty', as well as all economic reality, prevent any democratic or other influence by, of or for the people in any part of the Third World on any such decision which is vitally determinant of the economic welfare and political options for its people.

The Reaganomic response to the 1979–82 recession at the American presidency and Congress then set the stage for the major events in the world of the 1980s and into the 1990s. Contrary to the ideology of 'getting the government off our backs' and eliminating the US deficit and debt, Reaganomic military Keynesianism increased the budget deficit, promoted the trade deficit, trippled the foreign US debt to $3 trillion, and already in 1986 had converted the United States into the world's greatest foreign debtor. However, the pump-priming demand created through heightened military expenditures and domestic and foreign borrowing for the same by the United States maintained afloat not only its own economy in the 1980s, but also that of the entire West and of the East Asian NICs to boot. The costs were borne unwittingly and unwillingly by the then Soviet Union, Eastern Europe, the Middle East, Africa and Latin America, among others. The world recession since 1979, together with American economic policy, had already occasioned the decline in the Soviet Union's sources of foreign exchange through the export of oil and gold. Then, President Reagan's military spending on Star Wars and in support of 'regional' armed insurgencies against the governments of Afghanistan, Ethiopia, Mozambique, Angola, Nicaragua and others outcompeted the Soviet Union into bankruptcy and currency inflation. *Perestroika* and its failure, as well as the end of the Cold War and of the Soviet Union itself, were the economic and political results.

So was the 'revolution of 1989' in Eastern Europe. Its 'socialist' economies were caught up in the same debt crisis as Latin America and Africa, as we observed above. Eastern Europe suffered severe recession, and both Africa and Latin America experienced severe depression in the 1980s and sharp declines in their ability to compete in the world economy, if only because investment in new technology and human capital as well as social services were sacrificed to servicing the increased foreign debt.

In all three regions, the authoritarian governments and regimes that (mis)managed this economic and therefore also political crisis became totally discredited. Then they were, or are now being, replaced by 'democratic' ones instead – which have to continue to manage the same economic crisis. In the 1990s, severe economic depression is ravaging the republics of the former Soviet Union and Eastern Europe as well, without yet letting up in Africa and Latin America. China and India escaped many of the consequences of the crisis in the 1980s. However, their economies nonetheless suffered as they opened up to the world economy. Thus, China and India are now in more critical positions and may still also be visited by serious recession or depression in the 1990s. Moreover, the renewed world recession since the early 1990s could yet turn into a depression in the West as well.

Thus, Reaganomics and Thatcherism not only were supposed to, but also did, hit the poor hard, and much of the middle classes as well. However, the polarising effects of Reaganomics, Thatcherism and their carbon copies elsewhere which made the rich richer and the poor poorer were not limited to any 'domestic' or 'national' economies. The consequences were worldwide. In a single world economy, these are the costs borne by the weakest to support the benefits and policies of the strongest.

Yet no national, let alone world, electorate or democratically elected national or world parliament was ever given an opportunity to choose between this world-polarising economy and policy or any possible alternative. Liberal parliamentary democracy in scores of countries – and democracy in 100 countries – was even less able to!

To exercise any real democratic government by the people, of the people and for the people anywhere in the world, they would at a minimum have to have a vote for the American Congress and President, who make many of the economic and political decisions that vitally affect the interests of the peoples of the world. Yet, not even the 'foreign' right to vote in American elections would be sufficient to afford democratic control. For not even American voters can control Federal Reserve economic policy; and now its policy is also subject to conditions set by the Bank of Japan and the German Bundesbank – which in turn are also not subject even to their own electorates.

However, even the economic policies of the G-7, the G-3 or the G-1 are not autonomous, let alone democratically controlled. For if they were or could be, these policies could and would prevent the recurring recessions and inflations that they are 'supposed to' prevent or at least ameliorate. In fact, however, the course of the world economy is beyond the control of any and all policy makers, who mostly respond too little and too late and/or only make matters worse. (The *Washington Post*'s former financial correspondent Bernard Nossiter demonstrated this in his *Fat Years and Lean: The American Economy Since Roosevelt*, reviewed in Frank 1992a). If that is the sad record of economic policy makers in the centre(s) of the world economy, economic policy makers in the Third World periphery – including the (ex) 'Second World socialist countries'– are *afortiori* out to lunch when it comes to making and implementing economic policy.

Thus, the people or even their 'democratic' government in any Third World (and ex-Second World, now Third-Worldising) country lack the slightest control or even influence over the economy or economic policy at home, let alone abroad or in the world economy as a whole. So what sort of 'democracy' is that, which does not afford the people control or even influence over the most vital events and decisions affecting their lives? This liberal electoral democracy in 'sovereign' countries is still better than none at all of course, but it is not real democracy by the people, of the people and for the people in Lincoln's sense. Nor can it be. This sort of democracy can, however, especially when newly introduced after a long dictatorship, give some people a brief illusion of power and self-determination – until reality catches up with them, as it is already doing in Argentina, Poland and elsewhere.

Participatory Civil Democracy

Thus, liberal electoral democracy is not the be all and end all – even of democracy, let alone of history or its idea. Another increasingly important part of democracy are the non-party social movements, particularly in civil society, or what may be called participatory 'civil democracy' (Fuentes and Frank 1989; Frank and Fuentes 1990).

In the absence of political democracy in the East and also but less successfully so in the South, people had massive recourse to civil democratic social movements to lay the basis for electoral party democracy in the first place. All the New, Civic and other Forum movements in the former East Germany, Czechoslovakia and Hungary sought to maintain their identity and independence from the new political parties. Yet all these movements were soon overwhelmed by the electoral process and the imperatives of running the state.

Perhaps the blessings of multiple political parties (Hungary quickly had 50 of them!), elections and parliaments appear so important after so many years without them, that people tend to neglect the other equally important processes and institutions of civil democracy. In Latin America, social movements had less impact on bringing forth the turn to electoral democracy. However, they have also survived more and better since the onset of these democratic governments, since they are more concerned with people's economic survival, the threat to which remains or even grows.

It remains to be seen, however, whether the electoral and parliamentary democracy now touted by Fukuyama (Fukuyama 1992) and others can offer more opportunities for popular self-determination than this participatory civil democracy did. It can be argued that the new *de jure* electoral and parliamentary state institutions *in fact* serve effectively to *dis*enfranchise people in Eastern Europe and parts of the Third World, such as the Philippines and South Korea, again after their massive exercise of participatory democracy. How much democratic self-determination, *contra* Fukuyama, can these institutions guarantee and afford the people, especially if their economies are Third World-ised?

Therefore, it would be tragic now to abandon the conquest of this civil democracy to the blessings of the exercise only of political democracy through political parties, which contest elections for a government to run the state (as best it can under the external and domestic economic constraints).

For in the West and the South, civil democracy increasingly complements political democracy everywhere, precisely because of the limitations of the electoral process organised through political parties. Social movements arise and mobilise people for myriad economic, social, cultural and political causes and demands of the population, which elections and the government cannot provide or do not offer without the popular pressure exercised through this civil democracy. Indeed, it is again the economic crisis, especially in the South, which obliges people to organise and mobilise themselves in grass-roots social movements. These movements promote participant democracy and alternative production and distribution to defend livelihood and identity against the ravages of the economy and the neglect or domination by the state. Of course, as observed above, it was also first and foremost the economic crisis in Eastern Europe and the old Soviet Union which fuelled the social movements to demand and achieve some economic *perestroika* and political *glasnost* there. The need for the same or other social movements acting in and through civil society will also remain after the installation of elected governments based on political parties.

At the same time, such social movements in civil society, no less and often more than political parties in government, will also represent regional and ethnic or nationalist interests and demands. The best we can hope for is that each will recognise the others' equal right to existence within the political institutions of the state and the international community of states. The world's worst fears have been realised in the former states of Yugoslavia and the Soviet Union, where ethnic and nationlist groups have engaged in a renewed armed battle with each other in another process of balkanisation. However, this resurgence of nationalist and ethnic authoritarianism is the fruit of the aggravation of the same crisis in the world economy and especially in its Southern and Eastern sectors, for which economic privatisation and political democracy are now being ideologically sold and bought as the final sure-fire snake oil remedies, when in reality there is no end to history.

Summary

Like money, democracy is very desirable, especially when one does not have any. However, also like money, democratic decisions that are only in the hands of 'them' and not 'us' may also be used as instruments of oppression and exploitation. That is certainly the case when effective democratic control, like money, is monopolised by the few against the many. That is also precisely what the market does, especially the world market. The (world) market concentrates both money and decisions, democratic or otherwise, in the hands of the few at the expense of the many. The spread of political democracy in the South and East, however welcome for other reasons, is not powerful enough to impede, countermand, counteract, let alone eliminate, the economic forces operating in the world economy. These economic forces are far more determinant of people's welfare than their own decisions or those of their democratically elected governments. Moreover, many of these world economic forces are largely beyond anyone's control. Some of the appeal to political democracy is a cover-up for the inability to manage their own affairs, to which people in these democracies are exposed. Participant civil democracy in civil society is the people's answer and their alternative instrument of struggle.

References
Amin, Samir 1990. *Delinking: Towards a Polycentric World*. London, Zed Books.
Bello, W. and Rosenfeld, S. 1990. *Dragons in Distress*. San Francisco, Institute for Food and Development Policy.
Frank, Andre Gunder 1967. *Capitalism and Underdevelopment in Latin America*. New York, Monthly Review Press.
—— 1988. 'American Roulette in the Globonomic Casino: Retrospect and Prospect on the World Economic Crisis Today' in Paul Zarembka, (ed.), *Research in Political Economy*. Greenwich, JAI Press, pp. 3–43.
—— 1990a. 'Revolution in Eastern Europe: Lessons for Democratic Socialist Movements (and Socialists)' in Tabb, William K. (ed.) *The Future of Socialism: Perspectives from the Left*. New York, Monthly

Review Press, pp. 87–105. Also in: *Third World Quarterly* (London) XII, 2, April, pp. 36-52.

—— 1990b. 'No End to History! History to No End?' *Social Justice*, San Francisco, vol. 17, no. 4, December. Also *ENDpapers 21*, Nottingham, no. 21, autumn, pp. 52-71.

—— 1991b. 'The Underdevelopment of Development', *Scandinavian Journal of Development Alternatives*, Sept. X(3): 5–72. Published in Spanish in an expanded version as *El Subdesarrollo del Desarrollo: Ensayo Autobiografico con una Bibliografia de sus Publicaciones*. Caracas, Editorial Nueva Sociedad.

—— 1992a. Review of Bernard Nossiter's 'Fat Years and Lean: The American Economy Since Roosevelt', *Z Magazine*, Boston 5(1): 63–6.

—— 1992b. 'The Centrality of Central Asia', *Studies in History*, New Delhi, VIII(1): 43–97. Also in *Comparative Asian Studies*, Free University Press for Center for Asian Studies Amsterdam, Feb. no. 8: p. 68.

Frank, A.G. and Fuentes, M. 1990. 'Social Movements in World History' in S. Amin, G. Arrighi, A.G. Frank and I. Wallerstein (eds), *Transforming the Revolution. Social Movements and the World-System*.

Fuentes, M. and Frank, A.G. 1989. 'Ten Theses on Social Movements', *World Development* XVII, 2, February.

Fukuyama, Francis 1989. 'The End of History?', *The National Interest*, 16 (summer), pp. 3-18.

—— 1992. *The End of History and the Last Man*. London, Hamish Hamilton.

3. The Issue of Democracy in the Contemporary Third World*

SAMIR AMIN

The recent past has shown a global trend to democratisation of political regimes on a scale that may well become irreversible. In the socialist countries the trend has been forced upon the powers that be; they must acknowledge and adapt to its demands or perish. In Third World capitalist countries the call for democracy has not reached the same popular dimension and is frequently limited to the middle classes and segments of organised urban society – unions, for example. However, even on such a narrow scale the trend signals a qualitative leap in the extent to which democratic consciousness has penetrated the political system of a great many Third World countries. In the West a broad consensus embracing governments, public opinion and the media has emerged in support of this trend, particularly where it appears in the countries of the East and sometimes in the Third World – in the latter instance according to the reasons of state of interested parties.

This democratic trend has appeared concomitantly with another global evolution emerging in the 1970s and more so in the 1980s: a kind of generalised offensive for the liberation of 'market forces', aimed at the ideological rehabilitation of the absolute superiority of private property, legitimation of social inequalities and anti-statism of all kinds, and so on. Neoliberalism – the name given to the offensive – knows no frontiers and is deemed to have worldwide validity. 'Openness' (to capital and to 'information', that is, the dominant media) is synonymous with essential progress. Established powers everywhere seem to be falling in with the trend: in the West where social democracy has, in practice, lined up with the supposed demands

---

*This article is a contribution to a debate on the issue of democracy begun in the pages of the CODESRIA journal, *Africa Development*, No. 1, 1988. Translation from the French was by Michael Wolfers. It appeared in *Socialism and Democracy*, 12 (January) 1991, pp. 83–104. The editors would like to thank *Socialism and Democracy* for permission to reprint the article here. The essay is reproduced in the original version, written before the rapid collapse of many Communist regimes in 1989-90.

of this 'rationality' of the open market; in the Third World where the radical nationalist regimes all now seem prehistoric; and even in the socialist countries where entire sections of the ruling class have passed – or are in the throes of passing – from tactical retreat from their 'Marxism' to the revision or abandonment of it.

The coincidence of these two trends makes ours an era of intense confusion. The preponderant tolling of the bell, systematically drowning out all discordant voices and orchestrated by an unprecedented media campaign, sounds like a simple, unqualified, unilateral affirmation, taken to be self-evident.

The 'market' – a euphemism for capitalism – is regarded as the central axis of any 'development', and such development is seen as part of an 'ineluctable worldwide expansion'. The desirability of total openness to the forces governing worldwide evolution and simultaneous adoption of an internal system based on the 'market' are taken to be self-evident. Democratisation is considered the necessary and natural product of submission to the rationality of the worldwide market. A simple dual equation is deduced from this logic: capitalism = democracy, democracy = capitalism. By the same token, socialism is pronounced dead (and Marx of course along with it); its failure is complete, it has proven synonymous with inefficiency and autocracy. Similarly, 'national liberation' is proclaimed obsolete; 'nationalism' is accused of necessarily engendering a fatal backwardness in the sphere of international competition. These unilateral propositions, simple to the point of being simplistic and without scientific or historical foundations, seem to confuse even the ranks of those who in the socialist countries and the Third World fight for democratisation and social progress.

Three issues are worth examination in formulating a response to the questions raised by the democratic movement operating in the context of the capitalist offensive:

1.   the character of the new stage of capitalist transnationalisation – the issue here being whether openness to the exterior has in fact become 'ineluctable';
2.   the crisis of actually existing capitalism – the issue here being whether the crisis calls Marxism and socialism into question;
3.   finally, the various aspects of the relationship between democracy and social progress under contemporary Third World conditions.

The internal logic of the argument suggests tackling the three issues in that order, as the response to the first has implications for the others. This paper deals with the issue of democracy in the con-

temporary Third World and I shall make only brief mention of preliminary matters expanded elsewhere. I shall signal only such of my
conclusions as must be spelled out to situate my argument on the
matter directly at hand.

If the Third World countries have almost never seen their political
systems develop in the genuinely democratic manner (on the lines
of the developed capitalist countries of the West, since 1945 at least)
this is neither an accident nor a holdover from their 'traditional
culture'. Democracy here is incompatible with the demands of
capitalist expansion. What I call 'actually existing capitalism', that
is, capitalism as a world system and not as a mode of production taken
at its highest level of abstraction, has to date always generated polarisation on a world scale (the 'centre/periphery' contradiction). This
dimension has been underestimated by Marx and Marxism, and has
brought to the forefront of the historical stage not 'socialist' revolutions led by the working classes of the developed capitalist countries
but 'anti-capitalist' revolutions provoked by the polarisation inherent
in worldwide capitalist expansion, with socially intolerable consequences for the peoples of the peripheries and semi-peripheries of
the system.

The strategic aims of these revolutions entail delinking from the
logic of worldwide capitalist expansion. Implementation of these aims
supposes power based on 'national and popular' social hegemony
(and not the 'dictatorship of the proletariat' envisaged in the Marxist
tradition) that acknowledges a conflictual mix of aspirations of both
a socialist and a capitalist sort. The process of achieving these aims
entails in turn gradual and continual democratisation of society
through practical management of power and of the economy.

Regimes that emerged from so-called socialist revolutions (USSR,
China) began to create the necessary conditions to eradicate the legacy
of peripheralisation produced by capitalism, by abandoning criteria
of capitalist rationality and proceeding to internal social revolutions
that had tremendous impact. The national liberation struggles,
arising from a similar rejection of capitalist peripheralisation, have
not led to such significant advances, either in delinking or in internal
social transformation. The societies emerging from these struggles
in the Third World have so far remained subject to the law of
capitalist polarisation. National and popular revolution and delinking
are still the strategic aims of the fight for progress of the peoples on
the periphery of the world capitalist system. Progress in this regard
in the so-called socialist countries of the East as in those of the South
(the capitalist Third World) largely determines not only the future

of socialism on a world scale, but even of social progress pure and simple for the majority of humankind.

The central proposition I have sketched here would be invalid in the event that either:

1. the new forms of transnationalisation had rendered the national and popular strategies and concomitant delinking obsolete and made feasible a single path of development: the capitalist path within worldwide openness; and/or

2. the fundamental propositions of socialism (and of Marxism in particular) concerning the historical limits of capitalism and the forms of democracy developed on its basis were without scientific foundation, their utopianism being confirmed by the failure of their implementation in the socialist experiences.

One should not underestimate the extent to which worldwide expansion has entered a more intense phase, marked by qualitatively new characteristics, of which I would mention the following six:

1. replacement of national systems of production (founded on the logic of social agreements produced by national history) by a worldwide system of production that challenges these agreements;

2. the worldwide spread of finance capital;

3. the new technological revolution;

4. a worldwide culture produced by intensified communications;

5. the availability of weapons with a destructive power that forces a change in traditional diplomacy;

6. ecological interdependence on an increasingly global scale.

Does this mean that the new factors necessitate unilateral submission to unification of the world by the 'market'? Does this mean that the polarizing impact of capitalist expansion could be neutralised within the framework of national strategies willing to accept such a submission?

I have found it necessary to base my response to these questions on an analysis of the effects these developments have on the global structure of the labour force. From this angle the first three developments cited above combine to hasten the formation of a passive reserve army of labour exploited by worldwide capital, especially in the industrialising peripheries. Far from attenuating the polarisation inherent in actually existing capitalism, the new phase of worldwide expansion can only heighten the contrast through which it is expressed. Moreover, the military, diplomatic and cultural evolutions cited help shift the mechanisms through which the polarisation operates from the field of economic relations *stricto sensu* to the broader one of politics.

As a corollary, I have also concluded that strategies of surrender to these identifiable 'worldwide constraints' will lead to catastrophe. The alternative of a 'national and popular' response not only has no rival but is even more essential now than in the past. The forms it will take have still to be defined, although its broad outlines can already be perceived. In this perspective, the reconstruction of a polycentric world system seems to me a realistic option (in so far as it is feasible in the fairly short term), and the only one capable of restoring the necessary scope for autonomy to permit the social progress of all the partners.

The crisis of the socialist bloc societies is invoked in order to conclude that socialism is utopian, that capitalism represents an ageless reality, and that the Marxist critique of capitalism is erroneous. These confused notions, when subtly deployed, make it possible to sell the West's strategy, based on the equation market = democracy.

But this equation in no way holds. Bourgeois democracy is the product of the revolution that dethroned 'tributary metaphysics'. It establishes 'equal rights' and personal liberties, but not 'equality' (except under law). As late as the latter half of the nineteenth century, the labour movement could enforce unqualified political democracy and win social rights, but only in the framework of a compromise based on acceptance of capitalist economic management, a compromise itself made possible by global polarisation to the benefit of the industrial centre. Western democracy is thereby restricted to the political domain, while economic management continues to be based on non-democratic principles of private ownership and competition. In other words, the capitalist mode of production does not of itself require democracy but rather its characteristic oppression is hidden in economic alienation affecting the entire society. By contrast, the socialist project of a classless society freed of economistic alienation implies a democratic structure. Once capitalist reliance on competition is broken, social relations based on cooperation among workers, and no longer on their subjection, are inconceivable without a full flowering of democracy.

The crisis of socialist bloc societies does not invalidate these fundamental propositions, for the good reason that it is not a crisis of genuinely socialist societies, but of societies committed to a national and popular order based on a revolutionary refusal to surrender to the dictates of capitalist peripheralisation.

These societies currently have several sets of options that can be briefly indicated as follows:

1. Evolution towards bourgeois democracy or progress beyond it through the strengthening of the social power of workers in the management of the economy.
2. Restoration of an out-and-out 'market economy' or effective progress by way of a carefully controlled use of market forces through democratic planning.
3. An unguarded door wide open to the exterior or guarded relations with the surrounding capitalist world, albeit on the basis of increased trade.

The theoretical debate and political disputes reverberating through the socialist bloc countries are confused in part because ideological labelling as 'socialist' has obscured the genuinely 'national and popular' character of the historical revolutions establishing each of the regimes. But more pertinent is the fact that the conflicting forces of capitalism and socialism are meeting within genuine struggles. The forces anxious to 'restore capitalism' propose total acceptance of the 'market' (as a springboard for the restoration of private ownership) and of 'an open door to the exterior', with or without democracy (in the Western sense of the word) according to the tactical requirements of their project. If the socialist forces dither in their resistance to the project, and if they find it difficult to articulate a coherent alternative (on the lines sketched above), it is because the lack of democratic debate and the ideological fallacy already indicated are major impediments to action.

The conventional social theory offered as an explanation of the absence of democracy in the Third World is desperately hollow and repetitious. In their successive forms dictated by current intellectual fashions, these theories formulate and reformulate the paradigm of modernisation: the Third World societies are 'half traditional/half modern' (on the path to development and modernisation) and therefore preserve the tradition of the autocratic concept of power, being constrained by force of circumstance to democratise gradually as their backward economies 'catch up'. In this domain as in others, the capitalist road is the only one envisaged, and, furthermore, it is assumed that democratisation would necessarily result.

This thesis, hidden for a while by the success of the 'Third-Worldism' of the 1960s among Westerners, has recently reappeared in a Weberian formulation. Weber, as we know, distinguished supposedly traditional power, described as 'patrimonial', personalised and contrary to the concept of modern law, from 'bureaucratic' and depersonalised power, based on the concept of law.

In truth Weber's thesis is very Germanic in the sense that it projects particular characteristics of German history on to that of the whole of humankind. Power in precapitalist societies was not, as a general rule, either personalised or disrespectful of law. The example of the advanced tributary society provided by imperial China rests on an extremely impersonal mandarin bureaucracy. In pharaonic Egypt the Pharaoh Thutmose III of the eighteenth dynasty wrote to his vizier Rekheret: 'What he [the vizier] must do is to take the law into account'. Undoubtedly European feudalism of the early centuries (from the barbarian invasions of the thirteenth and fourteenth centuries) comes close to the Weberian model in one aspect: the personalisation of feudal power. But, in fact, the fragmentation of power, a precondition for its personalisation, merely illustrates the fact that feudalism is a peripheral variety of the tributary system and not the general rule of the precapitalist 'tradition'. It can also be seen that the system of power loses this personalised character in the mercantilist Europe of absolute monarchies. And the monarchical bureaucracies were similar to those of other advanced tributary societies, as contemporary observers were not slow to note. A distinct exception is that of Germany, clinging to the seigneurial stage.

However, the chief characteristic of tributary ideology is not 'patrimonialism', but 'metaphysical domination'. This is true in all cases, the advanced tributary forms, evidenced by Confucianism in China or Islam in the Khalifate, and the peripheral feudal forms. Except that the metaphysical domination operates in the latter case through the autonomous power of the Church, compensating for the failing of the state. Once again with the evolution from feudal Europe to absolute monarchies the Church–state fusion was close to the general tributary model, as is evidenced by the establishment of national reformed churches or even, in Catholic countries, tendencies such as Gallicanism represented in France.

Furthermore, the 'patrimonial' systems in no way disregarded the law. In the advanced tributary systems there was state law governing the whole of social life, as is evidenced, for example, by the *sharia* in Islamic countries. In the feudal peripheral systems, seigneurial power, even when personalised, was obliged to respect customary peasant right.

Is the modern concept of power, theorised by Weber and his followers, 'bureaucratic' in its main impact in contrast with the supposed 'patrimonial' concept? Certainly not, since the bureaucratic character is only a form in which it works. Its essential content is bourgeois, produced by the operation of bourgeois democracy – with the distinct exception once again of Germany, where the weakness of the bourgeoisie resulted, in the sphere of political power, in an 'enlightened despot' until very recent times. In this instance Marx seems to me to outshine Weber in his analyses of the German specificity. Here too, Weber extends a particular characteristic – certainly typical of Wilhelmine Germany but not of parliamentary England or the France of the Third Republic – to the West as a whole.

Weber's disciples (like Richard Sandbrook) have tried to apply this dubious historical thesis to explain specific characteristics of power in contemporary black Africa. (Sandbrook and Barker 1985), where in fact personalisation and disregard for law do seem to have marked a great many postcolonial systems. They merely attribute these characteristics to African 'tradition'.

But is the thesis of 'patrimonial power' valid for precolonial Africa? Undoubtedly the latter has certain features in common with feudal Europe: precolonial black Africa is pre-tributary, still largely at the stage I call communal; feudal Europe preserves communal forms that originated in barbarism, which explains the primitive and peripheral character of the tributary system. The analogy illustrates the significance of customary rights in the two cases and in the absence of a bureaucratic state law: with the proviso that the model of the Church is confirmation of the metaphysical domination governing this stage. By contrast, in Africa, the ideology of kinship – appropriate to the communal stage – still dominates the systems of legitimation of power. The ideology looks very like personalised power. But this is much less the case than might be thought, as the power must operate within the framework of a customary law acting as a brake on possible caprices on the part of the 'chiefs'.

As will be shown later, the contemporary authorities in Africa have little to do with this supposed legacy, long since discredited, particularly in the slave trade. As will also be shown, the question of possible charisma of leaders here, as elsewhere, has no 'traditional' roots. It is a modern phenomenon to which we shall return.

The neo-Weberian thesis is not the only form of expression of the broader paradigm of modernisation. Everyone will remember the Latin American *desarollismo* of the 1950s and 1960s arguing that industrialisation and bourgeois-style modernisation would of themselves bring democratic change. 'Dictatorship' was regarded as the residue of a supposedly precapitalist past. The fallacy in this ingenuous line of argument has been made clear by the facts. Industrialisation and modernisation in the framework of this bourgeois plan have merely produced 'modernised dictatorship' and replaced the old oligarchical and patriarchal systems with an 'efficient and modern' fascist violence. Peripheral development could take no other course, as it aggravated rather than reduced social inequalities.

The absence of democracy from the periphery of the world capitalist system is a constant that is not a residue of earlier eras but the inevitable consequence of the expansion of actually existing capitalism. International polarisation inherent in this expansion brings in turn a manifold internal social polarisation: growing inequality in income distribution, widespread unemployment, marginalisation and so on Making the world system the key unit of analysis responds to a social factor of crucial importance for an understanding of what is at stake in the struggles, namely that capital's essential reserve army of labour is to be found geographically in the peripheries of the system. The reserve army is certainly composed of a staggering mass of urban unemployed and underemployed (many times the number of unemployed in the West, even during times of crisis), but also of large segments of non-wage labourers, destined, in accordance with progress in these areas of activity, to be expelled in turn from their land or the so-called 'informal' urban activities that keep them busy. The integration – always very limited – of fractions of this reserve army into the active army occurs either through 'semi-industrialisation' characteristic of the genuine peripheries of today and tomorrow, or by international migration towards the centres. But this migration is always limited, among other things by the employment strategies of the centres, and concerns only an infinitesimal fraction of the worldwide reserve army. 'Liberalism', which has never envisaged completing its programme of liberalisation of exchange and capital flows by unlimited openness to labour migration, remains therefore a truncated swindle.

Hence instability is the rule in the political life of the peripheries. The background of vicious dictatorships (whether military or not) broadly amenable to the demands of the world expansion of capital is occasionally shaken by explosions that challenge them. Such explosions rarely lead to any semblance of political democracy. The most common model is the 'populist' response. This is found in regimes that genuinely address at least some aspects of the social problems and contemplate a development strategy capable of reducing the tragic consequences of peripheralisation. These regimes can be given credit for industrialisation (mainly by the state), nationalisation of sectors dominated by foreign capital, agrarian reforms, efforts (that are sometimes remarkable) in the field of education and health, and some social rights offering a degree of job protection.

But they have their historical limits: on the one hand they clash with dominant imperialism (quite simply because any policy of social progress at the periphery is incompatible with the demands of the worldwide expansion of capital), yet remain incapable of taking this conflict to its logical conclusion, which is delinking; on the other hand these regimes are not democratic. They have often been popular, and as we say, supported by the 'masses'. But these 'masses' are maintained in an amorphous passive condition, 'mobilised' to 'support' but not permitted to organise as an autonomous force in respect to the authorities. These regimes produced by a familiar situation marked by weak class formation embark on the national and popular transformation without being able to carry it through. Therefore the charismatic leader is a common feature of these populist regimes. This inherent weakness of the populist system, combined with external aggression, bring about its fall, most frequently resulting in a return to dictatorship.

There is a middle ground between dictatorships of the Right and/or populist popular movements on to which 'petty democracy' can sometimes sneak. I am referring to regimes that recognise the principle of multiparty elections, and grant a measure of free speech, but fall short of addressing fundamental social problems and/or challenging relations of dependence and subjection to the world system. The range of these situations is broad enough to include merely apparent 'democracies', with the authorities retaining the means – most frequently by electoral fraud – of holding on to power, and other regimes that will bow to the eventual outcome at the polls.

These 'democracies' are little more than an expression of the crisis of capitalism's usual despotic system. Latin America, South Korea and the Philippines provide examples of contradictions unresolved by such regimes.

Democratic systems imposed under such circumstances face a striking dilemma, an either/or situation. Either the democratic political system accepts surrender to the demands of world 'adjustment' – it could not then consider any substantial social reform and a crisis of democracy would quickly develop (as is already the case in Argentina). Or the popular forces take hold of the democracy and impose the reforms: the system would then come into conflict with dominant world capitalism and would have to shift from the national bourgeois project to a national and popular one. The dilemma of Brazil and the Philippines falls entirely within this contradiction. In Argentina it has already been seen how the electorate, wearied by the impotence of President Alfonsín's democracy, returned of its own accord to the populist sirens, this time under the guise of fascists openly submissive to foreign dictates!

The areas of the periphery most affected by capitalist expansion are in a more desperate plight. The parlous condition of the 'Fourth World' is not the outcome of a refusal to integrate into the international division of labour and a 'failed' attempt to delink. In fact the 'fourth world' that is talked of as something new is a constant feature of capitalist expansion. A clear and lamentable example of this former Fourth World is provided by the areas of slave labour in the Americas in the period of mercantilism: north-east Brazil, the West Indies (including Haiti). These areas were regarded as 'prosperous' in their day; and within that system they represented the heart of the periphery.

Later the new structures of capitalist development marginalised these areas, and they are today among the most grievously wretched parts of the Third World. The history of capitalist expansion does not only include the 'development' it has engendered. Capitalism has a destructive side too often omitted from flattering portrayals of the system.

Is Africa not now on the road to exclusion from the world division of labour because of a system that has consigned the continent to specialisation in agriculture and mining through extensive exploitation of the soils until they are exhausted, and the technological revolution that provides substitutes for some raw materials? Fourth World societies subject to a passive delinking through rejection cannot by definition solve their problems through open door policies. Recolonisation sweetened by charity is surely trying to conceal the explicit failure of the neoliberal solution. Here the 'usual' pattern of power is the Tontons Macoutes in Haiti, Somoza in Nicaragua and a disturbing number of dictatorships of the same stamp in contemporary Africa. The thesis of 'patrimonial' power criticised above was formulated in regard to such African regimes. At a superficial level it describes certain features of this kind of regime: extremely personalised (from head of state to petty administrator – the village tyrant), with utter contempt for any notion of legality and rights (including sacrosanct bourgeois property rights), to say nothing of basic human rights, along with widespread corruption. There has been a strong temptation to blame this supposed 'legacy' on African tradition. A hint of racism may underlie the insinuation. In fact it is no such legacy that produces the 'Fourth World' phenomenon, but on the contrary it is the present world system which produces this kind of power in the 'Fourth World.'

Is this 'Fourth World' dictatorial model a 'kleptocracy' – as Nzongola-Ntalaja (1987) described it – closer to racketeers and the Mafia than to any traditional chiefdom, since the latter was mindful of customary rights? In any event, regimes of this type are modern states perfectly operational in their own way. How could the authorities operate any differently under Fourth World conditions? The latter deprive the state of any possibility of basing its legitimacy on discernible development, and of finding a social base to carry the appropriate strategy through to a successful conclusion. Not only do the peasantry, the working class and the urban fringe know they have nothing to look forward to, but even the bourgeoisie is deprived of any prospect of meaningful development. All that remains is direct exploitation of power as a means of personal enrichment, or its indirect exploitation through the channel of pseudo-private economic activities whose profitability depends entirely on relations with the administration. Terror, corruption and extreme personalisation are therefore essential to the very operation of the system. Charisma – so often spoken of – has no place here: it is not a matter of charisma of leaders who have won genuine popularity at a moment of history as in the populist regimes, but of a pseudo-charisma concocted by the media and incapable of fooling the public. Superficially, the petty bourgeoisie might be regarded as the social base of these systems, in so far as broad strata share power and benefit from the state treasury. When this is not an illusion, the correlation reveals a measure of fascist incorporation of this social stratum. Their hopes have been dashed and in their powerlessness – in the absence of a revolutionary intelligentsia offering an alternative – they take refuge in power worship.

The main task of progressive forces at the periphery of the system nowadays is to assert the missing democratic component, not to substitute for the national and social aspects of national and popular liberation, but to reinforce them.

In fact, the old paradigm of national liberation largely ignored the democratic component essential for the pursuit of national and popular advance. Democratic consciousness may well be a new phenomenon; in the past, democratic demands were limited to particular segments of the urban bourgeoisie and were not vigorously expressed, except at particular moments of the radicalisation of anti-imperialist struggles (the Egyptian Wafd being one of the best examples). Moreover, this democratic consciousness stayed within the narrow limits of bourgeois liberalism. The dominant tendencies in the popular and radical movements of national liberation were more marked by a progressive social content than by the democratic beliefs of their militants, despite the sometimes ritualistic use of the term 'democracy' and even despite the more advanced conscious-ness of some segments of the avant garde. I do not believe it is a caricature to say that the peasant-soldier of the liberation army entering Peking in 1949 was thinking of land reform, but as yet unaware of the meaning of democracy. Today his worker or student son or daughter has new aspirations in that regard. The same was true of the Egyptian peasant, even the Wafd voter, and of many others no doubt.

But what democracy are we talking about? This is not the place to disparage the heritage of Western bourgeois democracy: respect for rights and the rule of law, freedom of speech, institutionalizing of electoral procedure and separation of powers, checks and balances. But we should not stop there. Western democracy has no social dimension. The people's democracies at moments of revolutionary social change (the USSR in the 1920s, Maoist China) have also taught us much about what 'people's power' should be, if we give this much abused expression its real meaning. To stop at Western democratic forms without taking into consideration the social transformations demanded by the anti-capitalist revolt of the periphery means holding on to a caricature of bourgeois democracy and thus ensuring alienation from the people and extreme vulnerability. For our democracy to take root it must, from the start, take a position that goes beyond capitalism. In this as in so many other domains the law of unequal development operates.

This is the prospect that imperialism cannot accept. That is why the 'democracy' campaign orchestrated by the West stresses some features of democracy and ignores others. For example, it equates multiparty politics with democracy. In contrast with the language of Western media about democracy, our thinking concerns democracy in the service of national liberation and social progress (and not in opposition to them, or overlooking them).

I would argue that 'Jacobin democracy', to borrow an expression from the French Revolution, is astonishingly modern. In each of the three great revolutions of the modern world (the French, the Russian and the Chinese), the play of ideas and social forces at moments of radicalisation has succeeded in moving far beyond the requirements of 'historically, objectively necessary' social transformation. Hence Jacobin democracy did more than merely establish 'bourgeois power'. Although this democracy operated in a framework of private ownership, its drive to establish power genuinely at the service of the 'people' clashed with its merely bourgeois needs. At this stage of social development the bourgeoisie looked for little more than the qualified democracy such as Britain, the United States and France practised in the nineteenth century. The bourgeoisie was furthermore willing to compromise with the monarchy and the aristocracy, as British history shows. The aspirations of the 'people' – namely the mass of peasants and artisans – went further. The people wanted something more than 'free trade'. This was true to such an extent that during the Convention they launched the remarkably modern slogan 'Liberalism [that is, economic] is the enemy of democracy!' This advanced slogan was a foretaste of a socialist consciousness yet to come (Babeufism is an example). In the same way, the USSR in the 1920s and Maoist China expressed a communist vision well beyond the requirements of the 'national and popular' reform on the agenda. Certainly these moments of radicalisation are fragile; in the end, narrower concepts more consonant with 'objective' needs win the day. But it would be quite wrong to underestimate their significance as an indication of the trend.

'Jacobin democracy', rejuvenated by radicalisation of the socialist revolutions of our times, is the democracy to which the popular classes of the contemporary Third World aspire – albeit in a confused manner. It is distinguishable from liberal bourgeois democracy, which ignores the dimension of necessary social reforms, just as it is distinguishable from the anti-democratic 'populist mobilisations' to which we referred above.

My proposition certainly pays no heed to fashion! The latter nowadays seeks to devalue moments of revolutionary radicalisation in the name of 'realism'. At the same time it draws themes from another tradition: that of the 'local democracy', familiar in English-speaking countries. 'Decentralisation' and autonomy of a dismembered and segmented civil society are often in this spirit proposed as realisable advances, potentially more fertile than the supposed illusions of 'statist' popular democracy. The trends in this direction, often tinged with religiosity, seem to me to suggest a strategy too strongly biased by 'anti-statism' to be genuinely up to the real historic challenge. Yet there is something to be learned from this movement; and a genuine dialogue is necessary here. That said, it is difficult nowadays to know if the social movements of all kinds presently existing at the periphery (and at the centre) are capable of making headway in answering the objective challenge.

Some of the movements seem to be dead-ends. This is the case with the religious fundamentalist renewals or 'ethnic' communal movements. As symptoms of the crisis and not solutions to it, and as expressions of disillusionment, they will collapse as soon as they have revealed their impotence in the face of the real challenge.

Other movements may, on the contrary, play a role in the reconstruction of a plan for society 'beyond capitalism' that resolves the contradictions actually existing capitalism is incapable of overcoming, by drawing on the lessons of the first steps in this direction. It seems to me that this occurs whenever the 'new movements' (or even the old ones) do not stand exclusively on the terrain of 'state conquest', but on that of another concept of social power to be won. The choice is not between 'struggle for power or struggle for something else' (what would the latter be?); but the question is for what kind of power the struggle is being waged. The organisational forms based on the prevailing 'traditional' concept of power (power = State) are inevitably going to lose much of their legitimacy once the peoples understand the conservative character of the state. By contrast, forms of organisation addressing the complex social content of the power to be developed will be increasingly successful. In this category the theory of 'non-party politics' may prove fruitful. The same may be said of 'anti-authoritarianism' in Latin America, in which Pablo Gonzáles Casanova (1988) sees the principal requisite of the 'new' movements: rejection of authoritarianism in the state, in the party and in the leadership; and repudiation of doctrinaire concepts in ideology. This is a reaction against the burdensome legacy of the continent's history, and undoubtedly this reaction will stimulate progress. But likewise, and for the same basic reason, feminism in the West, with its aim of attacking at least some of the roots of autocracy, stems from that same concept of social power. To some extent the West is in the vanguard of breakthroughs in social liberation. Whether these advances imply breakthroughs 'beyond capitalism', or remain absorbable by the social system, raises new questions. In the medium term at least, it would seem that a central capitalist position has so many strengths that the movements in question will not shake the foundations of capitalist management of society. The future of the 'new movements' remains uncertain. It is not impossible that they will wither away in the current crisis.

Can objective criteria be defined in such a way as to encourage the movement to take the essential national and popular direction? I believe they can, and I make the following preliminary comments.

The principal task is that of democratic repoliticisation of the masses. The latter had a view of independence as something to be regained. Once the aim was achieved, the language on which national liberation was based ran out of steam. Can the new repoliticisation be 'extra-party' or even 'anti-party' since parties have been devalued as a consequence of their post-independence behaviour? The question is open, although I personally am somewhat shocked at what seems to me a degree of 'paternalism' underlying the activity of many of the trendy 'non-governmental organisations'.

Secondly, democratic repoliticisation of the people must be based on reinforcing their capacity for self-organisation, self-development and self-defence. Obviously, the aim of self-development, through various forms of cooperation, co-management and popular management, provokes conflict with the state, since national and popular society remains the locus of objective class conflict: overt conflict if the state is neo-colonial, latent if the state is embarked on a national and popular programme. Through such actions, might it be possible, for example, to transform activities inaccurately described as 'informal' into a 'people's economy'? Under current conditions, these activities are fully integrated into the global capitalist system and fulfil precise functions of ensuring the reproduction of the labour force at minimum cost or supplying subprocessing of inputs at low cost. They are a necessary adjunct to ensuring the profitability of capitalist exploitation. Transforming these activities into a 'people's economy' would be fraudulent if this conflict of interests were not faced openly.

Thirdly, the kind of action envisaged here raises anew the question of relations between the 'movement' and the parties of the historical Left, and populism, established in the fight for independence or in the fight waged against the neocolonial system. It seems to be neither proper nor cogent to lump these parties – whatever their 'mistakes' and historical limits – with those who have been responsible for neo-colonial management. Similarly, the question once again arises of relations between the 'movement' and the new forces that have coalesced at one time or another on a national and progressive platform. I am obviously thinking of the organisations of anti-imperialist and progressive soldiers at the root of changes responsive to popular aspirations, even if the changes were inaugurated by *coups d'état* (Egypt, Libya, Rawlings' Ghana, Sankara's Burkina Faso).

Fourthly, analysis of the strategy of democratic repoliticisation implies the reintroduction of at least three broad debates of theoretical significance:

1. the debate on the role of the revolutionary intelligentsia as a social catalyst capable of drafting a concrete alternative plan and promoting the struggles for its implementation;
2. the debate on the cultural content of this alternative plan – its potentially universalist scope being essential in my opinion – its relations with the national cultural heritage and so on;
3. the debate on the long-term outlook: socialism or capitalism?

Although it is fashionable nowadays to deny the validity of such debates, I believe they are indispensable. Here I merely point them out, as I have discussed the details in my other writings.

Fifthly, current history offers some tentative examples of this direction. I am thinking here of the experience of Thomas Sankara's Burkina Faso, but of others even more abused by the dominant media of the West (Gadaffi-ism, for example!) Obviously, the first steps fall short of solving the fundamental issues of the relationship between the authorities and parties of the radical Left, the relationship to populism, to the soldiers, and so forth. However, the debate on these propositions should be opened.

Sixthly, I am not suggesting magic formulae to replace the necessary democratic dialogue between all the components of the movement. I am merely suggesting that if polarisation imposes 'alternative development', then the only options are acceptance of 'wealth' as the backbone of the aspirations to be encouraged, or its replacement by 'welfare'. To find answers to this dilemma we need to return to old papa Marx whose critique of the market ('commodity alienation'), far from being 'played out', is rejuvenated by the rediscoveries of the contemporary movement. A 'market' that has not to be 'controlled', but eliminated, albeit very gradually through the slow maturing of consciousness and practice and not by bureaucratic rejection.

In the final analysis the issue of democracy cannot be debated without reference to the philosophical bases of the various interpretations of democracy.

Contemporary interpretations, broadly typified by Anglo-American evolutionism and pragmatism, impoverish the debate by treating democracy as a set of narrowly defined rights and practices, independent of the desired social outlook. This democracy can then stabilise the society, by leaving 'evolution' to 'objective forces' operating regardless of human will. Furthermore, in the analysis of these objective forces the focus is on technical and scientific progress, while the social realities that hide behind 'market forces' are systematically ignored. Finally, the democratic transformation of society is regarded as being largely the product of evolution; hence the functional role of the revolutionary process in history can be played down.

I am in total disagreement with this line of argument. The analysis of economic alienation provided by Marx is in my view central to any scientific and realistic understanding of the mechanism of capitalist reproduction. It is the only analysis that places democracy in its true context, and grasps its stabilizing role. Along with Marx, the Frankfurt School and Karl Polanyi (1987), I find it impossible to interpret our world outside this analytical frame of reference. The method leads of necessity to a rehabilitation of the crucial function of revolutions, moments of qualitative transformation and crystallisation of potentialities inconceivable without revolution.

In this view, the contemporary world and the perception of its future supercession are the product of the three great (and sole) revolutions of the modern world: the French, the Russian and the Chinese. With Immanuel Wallerstein I attach qualitative significance to the break inaugurated by the French Revolution. For the break substitutes a system of secular legitimation of political and social action for the ancient religious legitimation appropriate to what I have called tributary ideologies. In that sense we can see the break inaugurated the later evolutions, whether of bourgeois democracy or socialism. The Paris Commune slogan in 1871 ('Neither God, nor Caesar, nor Tribune') was no accident; it flowed from – and was an extension of – the slogan of 1789 ('Liberty, Equality, Fraternity').

The stress on this ideological aspect of the French Revolution challenges the very concept of bourgeois revolution. The supposedly fundamental definition of class struggle opposes the oppressed and the oppressors in a given mode of production: peasants and feudal lords in one instance, proletariat and capitalists in another. Bourgeois revolution would then necessarily be a peasant revolution, socialist revolution a working-class revolution. But capitalism did not abolish feudal exploitation to replace it with an egalitarian society (the aim of peasant struggles); it established a new form of exploitation, the possibility of which had not even been imagined by the struggling peasants. The new capitalist society and the bourgeois class were established partly on the fringe of, or even outside, feudal society (comprising feudal lords and peasants), in the free towns, partly even within the peasantry, by new differentiations (rich peasants and landless peasants reduced to the status of farm labourers) produced by the extension of commodity relations, strengthened sometimes by the peasant struggles. As we know, this new capitalist society ripened slowly within the *anciens régimes*, which were social and political systems remaining essentially 'feudal'. The bourgeois revolution thus consisted of the political moment marking the abolition of the *ancien régime* and installation of a new kind of organisation ensuring the political dominance of the new economically dominant class. The bourgeois revolution is therefore not the starting point but the culmination of an already long history of capitalist development.

Coincidence between the peasant social revolution and the bourgeois political revolution has occurred in only one historical instance, that of the French Revolution (which is, therefore, the sole genuine revolution of the bourgeois state in history). Here, obviously, the bourgeoisie was forced into the alliance; its radical advances and retreats shaped the stages of the revolution itself and the later evolutions. There is, however, no comparable coincidence elsewhere. Not even in England. The peasant–bourgeois radical revolution of mid-seventeenth century England, perhaps because it came earlier (as is evidenced by its religious expression through religious rein-terpretation, whereas the French Revolution made politics secular; the first came before the Enlightenment, the second inherited it ...), was aborted at the end of the century to give way to the scarcely glorious 'Glorious Revolution' (not even a revolution!). And not even in North America. Liberation from the colonial yoke was a political act, without revolutionary social impact, since it merely confirmed the power of the merchant society already established as such in New England from the outside (it is significant that the American Revolution did not even raise the issue of slavery). And even more so Germany, Italy and Japan. The general rule is that capitalism develops independently of peasant revolution, even if in some instances peasant struggles have contributed to the particular direction and shape of capitalist civilisation. But capitalism is not developed without an 'agricultural revolution', in the sense of estab-lishing a landed bourgeoisie often of great landowners (ex-'feudal lords') driving away the surplus rural population in order to modernise in favour of a largely market production. In all these cases the bour-geoisie attacks the state, seizes it and changes society from above.

The very particular circumstances of the French Revolution explain its advances beyond the mere adjustment of relations of production to the demands of capitalist development: its secularised legitimacy; its universal concepts; the abolition of slavery it proclaims. These advances half-opened the window on a still distant future. Without the French Revolution, the utopian socialism of Marx would be unthinkable.

The Russian and Chinese revolutions also had a dimension of grandeur sometimes described as 'messianic'. Wrongly in my view, since the future they portend remains a realistic possibility, a necessity if humankind is to avoid barbarism. But it is clear that these advances, going even further than those conceived in Paris in 1793 and 1871 (since the worldwide spread of capitalism, on the one hand, and the phenomenon of Marx on the other, occurred in the interim), are not the simple product of objective demands for immediate social trans-formation on the agenda in Russia in 1917 and in China in 1949.

I maintain, therefore, that the three revolutions under discussion are the great moments when our vision of the modern world and its possible and desirable future was defined. I believe that finding previous moments as decisive means going back 1,500 – 2,500 years earlier; back to the times of the great ideological revolutions through which the crystallisation of tributary society is expressed, in our part of the world under the successive forms of Hellenism, Christianity and Islam, elsewhere under the forms of Confucianism and Buddhism. At the level of ideology – a dominant factor in precapitalist societies – they represented as gigantic a qualitative transformation as those wrought in our era by those three modern revolutions. It is also worth noting that these ancient revolutions went further than simple adjustment to the demands of social evolution: by proclaiming, for example, a universalism which the regional tributary societies did not require. The changes between the historic revolutions have been of local and minor significance, provoked merely by continual adjustment of various spheres of social activity to the constraints of 'evolution'.

The interpretation of democracy that is part of the analytical framework we offer here is very different from that of Anglo-American evolutionist philosophy. In our analysis, democracy becomes a destabiliser, the means by which concepts 'ahead of their time' continue to progress and spur on social action and progress.

The current offensive of the West, ostensibly 'in favour of democracy', has the merit of concealing this destabilizing tendency of democracy. I draw the conclusion that it is not really an offensive in favour of democracy, but an offensive against socialism. The cause of democracy – in its impoverished form as a means of stabilizing an alienated society – is then mobilised as a tactical weapon. And like all tactical weapons it is deployed with a grain of cynicism. What other explanation is there for the way the Western media, so touchy in its defence of freedom of expression in the countries of actually existing socialism, stood up for those defending the freedom of the Afghan mullahs who did not conceal that their programme aimed to close the schools (beginning with those for girls of course) that the infamous secularists in the pay of Moscow had dared to open? What other explanation is there for the way these media ignored the interventions of Western paratroopers coming to the rescue of African dictators at the end of their tether? What other explanation is there for the way the assiduous defenders of trade union freedom in Poland overlooked the fact that adjustment policies imposed on the Third World envisage the dismantling of trade unions?

References

Amin, Samir 1980. *Class and Nation, Historically and in the Current Crisis.*
New York, Monthly Review Press, and London, Heinemann.

—— 1987. *Ma bad al rasmalia (Post-Capitalism)* (in Arabic). Beirut. (See likewise on issues concerning the birth of socialism, my articles in Arabic in *al-Mustaqbal af'-Arabi*, no. 114, 1988, and no. 126, 1989).

—— 1988. *Al Intelligentsia (On the Intelligentsia)* (in Arabic). Qadaya, Fikriyya, Cairo.

—— 1989a. *Eurocentrism*. New York, Monthly Review Press and London, Zed Books.

—— 1989b. 'L'Europe et les rapports Nord-Sud', *L'évènement européen*, 7.

—— 1989c. *Nahw nazaria lil thakafa (Towards a Theory of Culture)* (in Arabic). Beirut.

—— 1990. *Delinking: Towards a Polycentric World*. London, Zed Books.

—— 'The End of National Liberation?' in S. Amin, G. Arrighi, A.G. Frank, I. Wallerstein, *Transforming the Revolution: Social Movements and the World-system*.

Erman, Adolf and Ranke, Hermann 1983. *La Civilisation égyptienne* (translated from German). Paris, Payot.

Etiemble, René 1988–9. *L'Europe chinoise*. Paris, Gallimard.

Gonzáles Casanova, Pablo, 1988. 'El Estado y la Politìca en América Latina'. UNU-TWF, mimeo.

Nzongola-Ntalaja 1987. *Revolution and Counter-revolution in Africa: Essays in Contemporary Politics*. London, IFAA.

Polanyi, Karl 1987. *La libertà in una società complessa*. Turin, Boringheri.

Sandbrook, Richard with Barker Judith 1985. *The Politics of Africa's Economic Stagnation*. Cambridge, Cambridge University Press.

4. The Struggle for Democracy in the New World Order*

NOAM CHOMSKY

If we are to address the topic of this paper in a constructive way, we must clarify what is meant by 'democracy', and in just what ways the world has changed. Investigating these questions, we find that the guardians of world order have sought to establish democracy in one sense of the term, while blocking it in a different sense. There is every reason to expect these dominant themes of modern history to persist under the changed conditions of the current era.

Under one interpretation of the term, a society is democratic in so far as members of the public can play a meaningful role in managing their own affairs. But from the first modern democratic revolution in mid-seventeenth century England, elite groups have commonly regarded democracy so understood as a threat to be overcome, not a prospect to be encouraged. The reasoning is straightforward: the rabble cannot be trusted, as demonstrated 350 years ago by its reluctance to place its affairs in the hands of the gentry and the army, who were 'truly the people', though the people in their foolishness did not agree. The 'rascal multitude' must be suppressed, just as it is proper 'to save the life of a lunatic or distracted person even against his will'. If the people are so 'depraved and corrupt' as to 'confer places of power and trust upon wicked and undeserving men, they forfeit their power in this behalf unto those that are good, though but a few', so the commissars of the day declaimed. The rhetoric may have changed, but the conceptions prevail (Morgan 1988; see also Hill 1975; Chomsky 1991).

In the preferred version of democracy, the rabble must be barred from interfering with serious matters. The basic thinking was lucidly articulated by Walter Lippmann, the dean of American journalism and a highly regarded progressive democratic theorist. 'The public must be put in its place', Lippmann wrote, so that we may 'live free

* This paper was originally presented at the Catholic Institute of International Relations (CIIR) conference 'Negotiating for Change: The Struggle for Peace with Justice', London, January 1991. The editors would like to thank CIIR for permission to reprint this essay here.

80

of the trampling and the roar of a bewildered herd'. If the herd cannot be subdued by force, then their thoughts must be efficiently controlled. The statist reactionaries, called 'conservatives' in one of the current corruptions of political discourse, are only more extreme in their contempt for the rascal multitude.

Lippmann distinguished two political roles in a modern democracy. First, there is the role assigned to the 'specialised class', the 'insiders', the 'responsible men', who have access to information and understanding. These 'public men' are responsible for 'the formation of a sound public opinion ... They initiate, they administer, they settle', and should be protected from 'ignorant and meddlesome outsiders', the incompetent public, so that they can serve what is called 'the national interest' in the webs of mystification spun by the academic social sciences and political commentary (Rossiter and Lare 1982).

The second role is 'the task of the public', which is much more limited, Lippmann explains. It is not for the public to 'pass judgment', but merely to place 'its force at the disposal' of one or another group of 'responsible men'. The public 'does not reason, investigate, invent, persuade, bargain or settle'. Rather, 'the public acts only by aligning itself as the partisan of someone in a position to act executively', once he has given the matter at hand sober and disinterested thought. The bewildered herd, trampling and roaring, 'has its function': to be 'the interested spectators of action', not participants. Participation is the duty of 'the responsible man' (ibid.).'

There is, to be sure, an unspoken premise. The 'public men' gain access to authority and become 'experts' in so far as they serve the interests of private power. That trivial truth must be suppressed – and if spoken, angrily denied – or too much of reality becomes exposed to view. It is best for the educated classes themselves to be immune from this self-understanding, so that they may better fulfil their function – and keep their jobs.

These ideas, described by Lippmann's editors as a 'political philosophy for liberal democracy', bear an unmistakable resemblance to the Leninist concept of a vanguard party that leads the masses to a better life that they cannot conceive or construct on their own. The 'specialised class' of 'responsible men', which is to manage the affairs of the public according to liberal democratic theory, corresponds to the vanguard of revolutionary intellectuals. The 'manufacture of consent' advocated by Lippmann and a host of other respected figures is the agitprop of their Leninist counterparts. Following a script outlined by Bakunin over a century ago, the secular priesthood in both of the major systems of hierarchy and coercion have regarded the masses as stupid and incompetent, a bewildered herd who must be driven to a better world – one that we, the intelligent minority, will construct for them, either taking state power ourselves in the Leninist model, or serving the owners and managers of the state capitalist systems if it is impossible to exploit popular revolution to capture the commanding heights. The transition from one camp to the other has often been quick and easy, which is understandable, since the doctrines are similar at their root.

'The responsible men' are to be the managers of the corporate, state, and ideological institutions, which are all closely linked. For familiar reasons, in a state capitalist democracy the range of operative choices is narrowly limited by the concentration of decision-making power in the state–corporate nexus; but for efficiency, values and beliefs should be structured to ensure that few are tempted to stray from these confines, or are even aware of them. As explained by Reinhold Niebuhr (Niebuhr 1932; see also Chomsky 1989; Fox 1985), the highly respected moralist and political thinker, the intelligent minority must devise 'necessary illusions' and 'emotionally potent oversimplifications' to keep the naive simpletons on course. Less discussed, because it strikes closer to home, is that the educated classes themselves must be deeply indoctrinated if they are to carry out their managerial role.

With some modifications, these principles apply to the Third World as well. Its population also has its 'function', but it is not quite that of the bewildered herd at home. And the modalities of control also differ; terror and violence are available to an extent not possible on the home front. In the global system established half a century ago, the Third World was to be 'exploited' for the needs of the industrial capitalist societies, and to 'fulfil its major function as a source of raw materials and a market'; the terms are those of George Kennan's State Department Policy Planning Staff with reference to Africa and South-East Asia, but the application is far broader. In Latin America, Kennan explained, 'the protection of our resources' must be a major concern, as elsewhere. Since the main threat to our interests is indigenous, Kennan continued, we must accept the need for 'police repression by the local government'. 'Harsh government measures of repression' should cause us no qualms as long as 'the results are on balance favorable to our purposes'. In general, 'it is better to have a strong regime in power than a liberal government if it is indulgent and relaxed and penetrated by Communists' (see LaFeber 1983). The term 'Communist' is used here in its familiar technical sense, referring to labour leaders, peasant organisers, priests organizing self-help groups, and others with the wrong priorities.

The right priorities are outlined in the highest-level planning documents. The major threat to US interests is 'nationalistic regimes' that are responsive to popular pressures for 'immediate improvement in the low living standards of the masses' and diversification of the economies. Such initiatives interfere with 'the protection of our resources' and our efforts to encourage 'a climate conducive to private investment', which will allow foreign capital 'to repatriate a reasonable return'. The threat of communism, as explained by a prestigious study group, is the economic transformation of the communist powers 'in ways that reduce their willingness and ability to complement the industrial economies of the West' (ibid.). This is the real basis for the intense hostility to the former Soviet Union and its imperial system from 1917, and the reason why independent nationalism in the Third World, whatever its political cast, has been seen as the 'virus' that must be eradicated.

By the same token, the 'legitimate' forces in the Third World are elements of the oligarchy, business community and military who understand and serve US priorities. The function of the population is to be pack horses; the function of the elites is to keep them under control. If these goals can be attained with democratic forms, that is fine, even preferable, if only for propaganda purposes. If not, then other ways must be found, and in the Third World domains there need be no delicacy about the choice of methods. The rascal multitude can be taught lessons in manners by terror bombing of the kind pioneered by Britain in Iraq 70 years ago; poison gas, as authorised at that time for use against 'uncivilised tribesmen' by a high official of the War Office, who advised that gas should cause a 'lively terror' and condemned the 'squeamishness' of those who questioned 'the application of Western science to modern warfare' (Winston Churchill); death squads, 'disappearance' and other devices of the neo-Nazi national security states favoured by the United States since the Kennedy years; and so on, in the familiar way.

Of course, a different formulation is required for the home front. First, the guise for intervention must be self-defence, a virtually invariant feature of statecraft. Second, the use of violence must be for noble objectives: freedom, justice, world order and democracy. But like all terms of political discourse, these have their special Orwellian meanings, constructed for the occasion. We are indeed inspired by a 'yearning for democracy', as the *New York Times* tells us, but for 'democracy' in the proper sense.

The conflict between the two conceptions of democracy has arisen with particular clarity in the 1980s and early 1990s in Central America and the Caribbean. Few corners of the world have been so dominated by a regional power, but no respectable commentator would hint that their circumstances might be related to this fact. As the 1980s began, there were signs of hope for an escape from the dark ages of terror and misery, with the rise of self-help groups, unions, peasant associations, Christian base communities and other popular organisations, often inspired by the 'preferential option for the poor' adopted by successive Latin American bishops conferences. These remarkable developments might have led the way to desperately needed social reform and to democracy – but democracy in the wrong sense, with the rascal multitude raising their heads.

These prospects elicited a stern response from the ruler of the hemisphere and its local clients, with a huge campaign of slaughter, torture and general barbarism. Early efforts in Nicaragua to direct resources to the poor majority impelled Washington to wage economic and ideological warfare, indeed outright terror, to punish these transgressions by destroying the economy and social life. The goal of these programmes, pursued with the general approval of the European allies, was to reinstate the 'Central America mode' and 'restore democracy', as government and media constantly proclaimed – but 'democracy' in the officially acceptable sense, with power in the hands of those who understand their function.

These measures achieved a good deal of success, sinking the region still deeper into suffering and misery, and leaving societies 'affected by terror and panic', 'collective intimidation and generalized fear' and 'internalized acceptance of the terror', in the words of a Church-based Salvadoran human rights organisation. Enlightened opinion views these consequences with satisfaction, in so far as the challenge to power and privilege is rebuffed and the targets are properly chosen: killing prominent priests in public view is not clever, but rural activists and union leaders are fair game – along with, of course, peasants, Indians, students, and other low-life generally. US Secretary of State George Schultz expressed the common understanding when he described the results in El Salvador as 'something all Americans can be proud of' – at least, all of those who enjoy the sight of tortured bodies, starving children, terror and panic, and generalised fear.

Secretary Schultz's remarks were made in the course of a lamentation on terrorism delivered at the very moment that the US was carrying out the terror bombing of Libya, killing many civilians to much applause at home. His pride in accomplishments in El Salvador that may bear comparison to Pol Pot's elicited no comment, because it is indeed shared in respectable circles, which understand, as well as Winston Churchill, the merits of a 'lively terror'. That understanding lies at the core of the traditional culture. In the early days of the

American republic, John Quincy Adams wrote an official letter in which he took note of the 'salutary efficacy' of terror undertaken, in this case, against the American Indians and runaway slaves who were the target of General Andrew Jackson's rampages in Florida, which virtually annihilated much of its native population and left the Spanish province under US control. This defence of brutal slaughter, Indian removal, slavery, violation of treaties and executive war impressed Thomas Jefferson as 'among the ablest I have ever seen, both as to logic and style', a judgement in which modern historians have concurred. So taken was Jefferson with this racist diatribe that he urged its wide distribution 'to maintain in Europe a correct opinion of our political morality', a plausible proposal, since the 'salutary efficacy' of terror has always been appreciated in cultivated European circles as well.

A qualification is necessary, however. In our humane and enlightened society, we do not engage in terror and slaughter for their own sake, merely because we find the practice amusing. Rather, these are means, not ends, and must therefore satisfy the pragmatic criterion of efficiency. We regard with abhorrence the Mengeles and Idi Amins who do not share these exalted values, which are upheld with particular dedication at the outer limits of Left-liberal humanist thought. Thus, when the State Department publicly confirmed US support for terrorist attacks on agricultural cooperatives in Nicaragua, Michael Kinsley, who represents these sectors in the US doctrinal system, wrote that we should not be too quick to condemn the official government policy. Such international terrorist operations doubtless cause 'vast civilian suffering', Kinsley observed. But if they succeed 'to undermine morale and confidence in the government', then they may be 'perfectly legitimate'. The policy is 'sensible' if 'cost-benefit analysis' shows that 'the amount of blood and misery that will be poured in' is balanced by the 'democracy' that it yields (where the concept of democracy is to be understood in the manner already discussed).

Given the same assumptions, it is natural that not an eyebrow should be raised when the leading journal of American liberalism, the *New Republic*, gives 'Reagan & Co. good marks' for their support for state terror in El Salvador as it peaked in 1981. The journal then, surveying the carnage three years later, advised Reagan and Co. that we must send military aid to 'Latin-style fascists ... regardless of how many are murdered', because 'there are higher American priorities than Salvadoran human rights'. Those familiar with our traditional values will find nothing to surprise them in such pronouncements, or in the fact that they go side by side with impassioned denunciations of the crimes of official enemies. Nor will they be at all surprised that a distinguished Cambridge University professor of political theory should praise President Bush for standing firm on 'our traditions', which 'fortunately, prove to have at their core universal values, while theirs are sometimes hard to distinguish with the naked eye from rampant (and heavily armed) nihilism' (John Dunn, *Times Literary Supplement*, 5 October 1990) – sentiments that will be much appreciated by those who have experienced our traditional values from the days when England, having pacified the Celtic regions with blood and fire, extended the reach of its benevolence to Asia, Africa, and North America. The achievements of our doctrinal system are wondrous to behold.

The Indochina wars are a remarkable example. After years of terror with tens of thousands slaughtered in an effort to undermine the diplomatic settlement, the US attacked South Vietnam outright in 1962, with extensive bombing of civilian targets as part of operations aimed at driving millions of people into concentration camps where they could be 'protected' from the indigenous guerrillas who, it was conceded, they were willingly supporting. There was scarcely a whisper of protest in the civilised West, because this was, after all, self-defence against 'internal aggression', as liberal hero Adlai Stevenson explained at the United Nations. And the US had no alternative, because it was 'politically weak' though militarily strong, as agreed on all sides. Negotiations were therefore unthinkable, as was any peaceful settlement, because 'the whale would swallow the minnow', as government scholar Douglas Pike explained, comparing the political force of the South Vietnamese enemy and the US clients. US aggression extended to all of Indochina, with consequences that are well known. Twenty-eight years after the outright US attack against South Vietnam, the phrase, or anything like it, is unpronounceable in mainstream culture. Discussing the 'lesson of Vietnam', the London *Economist* quite accurately distinguishes the conservatives, who believed the war could have been won, from the liberals, who disputed this tactical judgement. No other question can arise in a well-disciplined commissar culture, which has the pragmatic criterion as its core moral doctrine. Our traditional values thus guarantee that we can do no wrong, as a matter of definition and principle – except as a result of naivete and understandable error. Of course, to maintain this happy state we must have the power to stamp on the face of anyone out there who might question our nobility, and the savagery to do so with equanimity. That has never been a problem.

Appreciation of the 'salutary efficacy' of 'a lively terror' is one fundamental component of our traditional values; another is our 'yearning for democracy'. The latter is illuminated by the reactions to the achievements of the current 'free world' crusade for democracy. Take Honduras. The liberal press describes the presidential elections of November 1989 as 'a milestone for the United States, which has used Honduras as evidence that the democratically elected governments it supports in Central America are taking hold'. President Bush, meeting with Honduran President Rafael Callejas after his election, called his government 'an inspiring example of the democratic promise that today is spreading throughout the Americas.'

A closer look helps us understand the operative concept of democracy. The elections were effectively restricted to two candidates, one from a family of wealthy industrialists, the other from a family of large landowners. Their top advisers 'acknowledge that there is little substantive difference between the two and the policies they would follow as president', we learn from the press report that hails this milestone. Both parties represent large landowners and industrialists and have close ties with the military, who are independent of civilian authority under the constitution but heavily dependent on the United States, as is the economy. The Guatemalan *Central America Report* adds that 'in the absence of substantial debate, both candidates rely on insults and accusations to entertain the crowds at campaign rallies and political functions' – all familiar to a US audience, not by coincidence. Popular participation was limited to ritual voting. The legal opposition parties (Christian Democratic and Social Democratic) charged massive electoral fraud.

Human rights abuses by the security forces escalated as the election approached, along with attacks with bombs and rifle fire against independent political figures, journalists and union leaders. In the preceding months, the armed forces conducted a campaign of political violence, including assassination of union leaders and other extrajudicial executions, leaving tortured and mutilated bodies by roadsides for the first time. The human rights organisation CODEH reported at least 78 people killed by the security forces in the first six months of 1989, while reported cases of torture and beatings more than tripled over the preceding year. But state terror remained at low enough levels not to disturb respectable opinion, so Honduras merits only polite applause for our benevolence.

Starvation and general misery are rampant, the extreme concentration of wealth increased during the decade of 'democracy', and 70 per cent of the population are malnourished. Despite substantial US aid and no guerrilla conflict, the economy is collapsing, with capital flight, a sharp drop in foreign investment and almost half of export earnings devoted to debt service. But there is no major threat to order, and profits flow.

In short, Honduras is a praiseworthy democracy, and there is no concern over the 'level playing field' for the elections, unlike Nicaragua, where an electoral campaign opened just at the moment of this 'inspiring example of the democratic process'. Leaving nothing to chance, George Bush brought his candidate to Washington where the White House announced that US economic warfare would end if the population voted as the US demanded. This economic warfare had been condemned by the World Court and the council of the General Agreement on Tariffs and Trade (GATT), but such facts are irrelevant in the lawless and violent cultures of the West, and therefore passed without notice, along with the World Court condemnation of the 'unlawful use of force', which elicited scarcely more than a few condemnations of the World Court as a 'hostile forum' (*New York Times*), and hence irrelevant. Bush also announced that US support for its terrorist forces would continue, in violation of the World Court judgement and the agreements of the Central American presidents. That too was passed over in silence, along with the continuing terror itself. In keeping with our traditional values, it is entirely legitimate to tell the people of Nicaragua that they have a 'free choice': vote as we dictate, or watch your children starve. Departure from these assumptions was at the level of statistical error, apart from the remote margins.

Another remarkable insight into Western political culture is provided by the reaction to the February 1990 elections – the first free elections in Nicaragua since Somoza, according to the official canon. Under the headline 'Americans United in Joy', the *New York Times* turned to the sole remaining issue: who deserves the credit for the joyous outcome? Such headlines as 'United in Joy' are not entirely unfamiliar. They might be found in North Korea or Albania, for example. The issue was plainly contentious, at least in Nicaragua, but enlightened Westerners are happy to depict themselves as dedicated totalitarians, 'united in joy'. The attitudes are so deeply entrenched as to pass unnoticed.

The press hailed this 'Victory for US Fair Play', also frankly explaining how it came about. In a typical reaction, *Time* magazine described the methods used to achieve the latest of the 'happy series of democratic surprises': to 'wreck the economy and prosecute a long and deadly proxy war until the exhausted natives overthrow the unwanted government themselves', with a cost to us that is 'minimal', leaving the victim 'with wrecked bridges, sabotaged power stations, and ruined farms', and thus providing the US candidate with 'a winning issue': ending the 'impoverishment of the people of Nicaragua'. The only issue dividing conservatives and liberals, *Time* concluded with complete accuracy, is 'who should claim credit' for this triumph of democracy. A respected commentator on the presidency, Hugh Sidey, called for 'a little fairness' to Ronald Reagan, who had achieved the goals we unanimously sought at little cost. 'Compare Viet Nam', Sidey observes: '58,000 Americans killed, $150 billion spent, the nation rent in bitterness, a bitter defeat.' In contrast, the Reaganites ran a cost-effective operation, expending only trivial sums to cause Nicaragua some US$15 billion in damages and 30,000 killed outright, along with unknown numbers of others who died from disease and hunger. We may note, however, that Sidey is a bit unfair to the Reaganites' predecessors, who did, after all, succeed in murdering millions in Indochina and leaving three countries in total ruin, not a small achievement despite the excessive cost to the US.

Out of a macabre interest in the political culture, I did a detailed survey of reactions to the US victory; across the spectrum, they scarcely varied – apart from the debate over who deserves the credit.

Even El Salvador and Guatemala are described as democracies. Elite opinion takes considerable pride in having established and maintained these charnel houses, with 'free elections' permitted after a wave of slaughter, torture, disappearance, mutilation and other effective devices of control. Physical destruction of the independent media and murder of editors and journalists by the security forces passed virtually without comment – often literally without report – among their US colleagues, along with many other atrocities.

The basic doctrines are captured by Robert Pastor (Pastor 1987), who directed Latin American affairs for the National Security Council under the Carter administration and is an ultra-left super-dove by US standards. In an interesting book on US policy towards Nicaragua, he writes that

> the United States did not want to control Nicaragua or the other nations in the region, but it also did not want to allow developments to get out of control. It wanted Nicaraguans to act independently, *except* when doing so would affect U.S. interests adversely (his emphasis).

In short, Nicaragua and other countries should be free – free to do what the US wants them to do. They should choose their own course independently, as long as their choice conforms to US interests. If they use the freedom accorded them unwisely, the US has every right to respond in self-defence, though opinions vary as to the proper tactical choices. Note that the conception of freedom and indepen- dence corresponds closely to liberal doctrine concerning the domestic population, who are granted the right to ratify the decisions of their betters, but not to choose unwisely.

With the 'Central American mode' restored, the general elite reaction is gratification over 'something all Americans can be proud of'. 'For the first time, all five of the countries are led by presidents who were elected in contests widely considered free and fair', the *Washington Post* reported from Guatemala City in June 1990, expressing the general satisfaction over the victory of 'conservative politicians' in elections which, we are to understand, took place on a level playing field with no coercion or foreign influence. It is true, the report continues, that 'conservative politicians in Central America traditionally represented the established order', defending the wealthy 'despite their countries' grossly distorted income patterns'. 'But the wave of democracy that has swept the region in recent years appears to be shifting politicians' priorities', so the bad old days are gone forever.

The student of American history and culture will recognise the familiar moves. Once again, we witness the miraculous change of course that occurs whenever some particularly brutal excesses of the state have been exposed – and, by reflex, filed in the category of inad- vertent error. Hence all of history, and the reasons for its persistent character, may be dismissed as irrelevant, while we march forward, leading our flock to a better world.

To demonstrate that the new conservatives are dedicated populists, the *Post* reviews the conference of the five presidents in Antigua, Guatemala, in 1990. The presidents, all 'committed to free-market economics', have abandoned worthless goals of social reform, the news story explains. 'Neither in the plan nor in the lengthier and more general "Declaration of Antigua" was there any mention of land reform or suggestion of new government social welfare programs to help the poor.' Rather, they are adopting 'a trickle-down approach to aid the poor'. 'The idea is to help the poor without threatening the basic power structure', a regional economist observes, contemplating these imag- inative new ideas on how to pursue our traditional vocation of serving the suffering masses: a 'preferential option for the rich', overcoming the errors of the Latin American bishops (Hockstader 1990).

While the three-day conference of populist conservatives was taking place in Antigua, 33 tortured, bullet-riddled bodies were discovered in Guatemala. They did not disturb the celebration over the triumph of freedom and democracy, or even make the news. Nor did the rest of the 125 bodies, half with signs of torture, found throughout the country that month, according to a report from the Guatemalan Human Rights Commission. The report comes to us from Mexico, where the Commission is based so that human rights workers can survive now that the US has succeeded in establishing democracy in their homeland.

A few days after the encouraging *Washington Post* report on the Antigua meeting, an editorial in a leading Honduran journal, *Tiempo*, appeared under the headline 'Misery is increasing in Honduras because of the economic adjustment', referring to the new and so promising trickle-down strategy – in fact, the traditional strategy with its lethal features now more firmly entrenched. The main victims are 'the usual neglected groups: children, women, and the aged', according to the conclusions of an academic seminar, confirmed by 'the Catholic Church, the unions, several political parties, and noted economists and statisticians of the country'. Half the population live below the level of 'dire need'. Unemployment, undernourishment and severe malnutrition are increasing. The story can be duplicated throughout the region, indeed throughout the domains that serve 'the rich men dwelling at peace within their habitations', who thus have the right to rule the world, as Winston Churchill explained.

One should not underestimate the success that Western humanism has attained in the past decade, 'an unrelenting nightmare' for the poor, as the chairman of the Organization for African Unity observed at a UN conference that failed to convince the rich men, basking in self-praise, to more than double their aid to the 41 poorest countries to a munificent .02 per cent of their GNP. Throughout the decade, the World Bank reports, the share of the world's wealth controlled by poor and medium-income countries declined from 23 per cent to 18 per cent (1980 to 1988) while resources transferred from the 'developing countries' to the industrialised world reached new records, debt service payments exceeded new flows of funds by over US$40 billion, and new funds from the wealthy declined through 1989 (*Central America Report*, 5 October 1990; *Financial Times* 17 September (1990). In short, Reaganomics and Thatcherism writ large.

Central America, the prime focus of recent concern, tells the story well enough. The challenge to the traditional order was effectively contained. The misery of the overwhelming majority deepened while the power of the military and the privileged sectors was enhanced behind a facade of democratic forms. The hopes of the beginning of the 1980s are a fading memory. Some 200,000 people have been killed, and countless others maimed, tortured, 'disappeared', driven from their homes. The people, the communities, the environment were devastated, possibly beyond repair. It was truly a grand victory.

There is still some unfinished business, however. In Nicaragua, the goal of restoring the security forces to US control has not yet been achieved, and the United Nicaraguan Opposition (UNO) government is not sufficiently harsh and brutal for US tastes. And despite US pressures – among them, withholding of the trickle of promised aid – the government did not abandon the World Court case and its call for reparations. Of course, respectable Western opinion would not expect the US to observe the judgement of the World Court, but the affair did cause a flicker of embarrassment amidst the posturing about the sanctity of international law.

Problems persist in El Salvador too. The assassination of the Jesuit intellectuals in November 1989 caused some discomfiture, but only for tactical reasons, as demonstrated by the reaction to other ongoing atrocities. In October 1990, Congress withheld half of planned military aid, US$42.5 million, in protest over the failure to prosecute the assassins. The Bush administration protested, but not too vociferously. One reason, dutifully suppressed by the free press, is that the White House had arranged for the IMF to provide El Salvador with US$50 million two months earlier, funds intended to free an additional US$100 million from other private sources, along with US$100 million of debt rescheduling.

Since 1917, the use of force has been presented as self-defence against the Soviet threat – including intervention in Russia itself. Before the Bolshevik revolution, similar actions were taken, but in fear of other menaces. When Woodrow Wilson invaded Mexico and Hispaniola – where his warriors murdered and destroyed, re-established virtual slavery, demolished the political system, and placed the countries firmly in the hands of US investors – the actions were in self-defence against the Huns. In earlier years, conquests and interventions were undertaken in defence against Britain and the 'base Canadian fiends' it manipulated, or Spain, or the 'merciless Indian savages' of the Declaration of Independence – in reality, against whoever was in the way.

With the Cold War a fading memory, intervention continued as before. In the first act of aggression of the post-Cold War era, the US invaded Panama in December 1989, killing hundreds (possibly thousands) of civilians, restoring the rule of the 10 per cent white elite and ensuring its grip on the canal zone. Not even the most fertile imagination could conjure up a Russian threat, so other pretexts were concocted, no less ludicrous but more suited to the occasion. Ambassador Thomas Pickering even informed the United Nations that the US interprets the UN Charter as entitling it to use force to 'defend our interests' – a momentary lapse into realism, dutifully ignored by the faithful.

After the First World War, then, the traditional pattern of intervention continued, but with two basic changes. First, the US joined Britain and France as a major actor in the international arena. Second, its interventions were now in defence of civilisation itself against the challenge of the Bolsheviks.

The analytic framework devised after the First World War was extended to broader domains in the 1940s, as the US became history's first truly global power and turned to the task of constructing a world order in its interests. Industrial capitalism was to be reconstructed under the leadership of Germany and Japan, but now under US control. Within the general framework of liberal internationalism, US business was expected to flourish, finding ample investment opportunities and markets for its excess production, expectations that were largely fulfilled. The function of the Third World has already been discussed.

From the 1970s, the postwar system has been moving towards what is now called a New World Order – but one that bears little resemblance to the constructions of the ideologues, with their lovely phrases about peace, justice and the sanctity of international law. The basic contours of the actual New World Order were coming into focus at the end of the 1960s, with the emergence of a 'tripolar world' as economic power diffused within US domains. The collapse of Soviet tyranny adds several new dimensions. First, there are now prospects for the Latin Americanisation of much of the former Soviet empire; that is, for its return to its traditional quasi-colonial status, providing resources, cheap labour, markets, investment opportunities and other standard Third World amenities. This is a development that may have large-scale consequences. The United States is distinctly uneasy over the prospect of German-led Europe and Japan taking the lead in exploiting this new Third World.

A second consequence of the Soviet collapse is that the United States is more free than before to use force, the Soviet deterrent having disappeared. In any confrontation, each contestant seeks to play its strong cards, to shift the conflict to an arena in which it is likely to prevail. For such reasons, the US has always regarded diplomacy and international law as an annoying encumbrance, a fact familiar to those who follow the affairs of South-East Asia, Central America and the Middle East, among others. With the current configuration of US strengths and weaknesses, the temptation to transfer problems quickly to the arena of forceful confrontation is likely to be strong.

Furthermore, the United States intends to maintain its near monopoly of force, with no likely contestant for that role. One consequence will be exacerbation of domestic economic difficulties; another, a renewed temptation to 'go it alone' in relying on the threat of force rather than diplomacy.

The Gulf conflict brought these issues to the fore. Aside from Great Britain, which has its own interests in Kuwait, the major industrial powers showed little interest in military confrontation. The reaction in Washington was ambivalent. War is dangerous; but defusing the crisis without a demonstration of the efficacy of force is also an unwanted outcome. As for the costs, plainly it would be advantageous for them to be shared, but not at the price of sacrificing the role of lone enforcer. These conflicting concerns led to a sharp elite split over the tactical choice between the threat of force and reliance on sanctions, with the Bush administration holding to the former course.

In the New World Order, the Third World domains must still be controlled, sometimes by force. This task has been the responsibility of the United States, but with its relative economic decline, the burden becomes harder to shoulder. One reaction is that the US must persist in its historic task, while turning to others to pay the bills. Testifying before Congress, US Deputy Secretary of State Lawrence Eagleburger explained that the emerging New World Order will be based on 'a kind of new invention in the practice of diplomacy': others will pay the costs of US intervention to keep order (Curtius 1990). In the *Financial Times*, David Hale, a respected commentator on international economic affairs, describes the Gulf crisis as a 'watershed event in US international relations', which will be seen in history as having 'turned the US military into an internationally financed public good ... an internationally financed police force'. While 'some Americans will question the morality of the US military assuming a more explicitly mercenary role than it has played in the past', he adds, 'in the 1990s there is no realistic alternative' (Hale1990). The tacit assumption is that the public welfare is to be identified with the welfare of the Western industrial powers, and particularly their domestic elites.

The financial editor of a leading US conservative daily, William Neikirk of the *Chicago Tribune*, puts the point less delicately: the US must exploit 'virtual monopoly in the security market ... as a lever to gain funds and economic concessions' from Germany and Japan. The US has 'cornered the West's security market' and others lack the 'political will ... to challenge the US' in this 'market'. The US will therefore be 'the world's rent-a-cops' and will be 'able to charge handsomely' for the service; the term 'rent-a-thug' would be less flattering but more appropriate. Some will call the US 'Hessians', Neikirk continues, but 'that's a terribly demeaning phrase for a proud, well-trained, well-financed and well-respected military'; and whatever anyone may say, 'we should be able to pound our fists on a few desks' in Japan and Europe, and 'extract a fair price for our considerable services', demanding that 'our' rivals 'buy our bonds at cheap rates, or keep the dollar propped up, or better yet, pay cash directly into our Treasury ... 'We could change this role' of enforcer, he concludes, 'but with it would go much of our control over the world economic system' (Neikirk 1990).

A right-wing British perspective is added by Peregrine Worsthorne. Britain is 'no match for Germany and Japan when it comes to wealth creation; or even for France and Italy. But when it comes to shouldering world responsibilities we are more than a match.' The responsibility in the post-Cold War world is 'to help build and sustain a world order stable enough to allow the advanced economies of the world to function without constant interruption and threat from the Third World', a task that will require 'instant intervention from the advanced nations' and perhaps even 'pre-emptive action'. Only the US and Britain are qualified for the task of silencing any disturbing rumbles from the servants' quarters, a legacy of their heroic past and the 'national character' that distinguishes them from contemptible rivals such as Germany and France who lack this 'caring' nature (Worsthorne 1990)

These conceptions, though rarely put so bluntly, are widely held, and capture an essential element of Washington's reaction to the Gulf crisis. They imply that the US should continue to take on the grim task of imposing order with the acquiescence and support of the other industrial powers along with riches funnelled by the dependent oil-producing monarchies.

There has been much curious commentary about the 'wondrous sea change' at the United Nations (*New York Times*), now at last able to undertake its peacekeeping function with the Cold War over, no longer obstructed by the Soviet veto and Third World ranting. The facts, scrupulously avoided in the hundreds of articles on this topic, provide a different message, with no ambiguity. In the early years, the Soviet Union regularly blocked UN action, the organisation being virtually an instrument of US foreign policy. But as the world recovered from the war and UN membership broadened with decolonisation, the picture changed radically. From the beginning of the 1970s to the beginning of the 1990s, the US was far in the lead in Security Council vetoes and negative votes in the General Assembly, often alone or with some client state, on every relevant issue: aggression, annexation, international law, terrorism, disarmament and so on. During the same period Great Britain was in second place, France a distant third, and the USSR fourth, with one-seventh as many vetoes as the US. There is no reason to suppose that with the Soviet withdrawal from world affairs, the US and its British client will suddenly end their campaign against international law, diplomacy and collective security – which had virtually nothing to do with the Cold War, as a look at actual cases will show. Furthermore, the 'anti-Western' Third World rhetoric that is so commonly derided often turns out to be a call for adherence to international law, a weak barrier against the depredations of the powerful. In the case of the Gulf, the UN could act because for once it was not being blocked by the US and its allies, as in many other cases, some much worse. A good example is the near-genocidal Indonesian invasion and annexation of Timor, to cite just one atrocity still in progress, which occurred, as always, with the decisive support of the US and Britain.

In the post-Cold War period, the pattern continues without change. Between November 1989 and January 1991, four Security Council resolutions were vetoed, two condemning Israeli human rights abuses, two condemning the US invasion of Panama. All were vetoed by the United States, in one case joined by Britain and France, in another with Britain abstaining. The General Assembly voted two resolutions calling for adherence to international law, one condemning US support for its terrorist forces attacking Nicaragua, the other the illegal US embargo; the US and Israel were alone in opposition. A resolution opposing the acquisition of territory by force passed 151 to 3 (US, Israel, Dominica), another affirmation of the peaceful diplomatic settlement of the Arab–Israeli conflict that the US has blocked for more than 20 years. Nothing here has to do with the Cold War, the Russian veto or Third World psychotics. The tales about the UN have sometimes moved from merely misleading to plain deceitful: the cumulative total of vetoes from the 1940s are cited with the crucial matter of dates and circumstances suppressed so as to lend credence to the theses required by the propaganda system.

In accord with the pragmatic criterion, the use of force and terror is only a last resort. The IMF is to be preferred to the CIA and the marines, if possible; but it is not always possible.

Some of the new devices can be found in the Uruguay Round of the GATT negotiations for a New World Economic Order, now in disarray because of conflicts among the rich, but sure to be revived in one or another form. Western powers call for 'liberalisation' when it is in their interest; and for enhanced protection of domestic economic actors, when *that* is in their interest. The major concern of the United States in the GATT negotiations was not so much agricultural policy as the 'new themes', as they are called: guarantees for 'intellectual property rights', removal of constraints on services and investment, and so on; a mixture of liberalisation and protectionism, determined by the interests of the powerful. The effect of these measures would be to restrict Third World governments to a police function to control their working classes and superfluous population, while transnational corporations gain free access to their resources and monopolise new technology and global investment and production. The corporations, furthermore, are granted the central planning, allocation, production and distribution functions denied to governments, which suffer from the defect that they might fall under the baleful influence of the rabble. These facts have not been lost on Third World commentators, who have been protesting eloquently and mightily. But their voices are unheard – again, in accord with US traditional values.

We may also take note of the broad if tacit understanding that the capitalist model has limited application; business leaders have long recognised that it is not for them. The successful industrial societies depart significantly from this model, as in the past – one reason why they are successful industrial societies. The US became the breadbasket of the world and its greatest industrial power, instead of pursuing its comparative advantage in the production of furs, because of state subsidy, investment and protection – which, incidentally, increased sharply under Reaganite 'conservatism'. The sectors of the economy that remain competitive are those that feed from the public trough: high-tech industry and capital-intensive agriculture, along with pharmaceuticals and others. Departures are still more radical in most of the other state capitalist systems, where planning is coordinated by state institutions and financial-industrial conglomerates, sometimes with democratic processes and a social contract of varying sorts, sometimes not.

Japan and its periphery are a familiar case, along with Germany, where, to mention only one feature, the IMF estimates that industrial incentives amount to a 30 per cent tariff. Some comparative studies of Latin America and East Asia attribute the disparities that developed in the 1980s in large part to the deleterious effects of greater openness to international capital markets in Latin America, which permitted huge capital flight, unlike East Asian economies which have more rigid controls by government and central banks – and in the free market miracle of South Korea, which controls via punishment up to the death penalty.

The glories of free enterprise provide a useful weapon against government policies that might benefit the general population, and, of course, capitalism will do just fine for the former colonies and the former Soviet empire. For those who are to 'fulfil their functions' in service to the 'rich men dwelling at peace within their habitations', the model is highly recommended; it facilitates their exploitation. But the rich and powerful at home have long appreciated the need to protect themselves from the destructive forces of free market capitalism, which may provide suitable themes for rousing oratory, but only so long as the public handout and the regulatory and protectionist apparatus are secure, and state power is on call when needed.

The costs of the emerging world order will be obvious to anyone who surveys the immense catastrophes of capitalism in the past years, particularly the past decade, dramatically evident in the wreckage of the inner cities in the world's richest country and throughout the vast regions that have long fulfilled their service function – though some sectors, linked to the rich men who rule the world, do very well for themselves. But the wealthy and privileged will not escape unscathed. The physical environment to sustain human existence is severely threatened as policy is driven by greed, and weapons of mass destruction proliferate in large measure because of great power interests. There are also growing conflicts among the three major power blocs: German-led Europe; Japan and its periphery; the US and the trading and resource bloc it is seeking to consolidate in the Western hemisphere and the Middle East. In earlier eras, such conflicts led to global war. That will not happen in the present case, for two major reasons; the interpenetration of capital is far higher, so that state power has broader and more complex interests than in earlier periods; and modern weaponry is so awesome that wars can be contemplated only against opponents too weak to strike back.

We can make this prediction with complete confidence; if it is wrong, there will be no one to refute us.

Such factors as these will shape the new methods for continuing the war against the Third World, now in a different guise and with a more varied array of competing actors. Popular forces in the United States and Europe have placed certain barriers in the path of state terror, and have offered some help to those targeted for repression, but unless they gain considerably in scale and commitment, the future for the traditional victims looks grim.

Grim, but not hopeless. With amazing courage and persistence, oppressed people continue to struggle for their rights. And in the industrial world, with Bolshevism disintegrating and capitalism long abandoned, there are prospects for the revival of libertarian socialist and radical democratic ideals that had languished, including popular control of the workplace and investment decisions, and, correspondingly, the establishment of more meaningful political democracy as constraints imposed by private power are reduced. These and other emerging possibilities are still remote, but no more so than the possibility of parliamentary democracy and elementary rights of citizenship were 250 years ago. No one knows enough to predict what human will can achieve.

We are faced with a familiar choice: assume the worst, and it will surely arrive; commit oneself to the struggle for freedom and justice, and its cause may be advanced.

References

Chomsky, Noam 1989. *Necessary Illusions*. London, Pluto Press.
—— 1991. *Deterring Democracy*. London, Verso Press (US edn, New York 1992), Chapter 12.
Curtius, Mary 1990. *Boston Globe*, 20 September.
Fox, Richard 1985. *Reinhold Niebuhr: A Biography*. Pantheon, 1985.
Hale, David 1990. *Financial Times*, 17 September.
Hill, Christopher 1975. *The World Turned Upside Down*. Harmondsworth, Penguin.
Hockstader, Lee 1990. *Washington Post*, 20 June.
LaFeber, Walter 1983. *Inevitable Revolutions*. New York, Norton.
Morgan, S. 1988. *Inventing the People*. New York, Norton.
Niebuhr, Reinhold 1932 (reprinted 1952). *Moral Man and Immoral Society*. New York, Scribners.
Neikirk, William 1990. Business section, *Chicago Tribune*, 9 September.
Pastor, Robert 1987. *Condemned to Repetition*. Princeton, NJ, Princeton University Press.
Rossiter, Clinton and Lare, James (eds) 1982. *The Essential Lippmann: A Political Philosophy for Liberal Democracy*. Cambridge, Mass., Harvard University Press.
Worsthorne, Peregrine 1990. *Sunday Telegraph*, 16 September (reprinted in *National Interest*, winter 1990–1).

[handwritten note:] Extends the notion of elite-based power to an intl. context: developed nations are controlled in a way similar to Marcuse, this deceit is merely extended to the less developed nations.

5. The Tragedy of American Democracy

ROGER BURBACH*

On 30 March 1990, Secretary of State James Baker in a speech to the World Affairs Council in Dallas, Texas, made a little publicised but major policy address. He laid out new objectives for US foreign policy in the wake of the collapse of the Soviet threat and the virtual end of the Cold War. Basking in the belief that US, or Western-style, values had triumphed in Eastern Europe and stymied Soviet intervention around the globe, Baker proclaimed that this was no time for the US to declare 'mission accomplished, to tend our problems at home.' 'Beyond containment lies democracy' he asserted. The new US mission is the 'promotion and consolidation of democracy.' America could be the 'city on the hill' for the rest of the world if it pursued these objectives in the years to come.

Less than five months later, the United States embarked on a course in the Gulf that had nothing to do with democracy. As President Bush himself declared in August 1990, the United States was sending troops to the Gulf to defend the 'American way of life,' meaning that the administration was intent on securing the flow of oil in world markets to protect the US standard of living. A few months later when US objectives in the Gulf came under congressional scrutiny, Secretary of State Baker adopted an even cruder justification for the Gulf adventure when he asserted that 'American jobs' were on the line. Not a word was heard about democracy, as the United States sought to restore the Emir of Kuwait and to protect Saudi King Fahd and the sheikhs of the conservative Gulf states. President Bush did try to portray the conflict as one between good and evil by asserting that Saddam Hussein was a new Hitler the world could not tolerate. But unlike the first coalition that defeated Hitler, this one did not pretend to hold high the banner of democracy as an alternative to the dictators and despots of the Arab world.

* The author wishes to thank the Fund for Investigative Journalism for a grant that made possible much of the investigative research for this article.

The tragedy of American foreign policy today is that just as much of the world's population is throwing out old-style regimes of the Left and the Right and moving towards greater participation in the affairs of government and society, the United States is caught in a fundamental dilemma between its declared support for democracy and its perception of its economic needs and interests abroad. US leaders argue that there is no cleavage between the two, that democracy and free market capitalism are compatible, that the two go hand in hand. This is, however, a simplistic argument which ignores the reality that the two objectives are often in contradiction with each other.

To understand fully the American democratic tragedy, it is necessary to look first at the institutions and policies the Reagan and Bush administrations developed in the name of democracy. Next we will look at what impact these institutions and policies have had abroad, particularly in Latin America and Eastern Europe. Finally the very concept of US-style democracy will be discussed and critiqued, particularly as it relates to US foreign policy.

Reagan's Democratic Revolution

Contrary to the common belief that the Reagan administration did little in the way of developing the US concept of democracy, it actually moved on three fronts to use democracy as an ideological tool in US foreign policy (Nuñez and Burbach 1990; Epstein 1989). Initially when Ronald Reagan took office it appeared that the United States would jettison even some of the limited democratic principles that previous presidencies had espoused. The human rights, anti-dictatorial policies of the Carter administration were scorned from early on as being unrealistic and soft on communism. The fall of the Shah of Iran and the ensuing Iranian Revolution, the overthrow of Somoza and the triumph of the Sandinista movement in Nicaragua, and the guerrilla challenge in El Salvador were viewed as problems that had emerged because of the Carter administration's decision to undercut the old regimes in the name of human rights.

Jeanne Kirkpatrick's (1979) widely publicised article, 'Dictators and Double Standards' captured the early thinking of the Reagan administration. Kirkpatrick argued that there was a fundamental difference between the pro-United States authoritarian governments and the totalitarian, communist governments. The former were allegedly open to change and evolution in a democratic direction, while totalitarian governments, once in power, set up institutions that systematically repressed their populations in a manner that prevented the rise of any opposition or democratic movements. In line with this analysis, Secretary of State Haig announced that the United States would engage in 'quiet diplomacy' with authoritarian governments. In Central America, the Philippines, South Africa and other regions the United States would not openly denounce transgressions and violations of basic democratic rights, but it would supposedly work behind the scenes and negotiate privately with the errant governments to get them to mend their ways.

While the Reagan administration never formally renounced this approach, international realities compelled the United States to adopt a different tack. By the mid-1980s, US-allied authoritarian governments were under siege around the world. Under the auspices of Haig's replacement, Secretary of State George Schultz, the United States in fact began to pull the plug on many dictatorial governments in hopes of forestalling a victory by radical revolutionary movements. There is no doubt that in the cases of Marcos in the Philippines, Pinochet in Chile, Duvalier in Haiti and Stroessner in Paraguay, US actions and diplomacy were critical and decisive in their fall from power.

Simultaneously, what became known as the Reagan Doctrine led to a new interest in taking up the banner of democracy. Not content to accept the status quo in the Third World, where 14 revolutionary governments had come to power in the 1970s, the Reagan administration sought to roll back or overthrow Marxist and revolutionary governments by supporting armed internal opposition movements. Angola, Afghanistan and Nicaragua became the primary examples of this new policy.

To lend legitimacy to these armed movements, the United States proclaimed that it was intent not on restoring the ancien régimes but on establishing new democratic governments. Anti-communist guerrillas were labelled 'freedom fighters' and compared to the US founding fathers. In cases like Angola, Mozambique and Afghanistan it was difficult for much of the world to swallow these democratic claims, especially since the counter-revolutionary movements in these countries were bent on re-establishing the old hierarchical tribal orders rather than on securing democracy.

There is no doubt that Reagan's ideological campaign at least made it possible for the administration to mobilise international support and to endow the counter-revolutionary movements with a certain sense of legitimacy they otherwise lacked. Thatcher's Britain, Kohl's West Germany, the Papacy, and prominent international leaders all provided symbolic and even material support to Reagan's counter-revolutionary campaign in the name of democracy. And at the grass-roots level in some Third World countries, this campaign did win the 'hearts and minds' of local peoples. In Nicaragua, for example, many peasants rallied to the ranks of the counter-revolutionary forces because they really did come to believe that the Sandinista government was authoritarian, godless and anti-democratic. This was a distortion of reality but the point is that the Reagan administration, through its use of the democratic banner, was able to convince others that it was fighting for democracy and against totalitarianism.

Enter the National Endowment for Democracy

To counteract scepticism about the democratic content of Reagan's counter-revolutionary policies, the administration developed a new arm of foreign policy that was formally dedicated to building democratic institutions abroad – the National Endowment for Democracy (NED). In 1982, Ronald Reagan in a speech to the British Parliament proclaimed a new 'crusade for democracy'. During the ensuing year, funds were provided to plan and lobby for a bipartisan institution that would be charged with assisting pro-US democratic organisations abroad.

In the earlier Cold War years, the Central Intelligence Agency (CIA) under both Democratic and Republican administrations had often intervened in foreign elections and politics to support political forces and parties that were sympathetic to US interests. By the mid-1970s, however the assassinations, coups and other covert activities of the CIA had provoked a series of investigations and congressional hearings which led to legislation that formally curtailed the CIA's ability to intervene in political processes abroad.[1]

The Reagan administration, champing at the bit with these restrictions as it sought to engage the Soviet Union and the radical revolutionary movements, brought together with NED a group of political operatives and intellectuals who had been arguing for almost a decade for the establishment of a new public institution that would openly fund foreign political activities. Neoconservatives, some of whom had been socialists and even Marxists, became the driving intellectual force behind the National Endowment for Democracy. Given their backgrounds and experiences, the neoconservatives were ideally situated to take up the institutional work needed to merge democracy with fighting communism abroad. Allen Weinstein, the first president of NED and Carl Gershman, who replaced him in 1984 and who still heads NED, were both leading neoconservatives, with long track records of fighting communism, particularly in the trade unions and in intellectual circles.

The founding of the National Endowment for Democracy turned out to be a stroke of genius by the Reagan administration. It successfully mobilised bipartisan support for a foreign policy that was very partisan and that often came under criticism by Democrats for its virulent anti-communism and its use of surrogate military forces abroad. The Iran-Contra scandal and the ensuing congressional hearings represented the climax of this partisan struggle over foreign policy. NED, however, while pursuing the same intense anti-communist goals, managed largely to isolate itself from these political attacks by having leading Democrats on its board (like Walter Mondale and Edmund Muskie) and by limiting its funding activities to foreign political and civic organisations. Most of NED's funds were distributed by four mainstream organisations – the Free Trade Union Institute (an arm of the American Federation of Labor and Congress of Industrial Organizations, or AFL-CIO), the Center for International Private Enterprise (US Chamber of Commerce), the National Democratic Institute for International Affairs (Democratic Party), and the National Republican Institute for International Affairs (Republican Party). (See NED, 1988.)

NED's early years were largely uneventful as it provided limited funding to political organisations in Asia, Latin America, Africa and Eastern Europe. Its first big operation came in Chile, when Congress appropriated US$1 million for the 1988 plebiscite that was to decide whether or not the Chilean dictator, Augusto Pinochet, would remain in power. Fearing another Nicaragua scenario after a series of political riots and strikes in mid-1986, the Reagan administration wanted to secure Pinochet's removal from office before Leftist political forces gained the upper hand. Most of the funding went to support the moderate organisations opposing the dictator, particularly the Christian Democrats (who had originally supported Pinochet in the early years after his coup against the elected socialist President, Salvador Allende). When Pinochet was defeated in the October 1988 plebiscite, NED's prestige as an effective pro-democratic institution grew among Democrats and Republicans alike.[2]

Bush's Democratic Charge

When George Bush took office, he inherited a foreign policy that had been largely successful in wedding the concept of democracy to anti-communist campaigns around the globe. Many of the most troublesome dictators were gone, armed counter-revolutionary movements in Africa, Asia and Latin America had stymied the efforts of many Marxist and revolutionary governments to consolidate their rule, and the National Endowment for Democracy had helped generate broad bipartisan support for some of Reagan's policies abroad.

There were, however, two major areas of controversy and tension left over from the Reagan years – the Contra war against the San-dinistas, and the campaign against Panamanian strongman Manuel Noriega. In each of these cases Bush was able to build on the Reagan democratic legacy to win victories that had eluded the former President. In Panama, Bush used NED as well as covert funding to support the domestic opposition to Noriega in the May 1989 elections. A page was taken out of the book of the Chilean plebiscite, in that scores of bipartisan observers, including Democrats like Jimmy Carter, were funded to go to Panama to oversee the elections. When the results of the elections were annulled by Noriega after voting irregularities and political disturbances (some provoked by the opposition), the US observers unanimously placed the blame for the failed elections on Noriega's shoulders.[3]

Given the bipartisan consensus against Noriega and the almost universal antipathy towards him that was generated among the American public, it was relatively easy for George Bush seven months later to employ US military force on the North American continent for the first time since the 1930s to overthrow Noriega. After the invasion, Bush, who had been viewed as a weak president prior to this action, saw his popularity rise dramatically in the opinion polls. The success of this venture against a non-democratic ruler virtually ended the 'Vietnam Syndrome', as conservatives called it, and made it possible for Bush seven months later to send US troops to confront Saddam Hussein in the Gulf.

In Nicaragua, the Bush administration had to tread more cautiously, for a significant sector of the US public never supported the contras as 'freedom fighters', nor did they view the Sandinistas as hardline rulers who had to be removed by direct US force. Bush, however, astutely turned to the most untarnished arm of Reagan's foreign policy apparatus, the National Endowment for Democracy. When the San-dinistas, as part of the Central American peace process, announced that the Nicaraguan general elections would be advanced from November to February 1990, the Bush administration persuaded Congress to provide US$9 million to NED to support opposition to the Sandinistas.

There is no doubt that NED played a critical role in the subsequent defeat of Sandinista President Daniel Ortega. The 13 diverse parties – ranging from communists to conservatives – that joined together in a coalition to back Violeta Chamorro as the candidate of the United Nicaraguan Opposition (UNO) were held together largely by NED funding and cajoling from the US embassy in Managua. NED funding also had a major impact on the Nicaraguan public.[4] If the equivalent of US$9 million were spent in the United States on a per capita basis, it would come to a total of three-quarters of a billion dollars. Moreover, given the much lower per capita income in Nicaragua, this amount of funding could buy a lot more and have a much greater impact. Thus it was no surprise that many Nicaraguans, seeing the United States pouring funds into the coffers of Chamorro's political campaign, came to believe that a Chamorro victory would mean continued US largesse, plus an end to the long and bitter war with the Contras.

These twin victories in Central America, combined with the upheaval in Eastern Europe in the latter part of 1989, made the United States and the Bush administration appear almost invincible. Communist governments were gone or in disarray, pro-US democratic governments were in place throughout the western hemisphere except for Cuba, and the Cold War had come to an end with the United States appearing to be the decisive victor. A political sea change had occurred in the world. Small wonder that George Bush and Secretary of State Baker could wax euphoric, proclaiming total victory on behalf of the Western democracies.

But had US-style democracy really emerged triumphant? Had new, stable, truly democratic institutions been forged in the old authoritarian and totalitarian societies? When one looks in depth at what the so-called 'democratic revolutions' have really meant for much of the world, one can argue that the Reagan and Bush administrations have done virtually nothing to establish authentic democratic institutions abroad. On a rhetorical level they have simply taken advantage of the democratic aspirations of other peoples to advance capitalism and narrow US economic interests.

The Democratic Quagmire in Latin America

Today, after a decade of economic decline in Latin America and the Caribbean, the region's democratic institutions are extremely fragile and threatened by political upheaval. Only three countries in the region – Chile, the Dominican Republic and Colombia – had positive per capita growth rates in the 1980s (Castenada 1990). Much of Colombia's growth was due to the booming drug trafficking that brought foreign currency into the country for local investments while Chile was ruled by Pinochet, who had secured stability and economic growth on behalf of a small economic elite. The Dominican Republic had moderate growth, although it was concentrated in the low-wage export zones. No country in Latin America or the Caribbean with a democratically elected government could lay claim to being a model of an 'economic miracle'.

If there is one lesson that emerges from the 1980s in the countries to the south of the United States, it is that the much lauded policy of neoliberal economics has not strengthened democratic institutions. In the early 1980s, the International Monetary Fund (IMF) under the direction of US and other Western leaders began to impose a series of austerity measures on Latin America. Due to massive lending by Western banking institutions in the 1970s and a drop in the world prices of most primary products produced by Third World countries, Latin America found itself unable to continue paying its international debts in the early 1980s. The IMF in many cases agreed to help the countries restructure their debt loads, but only if they carried out neoliberal economic programmes. Social spending was severely curtailed, many state-owned enterprises were sold off, and protectionist measures were dropped so that foreign capital would have access to local markets and drive out 'inefficient industries' (MacEwan 1990).

Contrary to the rhetoric of the IMF and US leaders, these policies have failed. They have not induced economic growth in Latin America, only more suffering and economic deprivation for the bulk of the region's population. The foisting of neoliberalism on Latin America and the Caribbean explains in large part the political and social upheaval that is engulfing many countries. The violent food riots in Argentina, Brazil, Venezuela and the Dominican Republic in recent years were direct responses to IMF programmes. Anthony P. Maingot (1989, pp. 6–8), a long-time observer of the Caribbean who is no radical, argues that the situation is now fundamentally explosive throughout the Caribbean and that neoliberal policies have not worked. He states: 'There is danger that the new "neo-liberal" pragmatism can become another ideological ploy, no more useful than the socialist rhetoric of the 1960s and 70s. There might be danger in overstated rhetoric about privatisation and the market.'

Along with neoliberal economics, specific US policies have done little or nothing to nurture the development of democracy in the western hemisphere. The invasion of Panama, carried out in part to 'restore democracy', has not stabilised the country. In the wake of the invasion, the government of President Guillermo Endara enjoys little popular support. The political consensus in Panama is that if Endara had to stand in a plebiscite or elections, he would lose overwhelmingly. The basic problem is that Endara is viewed as a puppet of the United States who has been unable to improve the lot of the country's population. Sworn in as President on a US military base in the canal zone on the night of the invasion, Endara has been unable to build a local political base. A badly organised mutiny within the ranks of the restructured Panamanian security forces was suppressed only by the intervention of US army units from the Panamanian canal zone. Only continued US military support keeps Endara in power, while popular discontent continues to build.

Nicaragua provides another case study of how US intervention in the name of democracy has led to social and political disintegration rather than to the forging of new democratic institutions. Soon after the victory of Violeta Chamorro in the February 1990 elections, the UNO coalition that the US embassy had pulled together to back her split into contending factions fighting over the spoils of victory. Chamorro's Vice-President, Virgilio Godoy, has been a major antagonist of the new President's policies since the moment of her inauguration. He has formed his own paramilitary units, but, ironically, it is the old Sandinista army which has prevented Godoy from mounting any real military challenge to the Chamorro government.

The National Endowment for Democracy, having achieved its objective by securing the defeat of the Sandinistas, reduced its funding in Nicaragua to a mere trickle of what it was before. While the United States did make an emergency grant of US$300 million to the new government, these funds did not stabilise the country economically or politically. In fact Nicaragua is politically fragmented, with no group or political party able to control its destiny. Remnants of the Contras occupy roads and towns, demanding that they receive the financial aid that was promised them when they disbanded, Sandinista trade unions go on strike on a regular basis to demand that their wages keep pace with inflation rates, and in the countryside peasants take over new lands while old landowners return to try to take control of properties that were officially expropriated in the early 1980s. As one long term foreign observer of the country noted, 'Nicaragua is ungovernable. No one runs the place. There are only small local fiefdoms of control and influence'.[5]

Democracy and Double Standards

Mexico, rather than Central America as a whole, may provide the clearest case of where narrowly conceived economic and political interests have led US policy makers to adopt hypocritical and double standard policies. In Central America, one could argue that the spectre of communism and drug dealers compelled the United States to carry out policies that were of dubious democratic validity. But in Mexico there has been no real communist or national security threat; only political and economic forces have at times not been to the liking of the United States.

In the early and mid-1980s, the Reagan administration and neo-conservatives began to question the democratic credentials of the ruling Institutional Revolutionary Party, or PRI. Upset by the independent role Mexico was playing in the Central America conflict and by the country's long-standing protectionism, particularly of its petroleum resources, administration representatives began to point out that the PRI was a corrupt, authoritarian government that had manipulated elections since the 1930s to hold on to power.[6] The National Action Party, or PAN, a conservative opposition party backed by Mexican business interests, suddenly became the 'democratic darling' of the Reagan administration. By the mid-1980s the National Endowment for Democracy was funding individuals and organisations aligned with PAN.

However, the 1988 presidential elections in Mexico precipitated an about-face in US policy. At first, the United States applied pressure on PRI to hold fair and open elections. But then a political earthquake shook Mexican party politics when Cuauhtemoc Cárdenas, the son of a popular Mexican President of the 1930s, split the ranks of the ruling PRI and set up the Revolutionary Democratic Party, or PRD. The PRD campaigned on a platform of nationalism and democratic populism. In the ensuing presidential contest between the PAN, PRI and PRD candidates, it is unclear whether Cárdenas or Carlos Salinas de Gotari, the PRI candidate, won the majority of votes. However, what is universally acknowledged is that massive vote fraud was perpetrated by PRI and that Salinas de Gotari did not win the 51 per cent of the vote as the government-controlled electoral commission claimed.

In the ensuing uproar in Mexico over the election, little was heard from US policy makers. There were no NED-sponsored election observers who denounced the fraud, nor did the United States government make any public statements about the fairness of the elections. The fact was that, given the candidacy of the nationalist and Left-leaning Cárdenas, the United States preferred the victory of Salinas de Gotari. And to help ensure the stability of the new government when it took power, the Bush administration rushed in with US-backed loans. Since then electoral fraud has continued in state and local elections, particularly in southern Mexico where PRD is strongest. In subsequent gubernatorial elections, an opposition victory was recognised only in Baja California, where the conservative PAN party is strong and enjoys support from US business interests across the border. Even more importantly, repression and violence have grown throughout Mexico, with a number of PRD sympathisers and candidates being assassinated (Amnesty International 1991). However, the Bush administration was notoriously quiet in making any statements opposing the violence or the suppression of democratic freedoms in Mexico.

Economic Initiatives Take Command

Next to the US intervention in the Gulf to secure the flow of petroleum, the consolidation of economic interests in US foreign policy in the post-Cold War era is most prominently manifested in the Initiative for the Americas. Officially launched by George Bush during his whirlwind tour of key South American countries in December 1990, the Initiative calls for the creation of a free trade zone stretching from Alaska to the Magellan Straits. Occurring almost at the same time that the General Agreement on Tariffs and Trade (GATT) talks to expand free trade were failing, the strategic objective of the initiative is to create a US-led trade bloc in the western hemisphere that will rival the united European economic system and the emerging Japanese sphere of influence in Asia and the Pacific.

Unfortunately, the implications for democracy in the hemisphere of the free trade zone are largely adverse. Labour and citizen groups throughout the hemisphere, including the AFL-CIO of the United States, have come out squarely against the proposed free trade zone. They argue that US capital unfettered in the hemisphere will seek out the cheapest labour markets, undermine already weak trade unions and decimate many industries that are now located in the more advanced countries. The rebuttal by the supporters of the Initiative is that 'free trade' will benefit all, that industries in countries like Canada and the United States will modernise and move into high-tech areas, while millions of people in countries in Latin America will have higher paying jobs and greater economic security, which in turn will lend stability to democratic institutions.

However, the arguments of the Initiative's supporters are seriously flawed. The Initiative will concentrate economic power even more throughout the hemisphere, lead to the intensified exploitation of workers and undermine rather than sustain whatever democratic institutions may exist. One only has to look at economic developments in Mexico during the past decade to see how this dynamic works.

The United States in effect has for a number of years had free trade zones in Mexico, areas where US and foreign capital can move in and set up industries that export to the US market. When the debt crisis hit Mexico in 1982 and the Mexican peso collapsed in value, there was a large influx of US capital, as real wages dropped by over 50 per cent. In five years, the number of workers employed by the foreign industries more than doubled, so that by 1988 about 10 per cent of the total Mexican industrial workforce was employed by foreign manufacturers (*maquiladores*).

Wages and working conditions in the Mexican *maquiladores* were horrendous. As *Business Week* wrote in 1988,

> from the start, US employers turned to the most vulnerable – and cheapest – workers: young women and girls. Women represent two-thirds of the maquiladora labour force, and many are teenagers. The result is a labour force that's miserably underpaid – even for Mexico. In a country where one-half of the work force is unemployed or underemployed, the turnover rate runs 50% to 100% in many plants. (*Business Week* 1988, p. 62)

The Dominican Republic, the only country with a democratically elected government in the Caribbean and Latin America that had a positive per capita growth rate in the 1980s, also felt the bite of the *maquiladores*. Under the Caribbean Basin Initiative, which allowed countries in that region to gain access to US markets, the Dominican Republic set up seven free trade zones that employ 70,000 people and export US$200 million annually (*South* 1988, p. 44). Working conditions in the zone are horrendous, and the *maquiladores* have in no way precipitated economic growth in the rest of the country. Chronic shortages and economic misery make the Dominican Republic today one of the most explosive countries in the Caribbean. As one United Nations official on a visit to the Republic declared: 'Living conditions are wretched. The free trade zones only re-enforce the appalling situation that women and other Dominicans face on a daily basis.'[7]

One cannot ignore the fact that the free flow of trade and capital in the Americas could be of assistance to the peoples of the hemisphere because of the need for capital, employment and economic development throughout the Americas. But given the fact that US multinational capital would be in the driver's seat with the Initiative, it is the few rather than the many who would reap the benefits of a hemispheric market. One Brazilian legislator noted during Bush's December 1990 trip that the free trade proposal is called the 'Initiative for the Americas', and not the 'Initiative of the Americas'. This is a proposal conceived in Washington on behalf of US economic interests, not an initiative that is designed to build democracy or to arrest the growing poverty in Latin America and the Caribbean.

The Democratic Challenge in the East

Eastern Europe, rather than Latin America, may provide the major litmus test for judging the ability of the United States to foment democracy abroad. There, unlike Latin America and the Middle East, the United States has no substantial economic or commercial interests that should obscure or short circuit its commitment to democracy. And in Eastern Europe one finds new virgin democratic grounds, a region where the peoples have overthrown 'communist totalitarianism' and turned to the Western democracies for help in rebuilding their economic and political systems. The 'Revolutions of '89', which toppled governments in Poland, East Germany, Czechoslovakia, Hungary, Bulgaria and Romania, generated hope and admiration around the globe. Not since the days of the revolutions of 1848 in Europe, or the French Revolution of 1789, has such a democratic groundswell gripped the European continent.

Today, however, it is clear that the enthusiasm and aspirations of the Eastern Europeans have largely been stifled. The simple fact is that the events of 1989 did not lead to social and political transformations similar to the other great revolutions of the twentieth century (Russia, China and Cuba, for example) in which a renaissance occurred in the arts, education, culture, politics and society in general. One student of Eastern Europe asserts that the upheavals there were 'refolutions' not revolutions (Brunce 1990). There was a spontaneous popular outburst that toppled the older governments, but instead of completely sweeping out the old social and political order, the new governments carried out programmes that were largely reformist and did nothing to alter the social and cultural orders, in contrast to what had occurred in other revolutionary periods.

One could go even further and argue that the Eastern European revolutions are 'aborted revolutions'. The popular ferment of the early months was intentionally contained by the decision of the new Eastern European leaders and the Western democracies to steer the revolutions in old political directions. There was virtually no political experimentation, no attempt to tap into the democratic groundswell.

Instead, staid Western-style political regimes were set up in which the leaders of the new and old political parties of these countries began to bicker among themselves over the spoils rather than trying to encourage the unleashed political and social energies to invigorate society as a whole. Today, when one talks to people in Hungary, Bulgaria and Czech and Slovak republics, for example, one finds disillusionment and cynicism at the grass-roots level.[8] This lack of political hope, as well as deteriorating economic conditions, explains why the peoples of Eastern Europe are streaming abroad in unprecedented numbers. Many have no faith in the future of their countries: they only want to get out as fast as possible so they can begin to accumulate goods and commodities like their Western European cousins.

This stunted political environment cannot of course be blamed solely on the United States or the Bush administration. Given the crisis of socialism and the rejection of the old socialist model of revolution, there was little interest in experimenting with political models. The new political leaders, as well as the Western democracies, did not want to move Eastern Europe in political directions that would polarise the societies along class or social lines. For better or worse, political tranquillity was sought, and political experimentation was viewed as a passé approach.

One would expect that this restrained political environment would be an ideal laboratory for the United States to propagate a moderate, conciliatory approach to democracy. Throughout much of American history, US leaders have viewed with disdain the radical revolutionary upheavals in Europe and the Third World because they often threatened property and were violent and bloody affairs (Hunt 1987). However, in Eastern Europe the Bush administration did little to strengthen or build authentic democratic institutions. In general the United States supports the most conservative political forces in the region, often backing their efforts to impose conflictive, unconciliatory policies on their countries from above.

US activities in Bulgaria provide an insight into how the United States has often hindered rather than encouraged democratic development. Bulgaria was historically close to the Soviet Union because Russian armies liberated the country first from the Ottoman Turks in the late nineteenth century, and then from the Nazis in 1945. The postwar Communist government of Bulgaria, which was run by indigenous communists who had resisted the Nazis, enjoyed more popular support than most other Eastern European regimes. However, by the late 1980s the Communist government of Zhivkov had become entrenched and isolated, and so it also fell victim to the popular upsurge that gripped Eastern Europe.

In the first free elections, the resilience of a reformed communist party (renamed the Bulgarian Socialist Party) was demonstrated when it won over 52 per cent of the vote and a narrow majority in the new parliament. In the elections, the National Endowment for Democracy provided support for organisations aligned with the opposition United Democratic Front (which won 36 per cent of the vote). But US electoral observers recognised the fairness of the elections and did not question the right of the Socialist Party to form a new government.

But NED and its affiliated institutions, however, continued to pursue policies that aided the opposition and helped to destabilise the new government. As a NED representative in Washington flatly declared, 'We will have nothing to do with the Bulgarian Socialist party'.[9] Two key affiliates of NED, the AFL-CIO and the US Chamber of Commerce, acted in ways that also undermined the new government.

The AFL-CIO-backed Podkrepa (meaning 'Support'), is a small Bulgarian trade union which contains pro-monarchist elements. The largest trade union, the Confederation of Independent Trade Unions of Bulgaria (CITUB), which broke with the Socialist Party and adopted an independent role in Bulgarian politics, was opposed by the AFL-CIO. The US embassy justified this stand by arguing that CITUB had a 'political programme', and did not stick to bread and butter trade unionism.[10] When the new leader of CITUB, Dr Krustyo Petkov, visited the United States in late 1990, he was given the cold shoulder by the AFL-CIO. His requests for meetings with AFL-CIO leaders were summarily rejected. NED officials in Washington DC also refused to have anything to do with Petkov, even though he spoke out publicly against the shortcomings of the Socialist government.[11]

Meanwhile, the US Chamber of Commerce, building on the opening that it had secured in Bulgaria due to its work with NED, decided to undertake a study of the Bulgarian economy. A delegation of US economists, with virtually no experience in Bulgaria, were sent to prepare a report. With US embassy support, and after less than a month of work, they issued a 600-page blueprint for the economy which called for the immediate restoration of a free market economy and the institutionalisation of private property. A new constitution was also called for, modelled after the US system. Somewhat taken aback by the length and audacity of the report, the government released a 50-page critique that accepted some of the proposals and labelled others 'unrealistic'. The opposition Bulgarian Democratic

Union used the report as part of its general campaign to discredit the government and to attack the Socialist programme to stabilise the economy.

Challenged on all fronts, the Bulgarian Socialist Party was unable to run the country effectively. At the end of 1990, its cabinet fell and a new government was installed with equal representation from the opposition and the Socialist party. New elections in October 1991 – in the midst of an economic crisis – enabled the United Democratic Front to win a narrow plurality over the Socialist Party and to set up a very tenuous coalition government.

These sectarian US policies and the activities of NED-affiliated institutions are by no means unique to Bulgaria. Throughout Eastern Europe, the United States appears more intent on pushing politicians who back US views and support neoliberal economic policies than on fomenting authentic democratic institutions. In that part of Czechoslovakia which is now the Czech Republic, the US embassy is particularly supportive of Vaclav Klaus, the Finance Minister who is bent on privatising the economy along neoliberal lines.

Although the Civic Forum, which has strong social democratic tendencies and is led by popular playwright Vaclav Havel, is formally in power, the economic policies pursued by the country are largely dictated by Klaus. Social spending has been cut drastically, state enterprises are being sold off *en masse*, and the uninhibited market-place reigns supreme (Burbach and Painter 1991). The International Monetary Fund, as well as the United States, openly endorses Klaus's approach and makes it clear that continued economic support is contingent on the Czechs' adherence to the policies he has put in place.[12]

The 'Business' Corps and Latin Americanisation

In May 1990, while US leaders were still euphoric over the transformations in Eastern Europe, President Bush announced the formation of a Citizens' Democracy Corps to help 'develop democratic institutions and market-oriented economies' (*Focus on Central and Eastern Europe*, 1990). The new organisation was to assist and link up US private volunteer assistance programmes with organisations in Eastern Europe that needed help. One million dollars in startup funds were provided by the National Endowment for Democracy and another US$300,000 came from the Agency for International Development.

It was clear from the start that the Citizens' Democracy Corps had little to do with citizenship or democracy and a whole lot to do with building up private enterprise. 'Entrepreneurial know-how' and 'economic infrastructure' were seen as key qualities that had to be developed so that Eastern Europe could 'absorb Western investment and aid' (ibid.). In the United States, the Democracy Corps was tied directly into corporate America. Drew Lewis, a former high-ranking official of the Reagan administration and the chairman of Union Pacific Corporation, was appointed chairman of the Democracy Corps. As a staff member of the Corps proclaimed 'we need to reach out to the corporate world for support. Drew will make this happen.'[13] Peace Corps volunteers, who are in their greatest numbers in Latin America, were also dispatched to Eastern Europe. Here again the goal was not community development or to help in developing the social infrastructure (as had occurred in Latin America during the early Peace Corps years), but to help incorporate the region into the Western economy. For instance, the first 20 volunteers sent to Czechoslovakia were to teach English, 'a language that is needed for relating to our world', proclaimed one US embassy official in Prague. Other Peace Corps volunteers were sent to Eastern Europe to teach business skills.

Thus in Eastern Europe, whether one scrutinises policies in specific countries or new institutions, one finds no real commitment of the US government to building up the democratic infrastructure. The fundamental goal is to develop what US officials refer to as 'private enterprise and the free market'. And just as in Latin America, the economic doctrine of neoliberalism reigns supreme. Under the tutelage of the IMF and other Western institutions, social programmes are to be drastically cut, state-owned enterprises are to be sold off, and the law of supply and demand is made to reign supreme.

Eastern Europe is in effect being 'Latin Americanised'. As the austerity programmes take hold, we see widespread unemployment, a downturn in production and growing economic polarisation - all phenomena that have characterised Latin America since the early 1980s. Democracy, rather than being strengthened, is actually being undermined, as the peoples grow economically desperate and politically cynical. With no real ideological cement to hold the countries of Eastern Europe together, it is small wonder that old national and ethnic rivalries have exploded throughout the region, especially in the former Yugoslavia and the Asian republics of the former Soviet Union. Armed conflict has further accelerated the economic downturn.

This is the context for understanding US policy towards the former Soviet Union, particularly since the attempted coup in August 1991 and the subsequent collapse of the Communist Party. The failed coup and its aftermath made it clear that Russia was no longer a superpower capable of challenging the United States. But among Western leaders,

George Bush was the most hesitant to extend large-scale Western assistance to Russia. His concern was not the development of democratic institutions but whether the country's economy could be sufficiently revamped along 'free market' and capitalist lines so that it could 'effectively use' Western aid. Western European leaders, on the other hand, were overwhelmingly concerned about the political and social instability that would ensue if Western aid were not extended. The determination of the European leaders to get massive aid to Russia eventually forced the Bush administration to go along with the extensive relief programme.

But the Bush administration's main concern remained that of furthering the development of capitalism in the former Soviet Union. US corporate representatives are encouraged to be directly active in the relief process and to set up subsidiaries in the states of the former Soviet Union. And in the disputes among the various republics over autonomy and independence, the United States generally supports the 'central' government in Moscow because it believes that capitalism in general, and US capital in particular will have a greater chance of success if a larger market can be maintained. The various republics' demands for greater democracy and self-determination are viewed as 'centrifugal forces' that are contrary to the US interests of aiding the construction of a unitary capitalist economy (*Wall Street Journal*, 28 October 1991).

On Tragedies: Old and New

In 1959, William Appleman Williams published his seminal work, *The Tragedy of American Diplomacy*. He argued that the United States from the 1890s onward had pursued an 'open door' policy in foreign affairs, a policy designed to ensure that the markets of the world remained open to the United States. US leaders, Williams asserted, believed that democracy could survive at home only if foreign markets were found for the surplus production of the burgeoning US economy. The tragedy of this policy was that throughout the twentieth century the United States, in order to advance the open door and to preserve its own democracy, was driven to make war and to subvert popular, nationalist and revolutionary movements abroad that were bent on securing their own political and economic development.

Many have disputed Williams' thesis, arguing that there is no clear-cut link between economic interests and US foreign policy. Michael H. Hunt (1987) holds that a core of ideological perceptions, principally a sense of mission and national greatness, a sense of racial superiority, and a fear of revolution and social upheaval abroad have shaped US foreign policy. Other foreign policy analysts linked to New Right think tanks that emerged in the 1970s and 1980s have asserted that the US mission abroad has been honourable, that the United States has sought to expand democracy and human freedoms around the globe. Francis Fukuyama (1989), a US State Department official, has carried this perspective to its logical conclusion with his 'End of History' thesis. He argues that with the collapse of the Soviet threat and the triumph of democratic capitalism, conflict as we have known it in the past is at an end and that we are in a new era of tranquillity and social calm.

However, this article's survey of developments in Latin America and Eastern Europe since the end of the Cold War reveals that history as we know it has by no means ended. If anything social and political strife are in the ascendent, particularly in the Third World. William Appleman Williams' view of economic interests as being paramount in US foreign policy seems more valid than ever. In Eastern Europe, Latin America and the Middle East one finds the United States bent on implanting free trade and the doctrine of neoliberalism, all contemporary versions of the Open Door policy. *Vis-à-vis* the other great capitalist powers, Japan and a united Europe, economic interests are also in the driver's seat as the United States seeks to eliminate trade barriers to US agricultural, industrial and electronic products.

Contrary to Hunt's contention that ideology acts as an autonomous force in foreign policy, the end of the Cold War appears to have stripped away much of the ideological baggage that shaped US policy. Anti-communism is gone as a mobilising force. US leaders do try to assert that the US still has a special mission abroad (such as the New World Order), and, as we have seen, they continue to throw up the rhetoric of fomenting democracy abroad. But the American people by and large are not taken in by these proclamations. US policy is in effect driven by the relentless pursuit of US economic interests.

Since Williams wrote, the tragedy of American diplomacy has become even more pronounced. It is no longer just foreign governments and movements that suffer from the pursuit of narrow US interests – now the very content of US democracy itself is being threatened. During the past three decades, US leaders have proclaimed one mission after another in the name of democracy while systematically violating the US constitution and limiting democracy at home. The Vietnam War, the covert activities of the CIA in Chile, Cuba and Africa, the Iran-Contra scandal, and Bush's early assertion that he as Commander-in-Chief could go to war in the Gulf without the 'advice and consent' of Congress – these are the more salient examples of how US leaders have conducted foreign policy in an authoritarian manner, violating the constitution and making a mockery of democratic participation in foreign policy.

Simultaneously, the internal fabric of democracy has been unravelling. The ever-widening spectre of homelessness, growing drug abuse and addiction, the deterioration of the country's schools and hospitals, the largest per capita prison and paroled population in the industrialised world, the growth of hardcore unemployment, the ascendant role of rich corporate contributors in the political system, and the increasing alienation of the US people from their country's political system (as reflected in the continuing decline in the number of voters in election after election) – these are all factors that are undermining the vitality and viability of the US democratic system as we know it (Burbach and Nuñez, 1990). This internal erosion of US democracy may not be directly linked to foreign policy abuses, but the refusal of US political leaders to deal with domestic problems while spending billions on foreign conflicts and military budgets certainly contributes to the decline of the US democratic system. During the Reagan years the relationship between domestic decline and foreign adventurism was accelerated as domestic spending was frozen or curtailed while military spending soared. The election of Bill Clinton in 1992 was partly a reaction to the years of neglect of domestic issues during the Reagan and Bush presidencies.

If there is one bright spot in the tragedy of American democracy over the past three decades, it is that sectors of the US public have challenged the abuses of democracy by their leaders by forming broad-based citizen's movements. The Vietnam War marked the beginning of this process. Popular protests drove President Lyndon Johnson from office, and there is no doubt that public opposition to the war compelled President Nixon and Secretary of State Henry Kissinger to withdraw US troops from Vietnam.

In the 1970s, particularly during the Carter administration, the citizens' foreign policy movement became more sophisticated. Human rights organisations and citizens' lobbies in Washington fought for legislative changes and began to put forward new foreign policy agendas that were less concerned with communism and more attuned to the needs of Third World peoples suffering from oppression and economic deprivation.

The military build-up of the Reagan administration and its support for counter-revolutionary military forces in the Third World fuelled the further development of broad-based anti-war and anti-militarist movements at the grass-roots level. The nuclear protest movement, domestic opposition to US pro-apartheid policies in South Africa, and the non-intervention movements that sprang up around Nicaragua and El Salvador – these were all independent citizens' initiatives that often involved churches, city governments and town councils, local trade unions, women and gay activists, and in some cases black and Latino organisations (Burbach and Nuñez 1987). Democratic discussion and activism were taking hold in the United States, but they were in opposition to, rather than in support of, US policies.

Thin Democracy

In the final analysis, the nature of the United States' attempts to foment the development of democracy abroad are linked to the limits and conceptualisation of democracy within the United States. Unlike the situation in the early years of the republic, the United States no longer serves as the shining 'city on the hill' that inspires other nations to perfect or develop their own democratic institutions. Political theorists point out some of the inherent limits of the liberal democracy that is practised in the United States. Benjamin Barber (1984) has argued that the United States has a 'thin democracy', one in which the very content of democracy is shallow. Periodic elections are held, but US citizens as a whole have little interest in truly democratic, participatory politics because the institutions of representation tend to alienate and marginalise people. A 'strong democracy' can be developed only if the barriers between the formal democratic institutions and the citizens themselves are broken down.

The Italian theorist Norberto Bobbio (1989) has pointed to the tension between 'liberalism' and 'democracy' as a major factor in the democratic development of the United States and other Western capitalist countries. Liberalism, in the classic sense, has tended to hold up individual rights against the rule of the democratic majority. In recent decades the classic liberal, or neoliberal, has tended to focus in particular on property rights, viewing them as immune to the demands of the majority and as essential for social stability and economic growth. This liberal view is of course tied to neoliberal economics and the primacy of the marketplace. One editorialist of the *Financial Times* even went so far as to argue that elections are increasingly irrelevant and unnecessary because the average citizen in a Western democracy can go out and 'vote' in the marketplace every day.

William Appleman Williams, in the final years before his death in 1989, began to look inward, to local movements and participatory democratic struggles as the major forces that could change US society and end the tragedy of American diplomacy. Today, in fact, the principal challenge to both politics as usual and the neoliberal ideology is being mounted by the social movements. The civil rights movement, the women's and gay rights movements, the ecological movement, activists with disabilities, homeless activists, and of course the anti-war and non-intervention movements mentioned above – these are all part of a broader, grass-roots democratic process that is at work in the United States and in other parts of the Western world. Moreover, if there is one part of the Western political and social process that is being 'exported', it is these social movements. In Eastern Europe, for example, to the extent that there is political innovation and renewal, it is found in the incipient social movements that have sprung up around women's, environmental, homeless and disability issues.

As the twentieth century draws to a close and the global economic situation deteriorates, the strife and debate over democracy and democratic institutions will only deepen. In the United States, the issue will not be whether or not it can export democracy, but whether or not the grass-roots social movements can develop enough strength to maintain and expand democratic institutions at home and serve as an inspiration to peoples abroad. Only if these movements become ascendant can the tragedy of American democracy be brought to an end.

Notes

1 The hearings of the Church Committee of the US Senate were critical in shutting down some of the more abusive operations of the CIA.
2 Based on personal interviews conducted with NDI officials in Santiago, Chile, in October 1988.
3 A delegation of Latin American observers actually criticised the opposition as well as Noriega. They stated that evidence was insufficient to proclaim a Noriega victory or defeat.
4 See special reports issued by Accuracy in the Media. Also based on personal interviews conducted at time of elections.
5 Interview with Eric Holt-Gimenez, US Agricultural Consultant in Nicaragua.
6 Interviews with State Department officials in the mid-1980s, particularly Craig Johnstone, Deputy Assistant Secretary of State for Inter-American Affairs.
7 Interview with Lea Guido, United Nations Pan American Health Organization, December 1990.

8 Based on personal conversations conducted in Eastern Europe during September–October 1990.
9 Interview with Margaret Ferry, Public Relations official, National Endowment for Democracy, October 1990.
10 Interview with Rob Moore, US embassy official, Sofia, Bulgaria, October 1990.
11 Conversations with CITUB trade union officials, October–November 1990.
12 Phone conversations with US embassy officials in Prague. See also Chetka News Agency reports, Prague, Czechoslovakia.
13 Interview with Enud McGiffert, staff member of Citizens' Democracy Corps, October 1990.

References

Amnesty International 1991. *Torture with Impunity*. London, Amnesty International.

Baker, James (US Secretary of State), US State Department Bulletin, speech on 31 March 1990, Dallas, Texas.

Barber, Benjamin R. 1984. *Strong Democracy: Participatory Politics for a New Age*. Berkeley and Los Angeles, University of California Press.

Bobbio, Norberto 1989. *Democracy and Dictatorship: The Nature and Limits of State Power*. Cambridge, Polity Press.

—— 1990. *Liberalism and Democracy*. London, Verso Press.

Brunce, Valerie 1990. *World Policy*, summer.

Burbach, Roger and Nuñez, Orlando 1987. *Fire in the Americas*. London, Verso Press. See Chapter 4 for a discussion of the role of the anti-war and non-intervention movements.

—— 1990. 'The End of Socialism or the End of Western Domination?' CENSA *Strategic Perspectives*, No. 2, October, for a more extended discussion of democracy in the Western World.

Burbach, Roger and Painter, Steve 1991. 'Capitalist Restoration in Czechoslovakia', *Monthly Review*, April, for a more extended discussion of the situation in former Czechoslovakia and neo-liberalism.

Business Week (international edition), 14 November 1988. 'Will the New Maquiladoras Build a Better Mañana?' p. 62.

Castenada, Jorge G. 1990. 'Latin America and the End of the Cold War', *World Policy Journal*, Summer, p. 485.

Council on Hemispheric Affairs and the Inter-Hemispheric Education Resource Center, National Endowment for Democracy (NED) 1988. *A Foreign Policy Branch Gone Awry*, pp. 18–19.

Epstein, Barbara 1989. 'The Reagan Doctrine and Right Wing Democracy', *Socialist Review* 1/89, pp. 9–40.

Focus on Central and Eastern Europe (1990). A periodic update of US assistance to Central and Eastern Europe, US Department of State, Bureau of Public Affairs, May 22.

Fukuyama, Francis 1989. 'The End of History?', *The National Interest*, 16 (Summer), pp. 3–18.

Hunt, Michael H. 1987. *Ideology and US Foreign Policy*, New Haven, Conn., Yale University Press, for an excellent discussion of how the United States has historically opposed revolutions abroad; see especially Chapter 4.

Kirkpatrick, Jeanne 1979. 'Dictators and Double Standards', *Commentary*, June.

MacEwan, Arthur 1990. *Debt and Disorder: International Economic Instability and US Imperial Decline*. New York, Monthly Review Press. See especially Chapter 3.

Maingot, Anthony P. 1989. 'The Difficult Transition in the Caribbean', *Hemisphere*, Fall vol. 2, no. 1, pp. 6–8.

National Endowment for Democracy (1988). *Annual Report*. Washington DC.

Nuñez, Orlando and Burbach, Roger 1990. 'Legacy of the Reagan Decade', *CENSA Strategic Perspectives*, January. We discuss the use of democracy in Reagan's foreign policy. The evolution of the concept of democracy as seen by Reagan administration officials is also revealed in Epstein 1989.

Report of the Bulgarian Economic Growth and Transition Project. Prepared by the National Chamber Foundation, an affiliate of the US Chamber of Commerce. Directed and edited by Richard W. Rahn and Ronald D. Utt.

South, Business, technology, politics, leisure section, May 1988, 'Enclave of Entente', p. 44.

Wall Street Journal 1991. 'US Loses Hope that Coherent Economy Will Link Nationalistic Soviet Republics', 28 October.

Williams, William Appleman 1959. *The Tragedy of American Diplomacy*. Cleveland, Ohio.

Part Two

Case Studies from the Third World

6. Continued Counterinsurgency: Civilian Rule in Guatemala

RICHARD WILSON

Generals in Retreat?

The presidential inauguration of Vinicio Cerezo in 1986 promised to be a historic opportunity to disengage the Guatemalan military from the governing apparatus. At the time, Guatemala seemed to be keeping stride with the rest of Latin America by moving away from military dictatorships and towards civilian democracy. A flurry of edited volumes in the late 1980s assessed these transitions from military regimes to civilian democratic governments in Latin America (P. O'Brien and P. Cammack 1985; Lopez and Stohl 1987; O'Donnell, Schmitter and Whitehead 1986). In Lopez and Stohl (1987 pp. 33–55), the most pessimistic prognosis was reserved for Guatemala (see also Painter 1987). In this chapter, I argue that the harsh reality of so-called 'civilian rule' has vindicated this scepticism towards the unfolding of Guatemalan democracy.

When the Christian Democrats won the 1985 elections, they became the first civilian government to be elected in 20 years. They were only the second civilian regime since the CIA-backed coup of 1954 restored military rule (Schlesinger and Kinzer 1982; Aybar de Soto 1978; Immerman 1982). Ever since 1954, the Guatemalan military has been the pre-eminent institution of the state. The military's stranglehold on state power did not diminish during the five years of Vinicio Cerezo's presidency (1986–91). Far from forcing the generals into retreat, the Christian Democrats were willing accomplices to the military's counterinsurgency strategies.

Instead of evaluating the Guatemalan regime simply on the basis of whether it is civilian or military, we should look at the balance of forces in the ongoing guerrilla war. Historically, 'civilian' is not synonymous with a decreased level of hostilities between the Guatemalan state and its armed opposition. For example, the civilian government of Méndez Montenegro (1966–70), with the assistance of US Green Berets, presided over the murder of 8,000 peasants so as to eradicate some 500 guerrillas. This chapter proposes that the Guatemalan state fluctuates between two models of counterinsurgency, 'war and crisis' and 'Low Intensity Conflict'. A military *or* civilian government can implement either strategy depending on the situation in the civil war.

Throughout Guatemalan history, the military and ruling oligarchy have been unable to establish a national political consensus, due to its unwillingness to reform a rigidly stratified social structure. In order to protect the privileges of an agro-exporting elite, the security forces have played a pivotal role in the organisation of society, leaving the civilian organs of the state weak, unstable and without ideological legitimacy.

Traditionally, the status quo has been preserved by brute force and repression alone. So why, in 1986, did the military suddenly abandon its historical station and seemingly abdicate power?

There were three main motivations for the army to withdraw from open dictatorship. Firstly, the army no longer wanted to assume responsibility for the country's economic crisis. Secondly, the so-called political 'opening' created by civilian rule permitted a highly controlled reorganisation of trade unions and political parties, which were to be coopted by the state. This constituted an attempt by elites to undermine political support in popular organisations for the guerrilla 'Unity' – the Unidad Revolucionaria Nacional Guatemalteca, or URNG, comprised of four revolutionary organisations which unified under a joint command in 1982.

Finally, a civilian government allowed Guatemala to emerge from its isolation as an international pariah and bid for more international aid from the US and the European Community. The US encouraged the military to renounce power formally as part of its global policy of 'rehabilitating' authoritarian governments so as to present an acceptable face for the US Congress and the international community. US policy adeptly foresaw the strategic benefits of a Guatemalan government which would appear legitimate from outside, and yet preside over a virtually unchanged national power structure.

Vinicio Cerezo inherited the legacy of military domination, but he neither achieved, nor even attempted, any significant reform of political institutions or the economic structure. The Christian Democrats defined their policies solely in terms of not provoking a military *coup d'état*. Economic policy continued to favour the established interests of the elite and foreign investors. The newly legitimate government attempted to coopt the labour movement and other popular sectors, yet early on its policies alienated potential supporters of civilian democracy. At the same time, there were greater opportunities for the popular movement to increase its autonomy and organisation, albeit through bitter struggle.

In contrast to its dismal failures in domestic politics and the economy, the civilian regime triumphed in the key area of foreign policy. Cerezo campaigned effectively to improve Guatemala's international image and to restore bilateral aid from Europe and the US. The arrival of more international aid, however, did not create a space for the evolution of democratic institutions. Instead, it bolstered the army's ability to control the state and civil society. Vinicio Cerezo was not the harbinger of democracy, rather he was the caretaker of an entrenched social and economic crisis.

In 1991, for the first time in Guatemalan history, one civilian-elected president succeeded another. Did this peaceful transition of power constitute a consolidation of democracy in the country? This chapter argues that Cerezo's successor, President Jorge Serrano Elías, performed the same neutralised role within the narrowly defined parameters of a military-forged counterinsurgency state. Serrano's room for manoeuvre was even smaller than Cerezo's was before him, and his personal style was more autocratic and nationalistic. Under Serrano the military continued to dominate political decision making, a significant percentage of international aid was suspended, the economy was in shambles, and the International Monetary Fund played an increasingly decisive role in policy making.

The Emergence of Civilian Rule

Social injustice in Guatemala has its roots in colonial society and the Liberal reforms of the late nineteenth century, but the modern system of terror evolved out of the events of 1954. In that year, a US-backed coup installed General Castillo Armas in power, ending the '10 years of spring' (1944–54) when popular elected governments began a process of profound reforms. The Arévalo and Arbenz administrations legalised trade unions and undertook an extensive land reform which benefited some 100,000 families. These regimes challenged the multinational United Fruit Company and expropriated a portion of its idle land. As a result, the reformers incurred the wrath of the US and earned themselves the label of 'communists'. In reality, these administrations were social democratic and sought to 'modernise' Guatemala; to capitalise agriculture and expand industry at the same time as promoting greater social justice and national autonomy. As in the Bolivian Revolution of 1952, they challenged the hegemony of the entrenched landowning oligarchy, favouring instead the industrial and commercial bourgeoisie.

The 1954 military coup mapped out the future political landscape of Guatemala until the present day. Primarily, it entrenched an anachronistic agro-export system of production. In so doing, it secured the political and economic pre-eminence of the landowning class which clings on as the most powerful segment of the private sector. Agriculture continues to be the largest component of the GDP, dwarfing manufacturing production. Coffee is the largest export, bringing in five times the earnings of the next largest export, bananas. Over half of the working population is employed in agriculture, the majority as rural proletarians or pauperised smallholders.

After 1954, the armed forces became the 'guardians' of national security and proved themselves to be among the fiercest anti-communists in the hemisphere. The events of 1954 circumscribed in the extreme the territory available for open political discourse. The civilian governments of Méndez, Cerezo and Serrano proved that democracy cannot result from simply placing a civilian president into the petrified structure created in 1954. In none of these three instances did participatory democracy evolve peacefully out of the structures of terror fashioned by the military. The phenomenae of civilian governments punctuating the continuity of military power has been part of a repetitive cycle in Guatemalan politics since 1954. Without imposing any iron laws of political development, there is a distinct pattern of political oscillations in the counterinsurgency character of the state. Each cycle lasts roughly 12–15 years, and comprises two phases:

- Low Intensity Conflict (LIC). This is characterised by popular agitation and a relatively greater opportunity for political activity. The state attempts to coopt nascent working-class organisations. Such corporative tactics operate in a context of selective repression and continued low-intensity counterinsurgency efforts by the army. This strategy predominated in the years 1956–62, 1972–8 and 1983/4 to the present day.
- War and Crisis (WAC). Attempts at coopting the masses are abandoned in favour of an all-out repressive assault upon popular organisations. Generalised violence is prevalent in areas of guerrilla operations, especially against the civilian population. Guatemala was in the grip of this phase during the years 1962–8 and 1978–83.

Just as the civilian governments (such as Méndez 1966–70) can employ WAC strategies, so can military governments implement a LIC doctrine. The particular phase in the counterinsurgency cycle, then, is more determining of the character of a regime than its status as civilian or military. For example, the military government of General Laugerúd García (1974–8) was characterised by a Low Intensity Conflict strategy until its final months of office, when state repression intensified, culminating in the massacre at Panzós in 1978.

At each turn of the cycle, the crisis deepens and the existence of the state becomes more precarious. Each defeat of the opposition in the WAC stage is followed by the development of a stronger insurgent movement during the next LIC stage. After being utterly vanquished in the late 1960s, the rebel forces reorganised and continued to fight Latin America's longest running guerrilla war (over 30 years). By the late 1970s, the guerrillas countered with collaboration in parts of the western highlands and in the capital. They enjoyed support from urban trade unions and some elements of the churches. Both poor and wealthier peasants joined revolutionary organisations. Indigenous peoples (up to 65 per cent of the population), hitherto lacking any national political representation, identified with the guerrillas in many highland regions.

By the early 1980s, the anti-government forces were a serious threat to the state and the country was on the verge of insurrection. The guerrillas controlled one-third of the country and were on the brink of announcing a rival rebel government. Faced with such circumstances, the military unleashed one of the most vicious counterinsurgency campaigns in Latin American history. Once again Guatemala tumbled into the war and crisis stage in its counterinsurgency cycle.

The military envisaged a transition from the WAC stage to the LIC stage from the beginning of its declaration of total war on the rebels. This unique ability to integrate LIC and WAC phases into a single comprehensive strategy was one of the main reasons that the Guatemalan military succeeded against opposition forces to a greater degree than the Salvadoran and Somocista armies.

The military's *Plan for Security and Development*, introduced in 1982, proposed three stages for the transition from WAC to LIC. The strategic vision of the army called for elections after the defeat of the insurgency, and the installation of the army in the countryside under the guise of rural 'development'. Thus we should interpret civilian rule less as a gain for democracy over military dictatorship, and more as the final stage in the army's strategy to ensure the survival of the state. In essence, elections are a national security issue, rather than a standard of democracy upheld out of principle.

The army's three-stage plan is as follows:

- *Stage I* Total war ('Security')
  General Ríos Montt (1982–3). The military defeated the URNG guerrillas, who were driven back to their strongholds. Repression directed against the civilian population separated it from the armed rebels. The state repression levelled 440 indigenous communities, killed between 40,000 and 70,000 people and made internal refugees of 1 million people. The military enforced participation in armed civilian vigilante patrols – an army of occupation forged out of the population itself. These 'civil defence patrols' still serve as a front line against the guerrillas and a free labour force for the army's 'development' initiatives. The civil patrols are a system of auto-repression; through them the military compels villagers to monitor themselves. The patrols are a linchpin in the army's effort to control the rural populace.
- *Stage II* Military consolidation ('Development')
  General Mejía Victores (1983–5). This stage displayed the degree of political sophistication of the Guatemalan army. Using the ideology of 'development', it implanted itself in the countryside at all levels of rural society. Many of the internal refugees in mountainous areas had sought protection in zones of guerrilla control. The military's first task was to capture these resisting populations and control them in 'development poles', that is, 'model villages' along the lines of strategic hamlets in Vietnam. At their high point, 45,000 people were contained in these model villages. The civil patrols were consolidated to include some 900,000 highland indigenous men. As one of its final acts, before bestowing nominal power to a civilian government, the military granted itself a full amnesty from prosecution for human rights violations.
- *Stage III* Political consolidation ('Security *and* Development')
  Civilian rule (1986–present). This stage completed the transition from the WAC phase to the LIC phase. The military conceded formal political authority to the civilians, while retaining ultimate command of the decision making process. It remains firmly in control of the countryside and the running of the war. The police force comes under the domain of the Ministry of Defence and so cannot serve as a counterbalance to the army's monopoly on the means of destruction. Behind the mask of civilian democracy and development lies the face of undiminished army domination of society.

Since formally giving up power, the military has continued to overshadow state decisionmaking. The armed forces regularly allot themselves approximately 40 per cent of the national budget. This figure is not secured constitutionally, but no element of the state has the will or means to challenge it. Several army bases have mutinied during civilian rule, demanding more funds, which they subsequently received.

The Congress is unable to undertake the demilitarisation of society. The legislature has tried to return some state institutions to civilian control but has been stonewalled by the armed forces. In a classic example, the 'Law of the Army' went into effect in May 1991. Among other measures, it provided for the return of the National Geographical Institute to the civilian Ministry of Communications. The appointed day passed and nothing happened. The Minister of Defence publicly refused to hand over control of the Institute, saying that national security was at stake, and directed the legislators to go and rewrite their law. The meek Congress members huddled and decided to 'amend' the law to retain army control over the Institute. The military is brazen in its defiance of the civilian Congress and bullies civilian lawmakers when they step out of line.

The military does not control the judiciary through any formal channels, but the UN human rights expert Christian Tomuschat referred in 1991 to 'a *de facto* principle of impunity' for human rights violators (E/CN.4/1991/5 of 11 January 1991). Prosecutors who genuinely investigate abuses by the security apparatus have been harassed, beaten, kidnapped and killed. A climate of fear paralyses the judiciary and deters any autonomy on the part of the legal system.

The Christian Democrats presided over five years of a government and legislature which bent over backwards to comply with army dictates. The balance of power between civilian and military sections of the state was much the same when they left as when they entered office. During this period, they made little protest against army hegemony, having already resigned themselves to powerlessness before entering office.

Before 1986, the Christian Democrats preened themselves to appear acceptable to the army and the agro-export oligarchy. From being considered a party of the Centre-Left, they aligned themselves with the ruling class in the pre-revolutionary conditions of 1979–82. Such tactics characterise Christian Democratic practice in Latin America, especially in the cases of El Salvador and Chile. For the opportunity of limited power, they offered themselves as acquiescent hostages of army interests. This policy was explicitly stated by Vinicio Cerezo (1975), when he argued for an alliance between Christian Democrats and 'progressive sectors' in the army. During the 1985 presidential campaign, Cerezo gave prior assurances to the business community and landed oligarchy that there would be no agrarian reform, nor any renovation of the tax structure. In conclusion, the compromises made by the Christian Democrats before they came to power precluded any aspirations of meaningful reform of either the economic or political system.

Life and Death under the Christian Democrats

The extent to which democracy has progressed in Guatemala can perhaps best be measured by surveying the human rights situation; that is, the number of political killings and disappearances, press freedom, demilitarisation and freedom of association and organisation.

The level and intensity of political repression during the Cerezo regime did not indicate a significant improvement on previous prevailing patterns. According to the Mexico-based Guatemalan Human Rights Commission (CDHG), there were 2,429 extra-judicial executions and 559 'disappearances' during the Cerezo years. These are hardly the kind of statistics one expects in a flourishing democracy.

Figure 6.1: Guatemala – Extra-judicial Executions and Forced Disappearances, 1985–1990

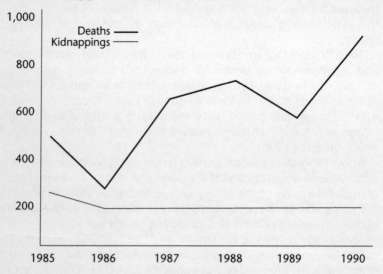

Source: *Central America Report*, vol. 18, no. 17, based on figures from the local press.

Human rights violations declined in frequency in the first year of Cerezo's presidency, but then escalated again in the following years. Since the structure of repression remains intact, it can be engaged at any time, and the intensity of violations fluctuates in peaks and troughs. After the attempted military coup in May 1988, the security forces stepped up their onslaught against any perceived opposition. The situation worsened dramatically in September 1989, when death squads declared an 'open season' on trade unionists and student leaders. This resurgence in violence was the result of another attempted coup in May 1989, when the WAC army faction demanded a clampdown on troublesome unionists and students. As in the early 1980s, the leadership of the student movement was decimated by death squad activity in the space of a few months. In August and September 1989, 15 members of the university student's union AEU were 'disappeared'; the majority were later discovered murdered with signs of torture.

The then human rights procurator, Ramiro de León Carpio (who became President in June 1993), reported 163 extra-judicial killings in the first six months of 1990, the election year. He attributed the majority of these to the security forces (*Inforpress Centroamericana* 2 August 1990, p. 13). The US State Department cited these attacks on universities and trade unions as its motive for recalling Ambassador Strook in March 1990. Such a move on the part of the US State Department is unprecedented in the history of Central America, although it has been seen by some as more indicative of US concern over the alleged drugs connections of the Christian Democratic presidential candidate.

Freedom of the press has been hindered and constrained under civilian rule. In 1988, the offices of the independent and investigative weekly *La Epoca* were bombed and one of its journalists was kidnapped and thrown down a ravine. In the same month the offices of the Cuban press agency *Prensa Latina* were bombed. In September 1990, the sociologist and reporter Myrna Mack Chang was assassinated as she left her office. Ms Mack had written critically on government policies towards internal refugees and street children (AVANCSO 1992). These events sent a clear message that serious investigative research would not be tolerated.

Up to now we have considered events primarily centred on the capital. Rural communities, however, have been subjected to the most extreme and hidden political repression. During the Cerezo years, 209 villagers were killed in massacres; the worst occurring at El Aguacate in 1988 and Santiago Atitlán in December 1990.

Although military control is not immediately apparent in the urban areas, it is thorough and undisguised in the indigenous highlands. There, civilian governments have left military authority unhindered in all security matters. Indeed, one of Cerezo's first acts as President was to open the new army-built model villages at Chisec. The army has saturated rural areas, exerting a comprehensive command over all realms of life, from religious practice to development initiatives (see Wilson 1991, 1993). Beatriz Manz (1988, p. 100) has documented how military authority permeates, overarches and dominates all other institutions in rural areas.

The civil patrols and model villages created during previous military governments still remain the cornerstone of a strategy designed to separate the guerrillas from the villagers, and to demolish any self-organisation by the peasantry. Village-level organisations which have survived hundreds of years of political upheaval have been swept aside. The civil patrols represent the most serious intrusion of the state into indigenous village organisation since the institutions formed by the Spanish Crown in the sixteenth century. To quote Amilcar Mendez, leader of the Council of Ethnic Communities 'Runujel Junam' (CERJ), the *campesino* human rights organisation:

> The basic structure of the patrols is one person watching over their neighbour, and their neighbour watching over them. It's the army's way of using the population as an unpaid labour force to control each other and act as informers. They are a duty imposed on the Indians (personal communication, 1990).

Though the patrols are voluntary according to the civilian constitution, the military has forbidden villagers to abandon this onerous task. At a patrol post outside a highland village, I interviewed two patrollers who assured me that the civil patrols were still mandatory by law:

> We would like to stop doing the patrol because it's boring and there haven't been any guerrillas here for nearly 10 years, but the army says no. It's still the law and so we have to fulfil our obligations.

In Guatemala, it is as if there are two legal frameworks; one for the Congress, constitution of the republic and international community, and another for the army, rural population and the exigencies of fighting a guerrilla war. In the capital the civilian deputies in the Congress can pass all the legislation they wish, but in the country-side the military is the final arbiter. Organisations such as the CERJ have raised people's awareness of their constitutional rights concerning the civil patrols in particular, but have lost many of their members to the death squads.

The civil patrol structure is not maintained by some ideological commitment to 'fighting communism', but through terror alone. Observers have interpreted the massacre at El Aguacate as a result of rural resistance to the civil patrols; villages around El Aguacate had been neglecting the patrols, so the military took action to reinforce the vigilante groups. The army murdered 22 men, orchestrated massive and immediate media coverage, and blamed the act on the guerrillas. The military then told surrounding villagers that 'the guerrillas' would do the same to them if they did not reorganise their patrols.

Military control of the countryside has not been a complete success, however. Indigenous peoples have pacifically resisted army measures and in some cases achieved a measure of autonomy. After the massacre in Santiago Atitlán in December 1990, the local community organised an effective campaign to have the large army garrison removed from their town. The civil patrols no longer function as a part of the local army base, but instead the municipality has its own independent peacekeeping force. Santiago is now an example to other indigenous communities, who are trying to regain self-governing rights undermined by military and other Ladino (non-indigenous) institutions.

Since the scorched earth policies of the early 1980s, the army is more entrenched than ever in rural power structures. This twisted vision of 'development' has granted the military more grass-roots control, but also contains within it severe drawbacks. More than ever, it is the army which is likely to be the focus of local discontent, rather than landowners and local elites as before. As a result, the army's plan of 'Security and Development' may have sown the seeds of further conflict by providing more grounds for Guatemalans to confront the military state directly.

The human rights record of the Christian Democrat regime was not that of a government which could control its security forces (Amnesty International 1989). From the beginning, Cerezo showed little willingness to confront the army over human rights abuses, making no effort to repeal the self-granted army amnesty. Nor did Cerezo endeavour to bring to justice officials involved in human rights violations during the early 1980s.

The judicial structure is ineffectual in pursuing army crimes to the top. Given the scale and long history of human rights violations in Guatemala, it is a staggering fact that no member of the security forces has ever served a full sentence for such an abuse since 1954. During the Cerezo years, only two police officers were jailed, for their involvement in the disappearing of students. Though sentenced to 30 years, they were released in less than two years. A human rights procurator was appointed and a congressional commission on human rights was formed; both have been vocal but are juridically toothless. Meanwhile, independent human rights monitors, such as the Relatives of the Disappeared (GAM) and CERJ, have been relentlessly persecuted by the security forces (America's Watch 1989).

The Christian Democrats were not the actual agents of human rights violations, but they were certainly aware of events. They never unequivocally denounced their military partners in government. Instead, government officials attributed virtually all acts of repression to the extremes of the political spectrum, who were supposedly intent on destabilising their 'democracy'. Cerezo's regime carried out an effective public relations exercise, diverting attention away from the true perpetrators of terror in society. Though they always portrayed themselves as Centrists sandwiched between the extremists of Right and Left, the Christian Democrats were in reality conscious accessories to the military's structure of political repression.

The Christian Democratic Work Ethic

In the early 1980s, the trade union movement in Guatemala was one of the most organised and radical in Central America, surpassed perhaps only by that in El Salvador. However, the state repression of the Lucas and Ríos Montt regimes devastated this sector, which only began seriously to reorganise in 1985, that is, *before* the advent of nominally civilian rule. This slow process of rebuilding from the grass-roots developed more rapidly than many expected, but it remained embryonic.

Little over 2 per cent of the workforce is unionised, mostly in urban areas. Few of the unions have a genuinely independent stance. The UNSITRAGUA (Unidad Sindical de Trabajadores de Guatemala) confederation is the most autonomous and militant, but unites only a handful of unions, with a total membership of about 35,000. It draws its strength from manufacturing industries such as textiles and bottling (including Coca-Cola), but also has bases on Izabal banana plantations. The other two confederations, CUSG (Confederación de Unidad Sindical de Guatemala) and CGTG (Confederación General de Trabajadores de Guatemala), are larger but more docile. The CUSG is linked to the US trade union federation, the AFL-CIO, and was formed by General Ríos Montt in 1983. The CGTG is formally associated with the Christian Democrat Party. In the countryside, the scope for organisation is substantially reduced, due to the war and army presence. The peasants' union CUC, however, re-emerged in 1988 and although it is still semi-clandestine, it has organised several extensive strikes on coffee and sugar plantations on the south coast.

On taking office, President Cerezo claimed that there was a new 'democratic opening' in the country and many international observers believed him. It is true that the labour movement has grown in strength, and organisations of shanty town dwellers, widows' groups (CONAVIGUA), peasant movements for land and indigenous groups (Majawil 'Ij) (re)entered the national political arena. Yet this was not without suffering constant, selective repression. One trade unionist from the UNSITRAGUA confederation told me, 'Cerezo did not give us an inch. What space there is now to organise, we fought for.'

In the beginning the Christian Democrat government tentatively tried to coopt the labour and peasant movements, but failed, through its inability to carry out any type of significant reform. Fundamentally, the economic recovery many had hoped for never happened. On the contrary, the economy continued to limp along, plagued by inflation, falling export earnings and a devaluing currency. When Cerezo left office, inflation ran at 60 per cent (*This Week*, 18 March 1991, p. 65), and the unemployment level hovered at the 45 per cent mark (Economist Intelligence Unit 1991, p.14). Real wages were driven down to levels lower than they had been in 1980. The growth of GDP per head stagnated, rising by only 0.8 per cent in 1989 (Economist Intelligence Unit 1990, p. 13).

Though GDP did not fall as it did under military rule, the elite's monopoly on national resources means that any growth is still not translated into better living standards for the majority. According to the Guatemala-based *Central America Report* (CAR) (*Inforpress Centroamericana*, 10 August 1990, p. 234), Guatemala heads the poverty index in Central America, with 87 per cent of the population living below the poverty level. More than any other issue, popular and labour protests coalesced around the Cerezo government's inability to improve the economic circumstances of the masses.

In his first years in office, Cerezo could have used the popular movement as a lever against the army, but instead he alienated it by repeatedly siding with the interests of industrialists or landowners (see Goldston 1989). In the true tradition of Guatemalan politics, the Christian Democrats never tried to build a power base outside the ruling class, nor did they cultivate a stronger labour movement for the future.

Independent trade unions showed their political maturity by moving with great caution and not allowing themselves to be swayed by the corporatist objectives of the Christian Democrats. Even the Christian Democrats' own confederation, CGTG, displayed surprising defiance at times. The Cerezo years saw an increase in white-collar trade unionism, with protracted and bitter strikes by teachers, bank workers and local government employees. However, the two strikes which most tested the civilian government's position on industrial unrest were those of the textile factory LUNAFIL (1987–8) and the glass-bottling factory CAVISA (1990). The government's response to such conflicts was characterised by prevarication and a lack of will to seek a negotiated solution. Both disputes led to lengthy factory occupations by the unions and, in turn, each was smashed in violent operations by the National Police. Overall, the Cerezo government maintained the repressive anti-labour policies of its military predecessors.

As the direction of the Christian Democrats' policies became clearer, the labour movement responded creatively by taking the lead in forming a broad popular front, called the UASP (Unity of Popular and Trade Union Action), which has challenged successive governments' political and economic policies. The UASP was formed in 1987 and is made up of trade unions, peasant leagues, human rights monitors, community groups, Christian and student groups and indigenous organisations.

Some founders of the UASP, such as UNSITRAGUA and the Relatives of the Disappeared (GAM), were formed in 1985 when the popular movement began to pick up the pieces from the early 1980s repression. Many other UASP groups formed after the transition from military rule. Though the real power of the UASP is small compared to the military and business sectors, it is an important base for popular initiatives. It serves as a central forum for the creation of an authentic popular opposition to formal political discourse. Importantly, the UASP links urban and isolated rural groups together. Though it is led by the Ladino trade unions, the UASP integrates several significant indigenous organisations, such as the widows' group CONAVIGUA and CUC.

In 1988, the UASP successfully organised several one-day mass work stoppages and gained concessions from the government on a provision for a minimum wage, and on electricity price increases. The UASP has broadened the scope of its campaign issues from economic questions to wider social inequalities. It has presented a programme for social change in Guatemala, including workers' rights, respect for human rights and an end to racism against the indigenous majority.

It has consistently argued for negotiations between the government and armed opposition to achieve a real and lasting peace.

Though it has not approached the level of organisation of the popular movement in the 1970s, the UASP represents a major achievement. It unites a broad range of different types of groups, channelling their voices into a collective strength. It is a basis for mass unity to challenge the government's discourse on democracy. At the same time, the UASP realises the limitations of its strength and moves cautiously within a hostile political environment. Although the labour movement has led a surprising regeneration given the circumstances, it recognises the extent to which it is still weakened by internal divisions and a lack of consolidated bases.

Technical Coups: Cerezo against the Ropes

The civil war raged on throughout the changeover from military to civilian rule. Since 1987, there has been a limited resurgence of URNG guerrilla forces. They operate in over half the country's departments and have opened several new fronts, one of which is in the capital. The URNG has been particularly successful in acts of sabotage against the economic infrastructure by demolishing major bridges and electricity pylons. Guerrilla forces claim to have caused over 1,000 army casualties in 1992, much the same as in previous years. This guerrilla expansion, combined with the failure of the army's 'End of Year Offensive' in 1987–8, has led to a deepening of inherent divisions in the army. Although the guerrilla forces do not represent a serious threat to the state, the army cannot wipe them out either.

Cerezo and ex-Defence Minister Gramajo were plagued by repeated coup attempts, the most important of which occurred in May 1988 and May and August 1989. Attempted coups are symptomatic of the deep splits which divide the economic oligarchy, military and political parties. There is a tendency for the LIC faction in the army to be allied with the industrial, commercial and financial sectors of CACIF, the confederation of Guatemalan industry. The WAC faction, however, maintains closer relations with UNAGRO, the agro-export grouping within CACIF. Each block has its representative political parties, which remain empty shells without a mass base.

In addition to these divisions along lines of counterinsurgency strategy, there is a divergence between the military and the ruling elite. The military has become Bonapartist in the sense that it is not completely beholden to the interests of the economic oligarchy. It has, during its decades in power, developed its own ethos and economic interests. The military owns and manages the national telephone, electricity and airline companies and has its own television channel. The military, and therefore the state, is not just a mere instrument of the ruling elite, but acts relatively autonomously. Smith (1990), for one, has provided a useful study of the concept of relative state autonomy in the context of relations between the state and indigenous communities.

At different phases in the Guatemalan political cycle, one or the other army faction is hegemonic. Periodically, the military goes down the road of Low Intensity Conflict and a corporatist solution to social tensions, but this inevitably fails when reforms are not forthcoming and the popular movement defies state legitimacy and power. At this point, the advocates of generalised violence gain the upper hand and the corporatist road is abandoned. The fate of the Christian Democrats depended on continued backing from the LIC faction in the army, and the ability of this current to maintain its hegemony within the state institutions.

The role of the military changes in different contexts; on the one hand it can act in complete accordance with the various factions in the ruling class, on the other it can function autonomously, according to its own interests. The divisions *within* the ruling class and *between* the military and dominant elite allow a certain flexibility to adjust to any changing circumstances in the counterinsurgency campaign, but these splits are also a source of chronic instability.

Although the military's strategies are usually functional to the preservation of Guatemala's own brand of capitalism, they can also be highly dysfunctional. The military has its own aggressive ethos and uncompromising principles which push it towards conflict and crisis. It is unwilling to negotiate any real reforms with the popular movement or armed opposition, even though some elements of the economic elite (such as in manufacturing and finance) would like to see a negotiated end to the war. The armed conflict is an immense drain on the economy and does not provide the conditions for stable capital accumulation. The war may have dammed the imagined 'red tide', but it has been no good for profits, and a small minority in the business sector feel that is better to have some accommodation and reform.

Given the army's role, I would argue that it is best to perceive the sporadic military uprisings during the Cerezo administration as 'technical coups'. The WAC faction in the army won its demands without formally deposing Cerezo. The coups were led by the 'Officers of the Mountains', base commanders in war zones, who are the shock troops of the WAC faction. The Officers of the Mountains fight in the front line against the guerrilla forces and advocate a full-scale military offensive against the popular movement and URNG. The antagonism of these sectors in the military towards President Cerezo and the LIC faction in the army, headed by Generals Gramajo and Bolaños, intensified after negotiations with the URNG guerrillas got under way.

With each technical coup, the power of Cerezo and Defence Minister Gramajo was eroded as the demands of coup instigators were granted in negotiations. The Officers of the Mountains forced the replacement of the low intensity faction Interior Minister Rodíl with the WAC faction stalwart Carlos Morales, an air force commander during the worst years of state repression. They also gained additional resources to combat the rebels and assurances that the trade unions and student groups would be dealt with more severely. It is ironic that 'democracy' has weakened the position of the LIC army faction within the state. Democracy permits a resurgence of the armed opposition which creates the conditions for the sweeping away of low intensity strategies and a return to total war.

Why did the Officers of the Mountains refrain from deposing Cerezo and directly seizing the reigns of state power? One of the main reasons is that the whole military feared that a coup, however desirable from the point of view of some, would ruin Guatemala's new image and possibly result in the curtailing of foreign aid.

Guatemala on the International Stage: From Pariah to Paragon of Virtue

Guatemala's foreign relations have been the most successful element of the military's plans for civilian rule. An improved international image has been a major advantage of Low Intensity Democracy. Having returned to the fold of 'civilised' nations, Guatemala benefits from the return of many non-governmental organisations (NGOs), large injections of foreign aid and training and armaments for the security forces. Thus section deals first with Europe–Guatemala relations and then discusses Guatemala's dealings with the US.

The improved relationship between Guatemala and Europe proved highly beneficial for civilian rule. The internationalism of Christian Democracy was certainly a significant factor, with European Christian Democrats heralding Cerezo as a bastion of democracy in the region. Shortly after attaining office, Cerezo secured a commitment of US$300 million in grants and loans from the European Community, in part due to lobbying by Christian Democrats (Painter 1987, p. 108).

Economic aid from the European Community to Guatemala doubled in the period 1984–7, from US$41 million per year to $82 million per year. Some member states are also individually furnishing significant levels of bilateral aid. Spain furnished US$71 million in 1989, and West Germany gave over US$175 million between 1986 and 1990 (Economist Intelligence Unit, p. 26).

Support from Europe came not only in the form of financial aid. The governments of Spain, Belgium (Christian Democrat) and Germany (Christian Democrat) engaged in training and supplying the National Police. The UK government also joined the chorus of approval for the civilian regime and renewed diplomatic relations with Guatemala after more than 20 years of severed relations over Belize. Economic ties between the UK and Guatemala began to solidify. British companies such as Courage, Range Rover and, until its demise, Polly Peck, all boosted their involvement in Guatemala.

Turning now to the US, relations between Guatemala and the US had been sour since ex-President Carter's implementation of a ban on military aid and lethal arms sales worth over US$13 million in 1977. Guatemala's rulers felt that the US had abandoned them in their darkest hour, and the fact that they emerged triumphant only heightened their sense of moral indignation. This history incited a prevalent streak of right-wing nationalism in elite circles, rendering Guatemala's oligarchy less compliant with US dictates than other Central American elites have been. Yet the Guatemalan ruling class has operated within the framework of US regional interests, even during the Carter years. Although overt US policy was at this time concerned with human rights violations, covert operations supported murderous scorched earth policies in the indigenous highlands. The Carter boycott did affect Guatemala's military capabilities, but countries such as Israel and Argentina quickly filled the vacuum by furnishing military hardware and training (Black 1984 pp. 164–8).

After the instalment of Ronald Reagan in office, the US sorely wanted to renew its direct influence in Guatemala. In the early 1980s the Contra war raged in Nicaragua and the US needed more allies in the region. The links between the countries began to thaw in 1982 after Reagan met Ríos Montt. On the issue of the Guatemalan government's human rights record, Reagan said he was 'inclined to believe that they've been given a bum rap'. Guatemala's elite then began to benefit from Reagan's Caribbean Basin Initiative and new loans from the World Bank and International Monetary Fund.

After the total war of 1982–3, the US State Department saw an opportunity to 'rehabilitate' the Guatemalan ruling elite so as to get aid packages past Congress. This was much the same policy as in El

Salvador, where the US played a more overt role in ushering out the military junta. The US did not need to play as active a role in the Guatemalan transition to 'democracy', since the ruling class there better understood how to maintain 'order'. Both the Guatemalan elite and the State Department agreed on the shift to a low intensity model of warfare. The Guatemalans needed little prompting from the US, since they knew when to devastate mass organisations and when it was safe to call elections and proclaim 'democracy' from the rooftops.

The transition from military dictatorship to Low Intensity Democracy was ultimately a decision of the national elite, according to its own criteria. Guatemalan government policies are not merely made in Washington. The US involvement in inspiring the sea change favouring democracy was not directly obvious, but more behind the scenes, and of course this changeover took place in a context of dependency on US trade, investment and covert military aid. As Chomsky (1989 p. 138) writes: 'Guatemala, another terrorist state, while not a mere creation of the US government, is still highly dependent on it to preserve its own system of military and class domination.'

The United States has very good reasons to be seen to side with 'democracy' in Guatemala. US foreign policy makers prefer client states to have at least a veneer of democracy (that is, a functioning, if mean-ingless, electoral system), though they will of course back blatant repression to protect their 'regional interests' (Iraq under Saddam Hussein until 1 August 1990, and General Pinochet's Chile throughout the 1970s and 1980s are but two examples). Since the US was routed in Vietnam, its foreign policy has generally favoured the Low Intensity Conflict model over direct involvement in guerrilla wars. El Salvador is the classic model of this strategy in Central America, allowing the US to play a deciding role in holding back a popular revolution without committing its forces, all the while paying lip service to human rights and democratic principles.

The United States capitalised on some semblance of electoral democracy in order to pass significant military and bilateral aid packages through Congress. In this way military and bilateral aid began to flow again before the 1985 elections, but became qualitatively greater after a civilian became President. Bilateral aid from the US to Guatemala rocketed to US$149 million in fiscal year 1989, tripling from $52 million in 1985, the last year of military rule (Economist Intelligence Unit 1991, p. 30).

US military aid remained at a relatively low figure (compared with that supplied to El Salvador), at approximately US$9 million per annum. Yet US arms sales to Guatemala, prohibited during the years 1977–82, soared under civilian rule. In 1989, the government bought 16,000 M–16 rifles and ammunition at a cost of over US$13.8 million, the largest purchase of hardware since the arms embargo was lifted in 1982. The US military presence in Guatemala deepened during the Cerezo years. In October 1987, US helicopters based in Palmerola, Honduras, airlifted Guatemalan troops from the capital directly into the combat zone of the Ixcán. Under the civilian regime, the United States added military advisers, augmented pilot training and provided medical assistance for combat casualties. Furthermore, this discussion of collaboration between the two countries' armed forces only includes documented, overt military aid.

Covert military aid has come not only through the more usual channels of CIA funds and proxy mercenary states, but also through the US drug enforcement programme. In the late 1980s, Guatemala jumped from nowhere to seventh in the Drug Enforcement Agency's (DEA) tables of world producers of heroin. The country is increasingly used by cocaine barons as a conduit to the US market. However, the highly inflated opium figure is seen by many as an attempt to legitimate the provision of hardware and finances to the Guatemalan military for its counterinsurgency war.

Outwardly at least, US involvement did not translate directly into complete Guatemalan compliance in foreign policy. On the one hand, Cerezo championed his doctrine of 'active neutrality' towards the regional conflict in Central America. Guatemala was not a front-line state against Nicaragua to the same extent as Honduras was. Much to the chagrin of the US, Cerezo supported the Arias Peace Plan and hosted the Esquipulas I and II meetings. On the other hand, the Christian Democrat regime played a pivotal role in providing logistical back-up for the Contras. Contra officers were trained in Guatemala and the army channelled Irangate money to the Nicaraguan counter-revolutionaries. However, the ideals of 'active neutrality' were transgressed when Guatemala sent crack commando troops to El Salvador during the offensive of the armed left-wing opposition, the FMLN, in November 1989.

The 1985 elections allowed the US government to cement relations with Guatemala. There was an increase in bilateral aid, as well as a deepening of the US involvement in the counterinsurgency war. President Cerezo was obliged to return such favours. Paradoxically, this meant that the Christian Democrat regime was more of an instrument of US interests in the region than some previous Guatemalan military governments were. From a low point in 1981–2, US–Guatemala relations steadily improved. The mending of bridges accelerated faster than ever after 1986, but the US has failed to exert the full political influence it would like to have in Guatemala.

Relations can only improve, however, as long as Guatemala pursues a low intensity model of conflict and maintains a civilian administration. Signs that the WAC faction is increasing its power in the country cause great concern to US foreign policy makers. The US State Department's frustration at the armed forces was expressed in 1990, when the US suspended military aid in an action which shocked many observers. In December, the House Foreign Affairs Committee approved legislation prohibiting military assistance and restricting Economic Support Funds (ESF) until it saw an improvement on human rights. The Bush administration opposed this measure, fearing that legislation would set a precedent in foreign policy, that is, a 'friendly country' might be denied economic and military funds because of a poor human rights record.

The US action was largely symbolic, since it deals with relatively small sums of lethal aid. It was obviously directed at the military since the suspension came at a time of changeover of civilian governments. So what message was the US State Department sending the Guatemalan military? The official version of events says that the suspension resulted from the refusal by the Guatemalan military to make progress on outstanding human rights cases. In particular, the State Department protested at the failure to prosecute the Special Forces for the killing of US restaurateur Michael Devine.

At another level of analysis, the US actions are designed to compel the Guatemalan military to clean up its act on drug running and to take part in negotiations with the URNG. This is in essence a conflict over strategy between the State Department and the Guatemalan military. The latter is moving more towards the WAC strategy by stepping up the repression and, until recently, refusing to sit at the same table as the guerrillas. The US, on the other hand, is strongly promoting Low Intensity Conflict, and so wants the armed forces to strive for a political defeat of the insurgency. That the Clinton administration plans to continue this basic strategy towards Latin America is apparent in the way that Bernard Aronson, Bush's Assistant Secretary of State for the region, was retained during the changeover of administations.

In general then, elections have been a successful strategy to gain international legitimacy, and this has translated directly into military and economic aid from the United States, and bilateral aid from Europe and Japan. Although it counts certain successes, this strategy has also brought increased dependency and external political influence for the Guatemalan state. The tendency for the landowning elite and army to swing back into WAC and try to defeat the rebels leads to tensions with international donors. Yet, the United States is not cutting off all aid, nor is it likely to. It will, however, use aid as a lever to push its counterinsurgency policy based on Low Intensity Conflict.

Government–Guerrilla Negotiations

Since the mid-1980s, the URNG has significantly widened the scope of its activities. At present, it is not a threat to the state, nor is it likely to become so. In the light of the Nicaraguan elections and developments within the Central American Left (especially the Salvadoran Democratic Revolutionary Front – FDR), the dominant tendency in the URNG favoured a political resolution of the conflict rather than a full-scale insurrection.

Armed struggle is seen as a lever to force the army and business sectors to the bargaining table, not as a means to seize state power. Recently, the possibility of a negotiated settlement to the armed conflict seems more likely than ever, yet still remote. Nothing is won at the negotiating table that has not been won in the battlefield, and at present the army is not pressured militarily to the extent that it has to yield its position.

Initially, dialogue between the URNG and the Cerezo government got off to a faltering start. Many observers suggested that government–rebel negotiations in 1987 sowed discontent in the ranks of officers, prompting the coup attempt of May 1988. The rebellion was led by Officers of the Mountains who are opposed to any talks with the insurgents. The threats of this WAC faction stymied any other attempts at dialogue. In August 1987, President Cerezo hosted the regional Esquipulas II peace process, seemingly without recognising that Guatemala was obliged to find a solution to its armed conflict. Negotiations were put on ice for the next few years.

The March 1990 meeting between the URNG and the National Reconciliation Commission in Oslo, Norway, set plans for a series of negotiations to end the war and write a new constitution. For each civilian government and the LIC army faction, the negotiations represent an effort to defeat the URNG politically. All factions in the military are unified in their vehement rejection of any perceived capitulation to the URNG, and are only coaxed into discussions in the belief that the guerrillas are about to abandon armed conflict.

A URNG representative in Europe summed up the rebels' position on negotiations as follows:

The government wanted to negotiate because it believes that the URNG is defeated militarily and because of the global political situation, given the events in Nicaragua and Eastern Europe. It extended the olive branch expecting us to reject it, thus giving them a justification to launch a final offensive. Yet we came willingly to Oslo with concrete proposals of our own, such as how to integrate the URNG into the electoral process, and this has caught them off balance. We want to split the negotiators from the non-negotiators, and massage the divisions (personal interview, 1990).

In June 1990, the first round of talks in the 'Oslo Process' were held between the political parties and URNG in Madrid, Spain The URNG agreed to cease offensive attacks during the 1990 presidential elections in return for future integration into the national political process. The second round of talks took place in September 1990 between the guerrillas and the private sector association CACIF and did not result in any agreement. The hard line agro-export association UNAGRO rejected the talks, refusing to take part in any low intensity diplomacy. In the April 1991 negotiations, the army sent high-ranking officers from the military high command who agreed to discuss the reformist agenda drafted in earlier meetings.

It is difficult realistically to assess the significance of these talks. Both sides claimed political victory. However, the URNG seems to be setting the agenda for future meetings, including sessions on human rights, constitutional reform, demilitarisation and land tenure. The rebels succeeded in widening the divisions in the ruling elite and isolating their fiercest opponents, the landowners. Divisions between the WAC and LIC army factions deepened, with the killing in May 1991 of General Maza Castellanos being interpreted as the result of his unbending opposition to negotiations with the guerrillas. While one group of officers agrees to discuss demilitarisation, the former Defence Minister General Mendoza has said about army reform, 'It will never happen so long as I am in control' (*This Week* 10 June 1991, p. 129).

The incorporation of the URNG into electoral politics seems particularly unlikely while the URNG and the military retain their military capabilities. If the army is killing Centrist and Centre-Left politicians, it is likely to direct an even fiercer repression at any electoral representatives of the URNG. The existence of the 1,000–2,000 guerrillas is the raison d'être of the 45,000–strong armed forces. One retired military officer has stated that without the active guerrillas, the army would be half its present size and the military budget would be correspondingly smaller. 'If we had no guerrillas, we might have to invent some', he quipped (*This Week* 20 May 1991, p. 109).

The guerrillas claim to be open to a negotiated settlement to the war, but they know that this depends ultimately on the position of the army. The military has made it abundantly clear that it has no intention of negotiating away power to the URNG, a position on which all factions agree. In its public statements, the army has continued to refer to a threat from Russia and 'Marxist-Leninist penetration' (*Inforpress Centroamericana* 9 August 1990, p. 3). The language of the Cold War is still alive and well in Guatemalan military circles, partly because the danger was never really external (that is, from the former Soviet Union). Rather, it comes from within and so is still a threatening reality. The progress in negotiations between the rebels and other elements in Guatemalan society has led to a hardening of military positions on the part of the army and the insurgents. As often occurs, negotiations result in intensified armed conflict, as each side seeks to improve its bargaining position. While rebel and army leaders shook hands in Mexico in April 1991, the air force (FAG) intensively bombed guerrilla positions in the Ixcán war zone.

The basis of recruitment for the URNG has not been removed, nor has the labour movement been placated with the guise of democracy. Low Intensity Democracy did not reduce the motivations for popular agitation against state authority combined with elevated levels of guerrilla war. As the war continues and the international image of civilian democracy is further tarnished, the prospect of open authoritarian dictatorship becomes more likely.

President Serrano: A Self-made Man?

In Guatemala, there are no political parties, only electoral campaign groups lacking both platforms and ideology.
(General Hector Gramajo, former Defence Minister,
conference at American University,
Washington DC, 27 May 1990)

This quote shows the respect which the armed forces accord to the electoral parties. The military openly sneers at the electoral process, knowing it to be a sham. Political parties, rather than elaborating independent programmes and creating a social base, vie for the army's favour. The narrow range of policies held by parties excludes the possibility of significant reform of the existing political order.

The majority of the population has little control over political parties, the leadership of which is drawn exclusively from the elite. Further, it is important to question the whole concept of participatory democracy in the context of mass illiteracy. Education is such a privilege that over 55 per cent of the population is illiterate. Among women and indigenous peoples this figure climbs to 80 per cent. The barriers of language and ethnicity also obstruct full participation in national politics.

There are 22 indigenous groups in Guatemala, a large number of whom are monolingual Mayan speakers, yet the constitution has so far only been translated into two of their languages. The Mayan groups of Guatemala have consistently been excluded from the electoral process. No parliamentary political party has ever organised a mass base in the rural communities since the parties have been the domain of non-indigenous Ladinos. We should bear this context in mind while assessing the 1990 presidential elections.

By early 1990, the possibility of democratic elections had already been marred by the high levels of political and social violence. Among the acts of politically motivated violence was the machine-gunning of a leading official in the Centre-Right UCN party, Otto Ruano Reyes. The Guatemalan press reported 198 assassinations in June 1990 alone, before the first electoral round began (*Noticias de Guatemala* no. 178, p. 6).

The surge in political killings resulted partly from the fact that the dominant groups were not united behind one platform. This is part of Guatemala's perennial problem of political stability: the parties have no real social base outside the elite, the elements of which are continually feuding for a transitional hegemony, without ever arriving at a stable consensus. This has been less of a problem in neighbouring El Salvador, where the right-wing Nationalist Republican Alliance (ARENA) has historically eclipsed all other political parties. Until the last few months of the 1990 elections, there was not a consensus in the army and oligarchy for any one presidential candidate. We can see, then, that there is no culture of democracy, in which people can freely express their beliefs without threat of reprisal and violence. In such a situation of generalised terror and domination, democracy cannot thrive.

In the first round in November 1990, the Christian Democrats were easily knocked out of the running. More than anything, this was a judgement passed by the impoverished majority on a party which had failed to extract the country from its morass of economic and political crisis. The outright winner in the January 1991 run-off was Jorge Serrano Elías, who received 68 per cent of the vote in an election characterised by high absenteeism, running at 55 per cent. Apathy in voting behaviour was most pronounced in the indigenous areas.

Serrano Elías is known as a conservative populist, an evangelical Protestant with neoliberal policies. He was the sole civilian in Ríos Montt's regime, heading the Council of State in 1982–3, during the worst years of the last war and crisis stage. He is CACIF's man, favoured by the industrial and finance sectors, but not by the landowning agricultural sector. The business community expressed their confidence in Serrano by repatriating capital to the country. In the context of Central America, Serrano's election completed the swing to the Right in the region; as part of the pattern set by the election of ARENA in El Salvador, UNO in Nicaragua, Callejas in Honduras and Calderón in Costa Rica. Serrano fitted perfectly into the US policy model for the region: economic liberalisation as a diversion from the urgent need for political and social reform.

Serrano inherited a government tarnished by corruption, with empty coffers, a growing budget deficit and a firm place on the international credit blacklist. The government budget deficit ballooned to US$409 million, with $125 million in overdue interest payments on the international debt (Economist Intelligence Unit 1991, pp. 25–7). Internationally, credit lines closed to Guatemala apart from a $12 million loan from the International Development Bank. The World Bank suspended all loans and classified the country as a bad debtor. The Banco Centroamericano de Integración Económica suspended disbursements in 1990. This made it harder for Serrano to rely on external assistance to shore up the economy. The country's economic debility meant that greater power was given to the International Monetary Fund (IMF) to determine the government's policies.

The Serrano administration desperately tried to placate the IMF, and sought to comply with any IMF dictates to reinstate previous levels of aid. The main IMF demands were the usual litany of liberal economics; austerity for the majority, cuts in the public sector and privatisation. The IMF called for reductions in government spending, controls on wages and a widening of the tax base. Serrano immediately set into motion these requirements by cutting public spending by 30 per cent in the first four months of his term (*ACEN-SIAG*, 20 May 1991, p. 3). He sacked over 10 per cent of government personnel and within two weeks of taking office had dismissed 3,000 public employees.

Early on, Serrano attempted to introduce a 'social pact' with the trade unions and business to accede to IMF demands to control worker wage levels and increase government revenue from business.

Through the social pact, the government hoped to raise US$180 million in taxes to meet its outstanding debt payments. The social pact was part of Serrano's corporatist strategy and it sought to tie both business and labour to the state.

Serrano's populist rhetoric wooed neither business nor labour. The unions rejected the new government's corporatist aims and pressed forward with wage claims. The trade unions remained wary. One unionist replied that Serrano planned to use his social pact as 'an instrument to neutralise the struggle of the popular classes' (personal interview 1991). The private sector was equally recalcitrant, seeing the social pact as a mechanism for increasing taxation. Although Guatemala has among the lowest levels of taxation in the western hemisphere, business adamantly refuses any attempt at fiscal rationalisation. Not even the military governments of Ríos Montt and Mejía could push through tax reforms. Serrano's social pact disintegrated before the end of 1991.

The IMF mandates also encountered antagonism from the armed forces. The army is often the first to oppose across-the-board cuts in government spending. The drain which the armed forces make on the governmental budget hinders the application of IMF measures, since they would involve cutting defence significantly. IMF demands for privatisation similarly challenged the army, since it is the main owner of state industries. We can see, then, how the IMF and international finance controlled the formulation of Serrano's policies, but their full implementation remains problematic.

Serrano's election was hailed by international observers as a victory for democracy. Yet President Serrano, like his predecessor, had to walk the tightrope between the LIC and the WAC faction in the army. The US acted early to buttress the standing of the low intensity doctrine and exert its influence through Serrano. Shortly after Serrano took office, US Ambassador Strook made an informal offer to reinstate military aid to Guatemala, conditional on progress in pending human rights cases. Serrano rejected the offer out of hand. To the applause of local editorial columns and the military, Serrano took a nationalistic posture, replying, 'We do not take orders from Washington' (*This Week* 14 February 1991).

Serrano had no success in reining in the security forces. The level of political attacks remained on a par with the worst figures under Cerezo, the most noted attacks being against social democratic politicians. The Guatemala-based *Central America Report* stated in May 1991 that 'clearly a campaign of repression has been launched against the unarmed left'.

The national newspapers linked the wave of repression with the negotiations between army and insurgency. The extreme Right feared that the meetings would lead to an integration of the guerrillas into the political process and acted to deny any room for manoeuvre on the Left. On the issue of negotiations with the URNG, Serrano publicly and personally committed himself to negotiations and was one of the authors of the 1990 Madrid accords with the URNG, but was later surrounded by army officers who deeply oppose them. Serrano was adamant that he was in charge of the armed forces, but was embarrassed when he announced his entire cabinet except the Defence Minister and the Interior Minister, whose posts he was still negotiating with the army.

Social reform hardly appeared on Serrano's agenda and any discussion of agrarian reform remained a recipe for political suicide. To date, civilian rule has not attempted to reform the skewed land tenure system, petrified social structure and white domination of the indigenous majority. As the fundamental structural conditions which give rise to social polarisation remain unchanged, so does the basis for relentless strife between the classes and ethnic groups.

Though governments may damp down the flames of social change during one period, the ashes only smoulder and catch fire at a later date. The army's strategy to use Low Intensity Democracy to defuse popular discontent, undermine guerrilla recruitment and coopt the labour movement has so far failed. Since 1954, no centre ground has evolved in the political spectrum, nor has any political party created mass bases of support outside the ruling class. A new government took office in 1993, but we will have to wait and see if its President shows any likelihood of breaking out of the cycle of LIC and WAC counterinsurgency strategies.

Conclusions: Low Intensity Deception

It is vital to recognise that the mere establishment of a functioning electoral system is not a sufficient criterion for announcing the existence of democracy. Before the international community heralds the consolidation of democracy in Guatemala, it must wait for civilian control of the armed forces, the establishment of rule of law in the country, real mass participation in politics and economic and social justice.

We should judge the authenticity of the transformation from military dictatorship to civilian elected democracy by the strength and organisation of the popular movement pressuring for change.

In Guatemala, there were no strong trade unions and other popular organisations left from the years of state terror to demand electoral democracy. In fact it was the defeat of the popular movement which meant that the state could afford to turn to Low Intensity Democracy. A false 'democratisation' was not led by the working class and peasantry, or even by the squeezed middle class, but by a dominant elite planning for the survival of a structure of inequality. Each civilian government has inherited the legacy of war and social inequality without the will or organised popular support to challenge the status quo.

Even though the mass of the population did not provide the catalyst for elections to take place, there was great euphoria in 1986 at the inauguration of a civilian president. This euphoria was quickly replaced by dashed hopes, as it was apparent early on that Vinicio Cerezo was strait-jacketed by the army and lacked the vision to free both himself and the country. Though Cerezo initially had a reputation as a Leftist and an independent, he moved to the Right until he was no more than the military's man of straw. Like other civilian leaders emerging out of a military-dominated past, Cerezo was caught in the iron cage of the Guatemalan power structure, where the state serves as a flexible instrument of continued counterinsurgency. Nor did Serrano escape this structural fate of Guatemalan civilian presidents. Ultimately, the Guatemalan military's strategy for Low Intensity Democracy has not brought peace, only a sharpening of political and social conflict and a heightening of tensions in the civil war.

We can only speculate on the long-term political ramifications of the population's experience of frustration at the political process. Part of the answer lies in the low turn out for the 1991 polls and the general disillusionment with party politics. Will recent experience cause apathy or lead to more armed struggle? The URNG has improved both its combative capacities and negotiating position during this latest LIC stage, but the guerrillas' strategy has distinctly changed. The trend is now more pragmatic; from armed struggle to take power militarily towards armed struggle to force negotiations.

In the end, only the popular movement and political opposition hold the key to a just peace, but the closer they get to attaining it, the greater is the likelihood of a return to the War and Crisis model of authoritarian rule.

Postscript: Prospects for Peace

The peace agreement in El Salvador led to hopes for a peaceful resolution to the 30-year war in Guatemala, but these are now fading fast. The Guatemalan negotiations reached an impasse in October 1991 over government opposition to disbanding the civil patrols and setting up a 'Truth Commission' to investigate human rights violations.

In May 1992, the pressure to restart the peace process increased. The URNG issued its 'Global Proposal', which advocated changing the order of the negotiation plans to discuss the imminent return of 45,000 refugees in Mexico, and the restructuring of the process to include all sectors of society.

This last proposal struck a chord in the popular movement. Civilian sectors produced a document demanding their participation in the negotiations. Popular movement activity escalated in July 1992 with a strike of 100,000 state employees from the FENASTEG union. Land invasions, *campesino* demonstrations for land and their violent repression led to the resignation of the Interior Minister Hurtado Prem.

The US has also pressured the government to restart negotiations. The gathering political determination to resolve the US debt has led to a reduction in expenditure in the region, especially direct military aid. US military aid to Guatemala has not been renewed since December 1990. The Clinton administration now wants demilitarisation in Latin America, leading to smaller armies which are locally financed, not dependent on US aid. The Guatemalan armed forces already devour over a third of the government's budget and the economy cannot support the larger army necessary for a successful counterinsurgency programme. Thus the Guatemalan government and army may have to yield to international pressure and negotiate. There is, however, an enormous tension between the US and the military elite who are resisting demilitarisation and loss of privilege. These officers, aggrieved at Bush's election defeat, are becoming increasingly more anti-US.

Where is the peace process going? It is extremely difficult to determine, since the political situation is very unstable. It appears doubtful that a peace agreement similar to that in El Salvador will be enacted.

At the beginning of the negotiating process the military was more united, since it approached talks as a way to give the URNG an honourable way out of the war. Since this scenario did not develop, the unity in the officer ranks has frayed, generating more factional disputes within the state.

Fragmentation within the army has resulted in continuing high levels of political violence as factions cultivate an atmosphere of lawlessness and impunity. The new President, de León Carpio, in his former role as Human Rights Ombudsman, recorded (conservatively) 6,295 human rights abuses in 1991. He affirmed that 'the wall of impunity continues to be unbreachable.' In 1992, the human rights office of the Archbishop in Guatemala City reported 204 extra-judicial executions and 499 assassinations.

A wave of bombings in the capital in 1992 seems to have been the responsibility of drug cartels linked to the army. They want to desta-bilise the government to create the atmosphere of political uncertainty necessary for their operations to continue within state structures. The air force is the section of the military which benefits most from drug money. It controls the airfields and reputedly earns US$150,000 for each drugs shipment that refuels. The air force is also the most vehemently opposed to negotiations with the URNG.

The political confusion caused by the bombings and general violence led to threats of a coup by those officers who wanted a more authoritarian state to stifle dissent within the state and society. Serrano, for his part, was increasingly plagued by attempted coups. The shifting allegiances and factionalisation within the army reached the point where there were few whom Serrano could trust. In December 1991 Serrano sacked his Defence Minister Luis Mendoza and the Army Chief of Staff Godoy Gaitán for allegedly plotting a coup against him with members of the WAC line. Godoy was also said to have been receiving kickbacks from coffee contraband shipments to the US and the now discredited Bank of Credit and Commerce International (BCCI).

Some of these coup attempts were reminiscent of the technical coups of the Cerezo years, since afterwards stiffer measures were agreed to in the counterinsurgency war. In May 1992, Serrano cut short his European tour after rebellion in the military ranks. As military pressure increased on Serrano in 1992, he repeatedly threatened to 'do a Fujimori'.

In May 1993, Serrano's threats became a reality. With the 'Fuji-coup' as the blueprint, Serrano and his military minders declared a state of emergency and suspended congressional powers. Police surrounded key buildings in the capital as television stations were taken off the air and newspapers closed down. There followed a crackdown on human rights organisations, but an attempt to arrest the congressional human rights procurator de León Carpio failed as he managed to flee over the back wall of his garden.

The coup was masterminded by a military wanting to take a tougher line against its internal critics, especially human rights organisations. Their cause has received greater publicity since Rigoberta Menchù won the Nobel Peace Prize in 1992. The WAC factions also sought to clamp down on growing trade union confidence and stem the influx of refugees returning from Mexico. The coup was favoured by those oppposed to all negotiations with the guerrillas and it is possible that the army planned to use this opportunity for an all-out assault on guerrilla strongholds.

By participating in the auto-coup, Serrano was reaching for the possibility of beefing up his own weak party political organisation. Like Fujimori, he came to power without a party infrastructure. Seeing how Fujimori increased his own party's control of the Peruvian congress, Serrano hoped to do same in the congressional elections that he planned after the coup.

Within five days, the Serrano auto-coup had failed because of a combination of immediate pressure from the US and popular protest in the streets of the capital. Fearing that Guatemala's events would derail the peace protest in El Salvador, the US threatened to block IMF and World Bank loans. This measure panicked the business sector, and when CACIF condemned the coup, the game was up. The military tried to re-instate constitutional rule with Serrano's vice-president as interim President, but these manoevres were rejected by Congress, which named its own presidential choice, the human rights procurator Ramiro de León Carpio. This was the best possible outcome of an attempt by the WAC faction to overtly control the state once again and launch an all-out assault on the guerrillas and popular sectors.

As this book goes to press, there seem to be more grounds for optimism about the political future of Guatemala. At least for the time being, open military dictatorship has been precluded. The WAC faction is in utter disarray and the military is more divided than at any point in recent history. Yet there are also reasons to be cautious, as the peasant leader Juan Mendoza commented to me, 'The army has its tail between its legs now, but they may have many other cards to play'. As the civil war carries on and social inequality deepens, de León's ability to challenge military power and address these issues depends much on the continued support of the international community. It remains to be seen if the events of summer 1993 will represent a democratic sea change in Guatemalan politics.

References

ACEN-SIAG Semanario informativo, diversos numeros, 1991. Guatemala.

Aybar de Soto, J. 1978. *Dependency and Intervention*. Boulder, Colo., Westview Press.

America's Watch Report 1989. *Persecuting Human Rights Monitors: The CERJ in Guatemala*. New York, America's Watch.

Amnesty International 1989. *Guatemala: Human Rights Violations under the Civilian Government*. London, Amnesty International.

AVANCSO 1992. *Donde Está el Futuro? Procesos de reintegración en comunidades de retornados*. Cuadernos de Investigación No. 8, Guatemala: AVANCSO.

Barillas, Danilo 1975. *Democracia Cristiana y su Posición ante el Ejército de Guatemala Hoy*. Guatemala City.

Black, George 1984. *Garrison Guatemala*. London, Zed Press.

Bowen, G. 1982 'Prospects for Liberalization by Way of Democratisation in Guatemala', in G. Lopez and M. Stohl (eds), *Liberalisation and Redemocratisation in Latin America*, pp. 33–55, Westport, Conn., Greenwood Press.

Cerezo, Vinicio 1975. *El Ejército Como Alternativa*. Guatemala.

CERIGUA Centro Exterior de Reportes Informativos Sobre Guatemala, Semanario Informativo, varios numeros 1990–1. Mexico.

Chomsky, Noam 1989. *The Culture of Terrorism*. London, Pluto Press.

Economist Intelligence Unit 1990. *EIU Country Profile Guatemala 1990–91*. London, EIU.

—— 1991. *EIU Country Profile Guatemala 1991–92*. London, EIU.

Goldston, James 1989. *Shattered Hope: Guatemalan Workers and the Promise of Democracy*. Boulder, Colo., Westview Press.

Immerman, R. 1982. *The CIA in Guatemala*. Austin, University of Texas Press.

Inforpress Centroamericana 1990, 1991. Semanario informativo, diversos números. Guatemala.

Junta Militar de Gobierno 1982. *Plan Nacional de Seguridad y Desarrollo*. Guatemala.

Lopez, G.A. and Stohl, Michael (eds) 1987. *Liberalization and Redemocratization in Latin America*. Westport, Conn., Greenwood Press.

Manz, Beatriz 1988. *Refugees of a Hidden War: The Aftermath of Counter-Insurgency in Guatemala*. Albany, NY, SUNY Press.

O'Brien, P. and Cammack, P. (eds) 1985. *Generals in Retreat: The Crisis of Military Rule in Latin America*. Manchester, University Press.

O'Donnell, G., Schmitter, P. and Whitehead, L. (eds) 1986. *Transitions from Authoritarian Rule: Latin America*. Baltimore, Maryland, Johns Hopkins Press.

Painter, James 1987. *Guatemala: False Hope False Freedom*. London, LAB.

Schlesinger, S. and Kinzer, S. 1982. *Bitter Fruit: The CIA in Guatemala*. Garden City, NY, Doubleday.

Smith, Carol A. (ed.) 1990. *Guatemalan Indians and the State, 1540 to 1988*. Austin, University of Texas Press.

This Week in Central America. Weekly reports 1991. Guatemala.

Wilson, R. 1991. 'Machine Guns and Mountain Spirits: The Cultural Effects of State Repression among the Q'eqchi' of Guatemala'. *Critique of Anthropology*. vol 11 (1), pp. 33–61.

—— 1993. 'Anchored Communities: Identity and History of the Maya-Q'eqchi', in *MAN: Journal of the Royal Anthropological Institute*. vol. 28, (1), pp. 121–38.

7. Argentina: Fragile Democracy[*]

MIGUEL TEUBAL

Introduction: from Alfonsín to Menem.

On 8 July 1989, six months prior to the date set for the conclusion of his term in office, President Raúl Alfonsín of the moderate middle-class Unión Cívica Radical (or Radical Party) resigned as President and transferred power to Carlos Menem of the labour-based Justi-cialista (Peronista) Party, the winner of the 14 May elections. While this was the third time in more than 40 years that the Peronistas were swept to power, it was the first in many decades that an incumbent civilian president chosen in free elections was succeeded by a popularly elected candidate of a rival party. Many observers looked upon this as an important landmark in the political development of Argentina: democracy seemed to have attained a certain 'maturity' since the change of government had been carried out without a military coup or the direct participation of the armed forces (see Potash 1989).[1] The transition from the Alfonsín to the Menem administrations cannot, however, be characterised as a smooth affair. The fact that Alfonsín was forced to resign prior to the conclusion of his term in office reflects, not only the failures of his presidency, but also the fragility of Argentina's recent democratisation process.[2]

The current democratisation process began in December 1983 when, after conceding free elections, the military government of the so-called Proceso de Reorganisación Nacional, (dubbed popularly as the *proceso*), one of the cruellest and most inept military regimes of recent times, finally came to an end. The return to a constitutional order had been greeted with widespread optimism by most sectors of Argentine society. Alfonsín had assumed the presidency after defeating Italo Argentino Luder of the Justicialista Party, dominated at the time by more right-wing factions. The election itself was an

* The main ideas of this paper were first presented at a Transnational Institute meeting in November 1989. I would like to thank Susan George for inviting me to the TNI, Joel Rocamora for suggesting that I write this paper and Barry Gills for very detailed comments on a previous draft which helped me improve it sub-stantially. Its structural analysis retains explanatory power as a critique of a failed process of democratisation.

161

important highlight in the political history of Argentina: it was the first time the Peronistas had lost a free presidential election; even many Peronistas of the lower classes had voted for Alfonsín.

The first years of the Alfonsín administration were marked by a relative flowering of democratic liberties. Nevertheless, unable – or unwilling – to cope with the pressures from the economic and military corporate establishments, or to respond to the social and economic demands of the vast majority of the population, Alfonsín soon began losing his early widespread support. By 1989 his government had become highly unpopular. The political climate of the presidential campaign in the early months of 1989 was reminiscent of the days of the waning Isabel Perón government prior to the military takeover of March 1976 and in many respects it was even more chaotic. Marked by ferocious hyperinflation with prices increasing exponentially, real wages falling, factories and business closing, unemployment increasing and financial institutions on the verge of bankruptcy, the government seemed to have lost control of the situation completely.

To many, these events formed part of an 'economic *coup d'état*'[3] by the corporate economic establishment (the so-called *nuevo poder económico* – Azpiazu, Basualdo and Khavisse 1986) that had been consolidated during the *proceso* years and had grown and been legitimised under Alfonsín. The pressures of the economic corporate establishment reinforced those of the military who, in 1989, continued to argue in favour of officers accused and/or condemned for human rights violations as well as for public recognition of the 'positive' role they had played in the 'fight against subversion' during the *proceso* years.[4] In May 1989, Alfonsín was also confronted with widespread looting of supermarkets and other shops, events which highlighted the fact that hunger and marginality had reached intolerable levels and had acquired a new political significance (see Teubal 1989).

These events came as a shock to the lame duck Radical administration. It reacted by applying repressive measures which took a toll of 14 dead and many wounded. A state of siege was declared, hundreds of people were jailed and *agitadores subversivos* (subversive agitators) were blamed for everything.

The possibility of an even greater *estallido social* (social outburst) similar to what had occurred in Caracas, Venezuela, earlier in the year led the government to adopt additional 'security measures' and to limit basic human and social rights further. It also contributed to Alfonsín's premature transfer of power to Menem after his intolerable loss of credibility.

The events of 1989 can also be looked upon as a means whereby the corporate establishment gave notice to Menem – the presidential candidate – of the need to fall in line with the types of policies it considered necessary if 'stability' was to be maintained.[5] After all, Peronism had never been trustworthy for much of this establishment. Past experience showed that Peronistas tended to place emphasis on government intervention, progressive income redistribution, labour welfare measures and overall nationalistic economic policies. Trade unions, in particular the upper echelons of the trade union bureaucracy, also acquired substantial political power under Peronista governments.[6]

These events of the transition period denote the profound crisis of 'Alfonsinismo' appearing as a prelude to the new conservative 'Menemista' regime. While they do not form part of a *coup d'état* in its traditional form – the military did not take power directly – many of the policies, and the institutional setting, the Menem administration was to pursue thereafter were, in many respects, in accordance with the objectives of the military and the different corporate establishments. Menem, for example, has pardoned officers condemned for human rights violations and has established a new and congenial relationship with the military. On the economic front, Menem has intensified the implementation of International Monetary Fund (IMF) and World Bank-imposed 'structural adjustment' policies. Because these policies are unpopular, Menem has imposed a series of measures limiting democratic liberties, restricting popular organisations – especially unions – and strengthening the executive at the expense of parliament.

The advent of democracy did not modify the essential nature of the 'regime of accumulation' installed in Argentina under the 1976–83 military dictatorship. Throughout the 1980s under both Alfonsín and Menem, IMF and World Bank-inspired 'adjustment programmes' were applied. These included: controls on wage increases (wages increased less than productivity and inflation), freeing up of labour markets, liberalisation of financial and capital markets, the maintenance of a regressive tax structure and subsidies to the large corporations, privatisations of different sorts, liberalisation of price and foreign exchange controls and so on. These policies led to important income, wealth and economic surplus transfers to the upper classes and large corporations, both domestic and transnational, increasing the regressiveness of income distribution, and contributing to the deteriorating living conditions of large segments of the middle and working classes. Despite these extreme adjustments which benefited foreign creditors, domestic financial interests and the *grupos económicos* (the so-called *patria financiera, patria contratista* and/or *capitanes de la industria*) the economy did not 'recover'. Productive investment fell, in both the state and private sectors, investment rates reached an all-time low and GNP and income per capita growth rates were on the whole negative. Capital flight and finance and speculative activities continued to be predominant features of the Argentine economy throughout the 1980s.[7]

The stability and sustainability of Argentine democracy appear to be in contradiction with these 'adjustments'. This is why Menem is so intent on consolidating a new regime of state power necessary to carry out his social and economic programme, even if this implies restricting the confines of democracy. While the current social and economic policies are extreme versions of previous 'adjustments' applied in Argentina since the mid-1970s, Menem is conscious of the need to pander to military and security, economic and labour corporate establishments congenial to his government. He complements this with a certain control of the media so that his programme can be enforced. In this sense, he has gone further than Alfonsín, who found it increasingly difficult to continue an economic programme which was incompatible with the consensus necessary for the maintenance of fully fledged democratic legality. While Alfonsín had put the maintenance of democracy on the agenda, and the need to manoeuvre *vis à vis* the corporate establishment so as to maintain essential liberties, Menemismo purports to be *the* political project of the corporate establishment itself. Menem simply tries to interpret the needs of the corporate establishment; many of his Ministers and government officials directly represent these interests.[8] 'Democracy' tends to be a subsidiary of his socioeconomic conservative programme which includes as part of its essential ingredients the maintenance of 'law and order' and a new-found subservience and alignment with the US.

Thus the question of democracy has once again been put on the agenda. To many, this is simply due to the fact that the Justicialistas whose 'democratic vocation' was never very strong, were voted to power (Cavarozzi and Grassi 1989 p. 3). In addition, questions have been asked about the earlier Alfonsín period. Why was any form of participatory democracy not consolidated during the Alfonsín years? What were the errors or limitations of the Alfonsín government?

The failure of Alfonsín is due in large measure to the idea that 'democratic stability' depended on his government implementing IMF and World Bank-type policies, and not carrying out reforms that could confront the corporate establishment. This meant that a series of necessary political, institutional, social and economic reforms were not carried out lest they be perceived as a threat to, or in confrontation with, the corporate establishment. In addition, the Alfonsín administration deliberately obstructed popular participation since this was seen as contributing to the instability or 'ungovernability' of 'democracy'. Both Alfonsín and Menem tend to dissociate 'democracy' from the economic power relations inherent in Argentina's class-ridden society. Both considered adhering to IMF and World Bank 'adjustments' as inevitable.

If the military did not intervene before the last elections, this was in part due to its continuing loss of prestige, but also to the fact that the corporate (mainly economic) establishment and the US government considered that more was to be gained via a freely elected government than otherwise. This constitutes a great difference from previous attitudes of this establishment towards the democratically elected regimes of Argentina. But while an important aspect of democracy is the absence of military rule, other aspects of formal democracy should also be considered. Even within the confines of a formal legality, democratic liberties can be considerably restricted, especially when this is considered necessary to carry out the designs of the corporate establishment as occurred towards the end of Alfonsín's administration and frequently occurs under Menem.

These observations lead us to some more general questions: what factors account for the evident fragility or apparent lack of sustainability of Argentine democracy? What are its social, economic and political foundations?

Class Formation and Capitalist Development in Argentina

The Foundations of Political Instability.

There are many interrelated factors that can account for the political instability of Argentina in the period from the military coup of 1955 to the most recent restoration of democracy in 1983:

1. competing interests among diverse bourgeois factions created a situation where no consolidated ruling class had hegemony, leading in various instances to one or other faction turning to the military to take over;
2. the threat which the advances of the working classes and their political and social organisations represented for these dominant elites;
3. the internal dynamic within the military corps itself.

We will look at each of these points in turn.

Competing Interests among Bourgeois Factions
Argentina in the 1960s and 1970s emerged with a heterogeneous structure of bourgeois interests, no peasantry to provide surplus cheap labour to the productive process (to some extent this was provided by immigrants from Paraguay, Uruguay, Bolivia and Chile) and a large (by Latin American standards) middle- and working-class strata associated with early urbanisation, a relatively extended domestic market and import substitution industrialisation (ISI). As far as Third World countries are concerned, Argentina had developed a relatively extended welfare state – particularly during the Peronista regime of 1945–55 – with measures favouring trade unions and the labouring classes in general. State intervention, credit facilities and other promotional measures initially introduced under the conservative regimes of the 1930s were thereafter used to enhance this popular and nationalist Peronist regime of the 1945–55 period. Some of these policies and measures were continued thereafter under succeeding governments.

In the 1950s and 1960s Argentina was already a dependent semi-industrialised capitalist Third World country containing a series of heterogeneous bourgeois interests. This resulted in a problem of hegemony: no bourgeois faction was capable of acquiring a nationwide hegemony for a long period of time and different 'ties' or 'stand-offs' characterised much of the political and economic developments of the period (Petras; Portantiero 1978). To a large extent, this was related to the complexity of Argentina's 'modernisation' and indus-trialisation processes. Two world wars and the Great Depression had demonstrated the vulnerability of the Argentine economy, due to its extreme dependence on a few export commodities and British markets. While there were many factors accounting for import sub-stitution industrialisation (ISI) in the interwar period – mainly prior industrial development and accumulated skills provided by massive immigration – this was initially visualised as a temporary policy designed to confront the crisis affecting Argentina at the time. The Peronista government of the 1945-55 period gave the economy renewed impetus as industrialisation was one of the main objectives of development policy. An industrial bourgeoisie based on the devel-opment of light industry, producing consumer wage-goods compatible with income redistribution policies, was enhanced. There also emerged an expanded urban industrial proletariat which rapidly developed its trade union organisations and acquired a certain autonomy. These factors contributed to the development of a large middle and labouring class society, with intermediary organisations of all sorts

(trade unions, cooperatives, neighbourhood organisations), constituting the basis of Argentina's dynamic and complex civil society.

An elaborate state structure based on the alliance of a 'national bourgeoisie' oriented towards the domestic market and the labouring classes
was also established. The state increased its control of key sectors of
the economy: railways and other public utilities were nationalised,
the banking system and foreign trade were controlled, and government
took direct charge of numerous private firms. It was within this
context that the conflicting interests of a 'national bourgeoisie' allied
with the working classes and the military versus the traditional agro-
export and landowning establishment, particularly of the Pampean
region, came out into the open. While urban industry thrived on the
basis of protectionist and nationalistic policies related to ISI and the
domestic market, the agro-export interests of the pampas – the so-
called traditional oligarchy – were subscribed to an economic (though
not necessarily political) *liberal* doctrine, and strongly confronted this
'national-popular' ideological matrix.[9]

After the first Peronista government was overthrown in 1955, a
new stage in the ISI process developed. The production of some
intermediary and capital goods and consumer durables oriented
towards the demand of more upper income strata were given pre-
eminence. The Argentine economy began integrating more fully
into the US sphere of influence. Automobile, chemical and petrochemical industries were established to a large extent with foreign
capital. The ascent of *desarrollismo* (developmentalism) in the late 1950s
and 1960s, based on foreign capital, implied the need to 'deepen'
the industrialisation process with the establishment of 'heavy industry'
(see Ferrer 1963) and the development of consumer durables and some
intermediary and capital goods industries dominated by foreign
capital.[10]

At the same time light industry – textiles, light metallurgical
products – in which mostly small and medium-sized firms were
dominant, but which was dependent on the domestic market and
the demand of wage earners, began losing out. Some of the traditional agro-industries of the interior – sugar and wine mostly – also
suffered important crises of overproduction. Hence, the 1950s and
1960s were marked by the increased rivalry of these diverse bourgeois
factions which represented contradictory interests. A new 'liberal'
alliance combined the traditional agro-export interests of the pampas
with foreign capital to confront the *national-popular* ideological and
political matrix and it frequently adhered to the 'stabilisation
programmes' propelled by the IMF.[11]

'Easy' ISI (that which established final consumer goods provided by light industry) can be associated with an accumulation process which in relative terms was 'socially and sectorally articulated'. Increases in real wages and in the share of wages in GDP implied larger markets for 'wage goods' industries: food, textiles, wood and furniture, light metallurgical products, household goods. As de Janvry and Sadoulet point out, in this model of accumulation:

> labour is simultaneously a cost and a benefit for capital: a cost in that all wage payments are a subtraction from profits, and a benefit in that the mass of wages paid creates the necessary effective demand for the products to be sold and for capital to return to the form of money. Growth and income distribution are, thus, indissolubly tied together in an ultimately progressive manner even if the nature of this relation is marked by serious class confrontations and recurrent economic cycles and crises'(de Janvry and Sadoulet 1983, p. 279).

In the 1960s these 'articulated ' sectors of the economy, coexisted with 'disarticulated' ones, not only with those forming part of the 'agro-export complex' but also with those related to the emerging interests of the new consumer durable industries (automobiles, petrochemical products) and foreign capital. The latter thrived with the application of programmes which reduced real wages, which caused large income transfers to the upper strata of society, thus increasing the regressiveness of income distribution. Foreign capital associated with the production of consumer durables for the upper classes and the agro-export complex associated with the agricultural exports of the pampas became the main beneficiaries of this trend towards a more 'disarticulated' accumulation model. As de Janvry and Sadoulet point out:

> Under pure social disarticulation, by contrast, labour is only a cost to capital. Non-workers' incomes create both the source of savings and the expanding final demand for the key growth sectors. Repression of workers' wage demands becomes a condition to accelerate growth as this expands simultaneously the capacity to produce and the capacity to consume of the economic system. Growth finds its roots in increasing inequality, and the only limit to inequality is the relative power of labour versus other classes. This relation tends to become institutionalised in repressive and non-democratic forms of government. (de Janvry and Sadoulet, 1983 p. 279)[12]

In the period we are considering, no clearcut hegemony was established between these diverse bourgeois factions with contradictory interests. While the 'articulated alliance' thrived on the basis of protectionist and nationalistic state policies related to ISI and the domestic market, the 'disarticulated alliance' adhered much more to the 'stabilisation programmes' propelled by the IMF. Needless to say, this lack of hegemony of any one of these bourgeois factions and alliances contributed to the succession of civilian and military regimes.[13] To this must be added the fact that the upper echelons of the economic and corporate establishments felt threatened by the advances of the 'national-popular' alliance within the context of the succeeding democratisation processes. Free elections and institutionalised democracy led to the victory of Peronism, which had developed policies and a form of state intervention that favoured the 'articulated alliance'. Peronista governments and programmes confronted the landowners of the pampas (via the application of land taxes and controls on foreign trade), foreign capital (via nationalisation of public services) and finance capital (control of bank deposits and credit policy), and favoured the labouring classes in general. Radical governments (like the Illia government), though much more liberal in their economics, also maintained a certain continuity with ISI policies.

The military coup of 1966 installed the first so-called 'bureaucratic-authoritarian' regime (O'Donnell 1979), reflecting the increased power attained by a highly oligopolised and transnationalised bourgeoisie. Under this regime, decisive weight was given to a transnational stratum of experts in metropolitan economic orthodoxy and 'specialists' in coercion. Many of the institutions of democracy and various channels for the representation of heterogeneous interests were liquidated. Popular sectors, especially the working classes, as well as small and medium-sized businesses, were excluded socially. Transnationalisation of the economy and denationalisation of society thereafter proceeded at a more rapid pace (see Cumings 1989, following O'Donnell).

During the post-1976 *proceso* years these trends deepened and attempts were made to break fully with the remnants of the 'articulated' regime of accumulation.[14] The power of the *grupos económicos* was increased, mostly due to increased financial and speculative activities resulting from an expanding foreign debt. The economy attained a greater *apertura* (opening) and transnationalisation, especially in matters pertaining to finance capital, all of which led to its increased 'disarticulation'. This new regime of accumulation was the most serious attempt to break the perennial 'tie' which had previously characterised Argentina's socioeconomic and political processes.

Perceived Threat from the Working Class and Other Organisations
During this period, one factor that was perceived by dominant elites to be a 'threat' to the stability of democratic regimes, was the significant advances attained by the labour movement, in particular during the Peronista governments. The labour movement had become highly organised, attaining a relatively high level of social solidarity associated with an elaborate and institutionalised (by Third World standards) welfare state, all of which post-1955 governments tried unsuccessfully to disarticulate. Ideas concerning income redistribution and basic welfare measures had become important components of Argentine society and were considered a threat by the dominant elites.

The fact that the labour movement since 1945 was almost wholly dominated by Peronism,[15] and not by the socialist or communist political tendencies prevailing in Chile or Uruguay, did not impede Peronismo from becoming 'el hecho maldito de la burguesía Argentina' (the bugbear of the Argentine bourgeoisie). For many years, Peronism and anti-Peronism divided Argentine society ideologically despite the many converging objective interests of Radical and Peronista parties. The coups of 1962 and 1966 were carried out to a large extent to impede the ascent of Peronista candidates. During the 1958 and 1963 elections the Peronista Party was banned. It was only after the failure of the military regime of the so-called *Revolución Argentina* (1966–73) and mass protest that the Peronistas were fully legalised, permitting them to attain power once again in 1973.

The opposition between conflicting bourgeois interests and a strong labour-based movement was shaped by the lack of institutionalisation of democratic liberties and institutions. With no party interests to represent them directly, the dominant elites involved the armed forces in successive military coups. In reality, dominant interests felt threatened by the emergence of democratic regimes and their socioeconomic policies. 'Democracy', even in its more formal terms, was also deprecated by much of the political establishment and trade union bureaucracy. Many of the trade unionists and politicians of the traditional parties went along with these elites and frequently induced the military to intervene and interrupt civilian rule.[16]

In the late 1960s the beginnings of a new phase in the development of Argentine society seemed to be emerging with the crisis of the old order, and with vast numbers of the middle and working class leaning towards the popular and revolutionary movement. Argentine society was in great ferment, due in large measure to the influence which international revolutionary events exerted on the constituencies of the trade union movement, the Peronista and Radical parties, the student movement, the Catholic Church and other parts of the Left. The *Cordobazo* of 1969 symbolised the explosiveness of the situation, which were thereafter extended to many cities. It was in this context that various urban guerrilla groups began operating. The 'revolutionary violence' of these groups was a response to the lack of democracy and channels of participation in Argentine society at the time. Nevertheless, the guerrillas of the early 1970s soon became disassociated from the labouring and popular masses. After 1973, their existence was used to justify increased military intervention and the particularly ferocious character of the post-1976 military regime.

The Military
Other factors which contributed to the political instability of Argentine society in the 1950s and 1960s were the changes in the strategy, organisation and professionalisation of the armed forces. In the early years of the century, the army had followed the German army as its model, establishing close contacts with it. This induced the Argentine military to develop its own armaments industry and to favour industrialisation as well. In the 1920s, the army was instrumental in the establishment of state-controlled steel, petroleum and chemical industries. During the Peronista years, the army maintained a statist and nationalist strategy associated with the need to attain a certain self-sufficiency and autonomy in 'basic' industries. In the 1960s, a change of strategy was begun: the armed forces redefined their role within a Cold War framework, in the process setting themselves clearly within the Western camp. This led them to establish closer relations with the military academies of the United States, and to adhere to US-dominated continental defence treaties.

In 1963, the more 'legal' armed forces emerged triumphant in the intra-armed forces conflict of that year. Thereafter, the army, but also the navy and air force, increased their 'professionalisation' and internal cohesion. They also adhered to Franco-American doctrines of national security and became increasingly preoccupied with internal repression. In this framework, domestic conflicts were visualised as manifestations of the fight against communism (see Cardoso 1979 p. 44). Seeing themselves as bulwarks of Western Christian civilisation, they assumed a quasi-fundamentalist outlook, defining their role as a special corps destined to save society from 'subversion'. This was related to the political instability of the time and the threat from the advance of Peronism and the labour movement. But it also had to do with the internal dynamic of the military corps itself, particularly the view that it could act as a 'military party'. The coups of 1966 and 1976, establishing the 'author-itarian-bureaucratic' (O'Donnell 1979) military regimes of 1966–73 and 1976–83 respectively, were due in part to this newly developed 'professionalisation' of the armed forces as well as to the other factors characterising these regimes.

The *proceso* years (1976–1983)

The military once again took charge of government in 1976. The Peronista government of 1973 had initially attempted to restore the 'national-popular' alliance, combining it with a much more industrial-export orientation. After the death of Perón in 1974 and the takeover of Isabel Perón, a total changeover of economic strategy was instituted. While the Cámpora and Perón governments of the 1973–4 period had supported a 'social pact' between the major components of the national-popular alliance, Isabel Perón supported the 'liberal' economic factions. Her government was supported mainly by the right-wing and fascist segments of the Peronista movement. The Isabel Perón government ended in total failure, due to conflicts between different factions of the Peronista movement and a deteriorating social situation which threatened the dominant corporate establishment.

It was in this context that the military intervened once again. By then, the military had developed a new *esprit de corps* based on the 'fight against subversion' and the decay of the Isabel Perón government. The internal cohesion of the armed forces was maintained by a reign of terror. Wholesale kidnapping, torture and disappear-ances were rife in the *proceso* years. Another major feature was the changeover in socioeconomic strategy and capital accumulation. An open-door policy towards international capital, as well as policies which supported speculative and financial activities sustained by an increased foreign debt (which grew from about US$7 billion in 1976 to more than US$43 billion in 1983), contributed to the changing structure and accumulation regime of Argentine society. Underlying these changes were certain 'modernisation' strategies which favoured the *nuevo poder económico*, the upper bourgeoisie and the segmenta-tion of the labour movement, with the cooption of labour leaders and disruption of labour solidarity.

Thus, during the *proceso* years a more fully socially 'disarticulated' accumulation regime was instituted. It was based on the predomi-nance of speculative and financial activities, and on increasing foreign indebtedness and the 'opening' of the economy to international finance capital. As Villarreal (1985) points out, while the upper segments of the bourgeoisie acquired a certain homogeneity, the dominated classes and segments of society were increasingly 'disarticulated' and became much more 'heterogeneous'. This accumulation regime also subordinated the bourgeois interests of the 'national-popular' alliance – the small and medium-sized firms – and tended to create a 'surplus labour economy', increasing self-employment and a host of precarious new activities in the 'informal' sector of the economy.

The ferocity of the military regime was soon to elicit widespread opposition. On the one hand, contradictory bourgeois entrepreneurial interests began confronting the speculative nature of the government's programme. The labour movement increasingly presented a united front against the military (see Godio 1991). One of the more important developments which heightened opposition to the regime came from the newly formed human rights organisations. The numerous groups which began opposing the barbarity of the military regime, led by the *Madres de Plaza de Mayo* (Mothers of Plaza de Mayo) had a profound moral effect on society, and greatly contributed to the delegitimisation of the military regime. The Malvinas adventure was the 'drop which overflowed the cup'. Thereafter a completely discredited military had no choice but to hand over power to a democratically elected civilian government.

The Alfonsín Administration (1983–1989)

During his 1983 election campaign, Alfonsín promised that the burden of foreign debt would not be transferred to the people, that real wages would be increased and the economy reactivated. In essence, the economic policy of the military regime would be discontinued. Alfonsín also promised that he would bring to trial the military officers who had ordered the wholesale violation of human rights. He usually ended his campaign speeches with a recital of the preamble of the 1853 constitution, which mandates the maintenance of a representative, republican and democratic form of government. Indeed, the first years of the Alfonsín administration were marked by a relative flowering of democratic liberties. Freedom of speech prevailed to a large extent. Progressive radio and television programmes were popular and there was, on the whole, no censorship. Parties organised freely and, after certain initial difficulties, trade unions did so as well. The independence of the judiciary was restored.

Throughout the Alfonsín years two basic issues were to elicit much controversy: one concerned trials for human rights violations during the military dictatorship; the other, the implementation of economic policies which responded increasingly to the dictates of the IMF with consequences that violated basic social rights and alienated support among large segments of the population. Both issues were to be important testing grounds for Argentine democracy.

The Human Rights Issue

After a long and widely publicised trial, almost all the members of the military juntas of the post-1976 military regime were condemned. Concurrently, a Comisión Nacional de Desaparición de Personas (National Commission for Missing People, CONADEP) was instituted which investigated human rights violations due to the 'excesses' of the armed forces in the 'anti-subversive war'. The strategy of the new civilian administration for the handling of human rights violations issues was to limit trials to a number of senior officers and to complete these trials as soon as possible, so that thereafter it could bring about the reconciliation and integration of the armed forces within the constitutional order. Nevertheless, the existence of an independent judiciary that was created by the restoration of democracy frustrated these plans. While initially only the members of the military junta and some other notorious members of the *proceso* were brought to trial, private citizens submitted denunciations against some 2,000 members of the armed and security forces. Civilian judges in many parts of the country summoned active duty officers for questioning. This was a process which Alfonsín had not expected, one which went much further than had been initially planned.

Concerned that the indefinite prolongation of the trials was endangering his efforts to promote national reconciliation and the acceptance by the military of its role in a constitutional order, President Alfonsín called on Congress to legislate a terminal date for the initiation of new trials. Passed by Congress on 23 December 1986, this law of *Punto Final* placed a 60-day limit on civilian courts for questioning military personnel about their participation in the repression. Anyone not summoned at the end of the period was exempted from criminal prosecution except in cases involving children or where the accused had fled. While the new law had the purpose of reducing to a minimum the number of new trials, it had a reverse effect: federal prosecutors worked intensely to summon military personnel who had been named in the denunciations; between 200 and 300 additional officers, most of whom had been in the junior grades between 1976 and 1982, were thus found subject to prosecution rather than the handful that the administration had anticipated.

In 1987 and 1988 several uprisings by fundamentalist military factions took place. The government responded by mobilising the population in defence of democracy, but in essence finally gave in to most of the military's demands. Under pressure by the executive, the law of *obediencia debida* was passed by Congress. Responsibility for human rights violations was placed exclusively on higher ranking officers. All military and security personnel below the level of zone commanders were absolved from criminal liability for their conduct during the repression. The military reaction against what they regarded as Alfonsin's 'anti-military' campaign only increased. As was mentioned previously, pressure from the military was an important element in the weakening of the Alfonsín regime.

The Economics of Democracy

Alfonsín's first Economics Minister, Bernardo Grinspun, applied policies which were not congenial to the IMF and foreign banks. Wages were increased beyond inflation rates and attempts were made to negotiate foreign debt servicing directly with foreign banks, that is, without the prior application of IMF-inspired 'adjustment' policies. The government was unable to control the local economic establishment and failed to acquire support abroad, in particular among European governments, for its programme. Inflation rates got out of hand in early 1985 and Grinspun was replaced by Juan Sourrouille, an efficient technocrat, who took charge of the Economics Ministry almost until the end of the Alfonsín presidency.

Sourrouille followed IMF adjustment policies almost to the letter. He imposed controls on wage increases, freed up labour markets and liberalised financial and capital markets, as well as maintaining a regressive tax structure and subsidies to the large corporations. All these measures formed part of what one author dubbed a 'Hood Robin' policy, that is, 'taking from the poor to give to the rich' (see the various articles by Horacio Verbitsky in *Página 12)*. Transfers to the upper classes and large corporations increased the regressive nature of income distribution. The 'socially and sectorially disarticulated' regime of accumulation established under the military dictatorship was intensified, increasing greatly the inequalities of Argentine society. No important reforms were introduced in the economic system inherited from the military dictatorship, since these were construed to be anathema to democracy itself.

Sourrouille's moment of glory came in 1985 when the Austral Plan was instituted: inflation was curbed – at least temporarily – via a price, wage, public utilities and foreign exchange freeze.[17] The Austral Plan contributed for a time to Alfonsín's popularity. But after a year or so inflationary pressures intensified and subsequent 'adjustments' exerted negative effects on growth, income distribution and wages. These policies understandably generated opposition. The General Confederation of Labour (CGT) staged 13 general strikes against the Alfonsín–Sourrouille administration. Nonetheless, the government continued inflexibly pursuing its policies. It insisted that no 'serious' alternatives were viable, and that these 'adjustments' were inevitable.

The more concentrated segments of the economic establishment, large corporations and conglomerates, were the main beneficiaries of the liberalisation and 'deregulation' policies of 'structural adjustment'. A highly regressive tax structure was not reformed, although large corporations paid relatively few taxes and tax evasion was (and is) pervasive. Subsidies to the large corporations and foreign banks continued to constitute a large part of government expenditure. They replaced the series of welfare measures that had traditionally favoured Argentina's salaried working and middle classes. Not only was little done by way of reforming the economic structure that had been consolidated during the military dictatorship, but the foreign debt was not tackled either. These became the weak links of Argentina's democratisation process. Economic policy became its Achilles' heel to the extent that vast portions of the population were marginalised and dissent became increasingly endemic.

In this respect the Alfonsín administration maintained a certain continuity with regard to the economic policies of the previous military regime. In essence, the 'liberalisation', 'outward orientation' of the economy,[18] and primacy given to speculative and financial activities led to the continuing disarticulation of the economy and society. This was particularly critical for a country in which the 'articulated' social segments have traditionally been important components of the Argentine economy.

While these policies corroded the legitimacy of Argentine democracy, and isolated the Alfonsín government, they did not contribute in any significant degree to capital accumulation. The enormous transfer of resources to upper income groups and corporations did not result in increased productive investments, which fell dramatically throughout the 1980s. These 'Hood Robin' policies only elicited perverse reactions from their beneficiaries. The large corporations were the main beneficiaries of foreign debt transactions, government subsidies and overall policies. Yet the enormous income transfers, as well as interest, profits and rents earned, were in large measure transferred abroad or consumed conspicuously, instead of being invested productively. The few manufacturing undertakings that did take place – paper, petrochemicals and oilseeds – were only marginally labour-intensive and did not contribute to any significant degree to overall growth or reactivation of the economy. Even from the perspective of establishing an industrial strategy for integrating into the world economy, the policies applied in this period were a total failure.[19]

Using macroeconomic and social indicators, the Alfonsín administration had one of the worse records of recent decades, much worse than prior democratic governments and worse still than almost all other Latin American countries in these same years (except, for example, El Salvador, Haiti and Peru). Official data, as well as those of UN agencies, show that under Alfonsín GNP stagnated, income per capita fell, income distribution worsened, the share of wages in the GNP reached a very low level, real wages continued falling, the rate of unemployment and underemployment increased substantially and poverty and marginality became 'structural features' of Argentine society. Despite an initially higher degree of welfare (a lesser degree of poverty) compared with other Latin American countries, the Argentine economy became increasingly 'Latin Americanized' – suffering an 'acute process of underdevelopment' (see data presented in Teubal 1990; based on Economic Commission for Latin America and official Argentine data).

Democracy under Alfonsín

One of the main tenets set forth by the Alfonsín administration was that democracy was only possible within the narrow confines of a policy of non-confrontation with essential parts of the corporate – economic, military and Church – establishment. This meant that no important reforms in the power structure were made lest these caused undesirable reactions. Thus, for example, no important tax reforms were enforced, nor were military education or military service reformed. Economic policy was aligned with the dictates of the IMF. Only when the reasons for a military coup were excluded from the agenda would democracy be safe. This implied limiting the participation of popular, trade union and intermediary organisations in decision making.[20] Social and economic reforms were perceived as a challenge to the corporate establishment. Reference was frequently made to the 1973–6 period, when the 'excesses' of popular participation had supposedly led to military dictatorship.

Democracy implies also the extension of parliamentary practices and the primacy of political parties. Despite much rhetoric, the legislature did not acquire a very active role during the Alfonsín years. Important labour laws passed by Congress were vetoed by the President. Many matters concerning, for example, foreign debt were never even decided upon by Congress. Different economic programmes of the period, 'the overall strategy and most of the economic policy initiatives of the Alfonsín government were the result of unilateral decisions taken by Sourrouille and his team of *técnicos* and then announced on television' (Smith 1989 p. 33). The preponderance of executive power over the legislative branch made it difficult for the parties and the party system to serve as legitimate, institutionalised mechanisms for the mediation of social conflicts and the articulation of the legitimate interests of collective actors in civil society with respect to key questions of macroeconomic policy making. The experience of the Austral Plan, the Australito, and especially the disaster of the Plan Primavera, reinforce a belief that technocratic modes of policy making limited to the corridors of executive power are deeply antithetical to democratic consolidation (Smith 1989 p. 33).

One of the reasons given for the numerous military coups that have plagued Argentina in the past half century is the absence of a conservative party capable of winning elections which would respond to the demands of the economic establishment (see Rouquié 1983 p. 385; Rouquié 1982). The Alfonsín government did much to help consolidate the Unión de Centro Democratico (UCeDe) as such a party, as a conservative alternative to both Radical and Peronista Parties. The Radical and Peronista parties competed for such a role, adopting economic orthodoxy as their main economic philosophy and generally moving to the Right. This strategy, however, weakened the political parties because it made it difficult for them to respond to the demands of their social base. To this day, political parties are characterised by extreme verticality, lack of mass participation and a certain *clientelismo*. They have become purely electoral machines, limiting participation to decisions of secondary importance (see Auyero 1989).

If democracy implies the democratisation of the economy and society, then Argentina in these years did not become structurally more democratic. While the traditional power structure was consolidated, small business and the working and middle classes lost out substantially. The popular mobilisations characterising the first years of the Alfonsín administration did not result in important democratic and social reforms. This in large measure can be related to the limitations of the governing party and of Alfonsín himself. There was no mobilisation to reform the structure of state power and reduce the influence of the entrenched corporate interests. Reforms in the military structure most probably could have been carried out during the first year when widespread support for the Alfonsín administration prevailed. Other policies which could have led to a more 'articulated' economic policy, and incorporated and addressed the interests of small business and popular classes, would also have signified a more united 'civil society'. But as we mentioned previously, mobilisation was perceived as dangerous, as something that could get out of hand.

At the beginning of the Alfonsín government, some theorists argued for a 'democratic popular-liberal' pact. Others, such as Borón, said that no constitutional legality can subsist without social reform policies to sustain it:

> These reforms are necessary because we know that the market, left to its own, will never carry them out. Latin American countries are confronted with a series of dilemmas which must be resolved if the project of redemocratisation is to have a certain continuity. In the first place, one must consciously choose between reformism or conservatism. The first is a necessary condition for democratic progress; the negation of reform will accelerate political decadence and precipitate a return to despotism. If the present processes of transition to democracy, faced with pressures from bankers and the dominant circles of international capitalism, do not incorporate a reformist project, we will have to conclude that the viability of democracy is seriously in question. It would not be an imprudent exaggeration to say that its defeat will be inevitable and another period of political crisis and authoritarian restorations will be opened ... To begin the process of social reform is the only creative alternative that can be opened at the present conjuncture. If this develops successfully, a better society may result with new protagonists capable of controlling the state democratically and promoting justice and liberty for all citizens. (Borón 1986, pp. 293–4; my translation)

The Politics and Economics of Menemismo

In much the same way as Alfonsín, Menem promised much during the election campaign. Menem, for example, promised that he would have Congress discuss the issue of the foreign debt. 'I will recommend the following guidelines: we are to declare a moratorium, we will seek to get foreign creditors to condone part of the principal and we will seek a reduction in interest rates. We will see to it that in the next five years not a single liquid dollar will leave the country' (my translation). The Justicialista Party also wrote into its platform the need for a *Revolución productiva* (productive revolution) and a *salariazo* (large wage increase). It was agreed that the economy should be reactivated (that production should be given precedence over speculative and financial activities), and that real wages should be substantially increased. Following what appears to be a trend in Latin America and the Caribbean if consideration is given to policies implemented by Michael Manley in Jamaica, Carlos Andres Pérez in Venezuela, Fernando Collor de Mello in Brazil and Alberto Fujimori in Peru, Menem was soon to present a complete *volte face* with regard to what he had promised during his presidential campaign.

While a conservative adjustment had been expected, in particular after the hyperinflationary hecatomb of mid-1989, the extreme nature of Menem's economic programme came as somewhat of a suprise. During his presidential campaign Menem had spoken of the need to take into account the interests of workers and popular classes, small business and rural areas. Once in office he set these objectives aside. His extreme adjustments overtly favoured the more concentrated economic and financial corporate elites, including foreign banks, the main beneficiaries of previous policies. The first two Economics Ministers appointed by Menem were ex-employees of Bunge and Born, the large grain transnational originally based in Buenos Aires, a fact quite extraordinary for a Peronista government. When the first Economics Minister of the Menem administration died, less than a week after being sworn into office, another employee of Bunge and Born, Rapanelli, was appointed.

With these appointments Menem began the application of an extreme 'adjustment' programme which was soon to be given 'shock' treatment – 'without anesthesia or parachutes'. The adjustments beginning from mid-July 1989 onwards were extremely severe, not only for the lower classes but also for vast segments of the middle classes. Public utility rates were increased by some 500 per cent, prices were liberalised and increased and the foreign exchange rate was pegged at a very high level. In the meantime, wages were controlled and rapidly lost their purchasing power in a hyperinflationary context.[21] According to government strategy this was followed by a series of 'structural' adjustments (wholesale privatisations) which created a 'shock of confidence'. This would supposedly reverse capital flight and induced massive inflows of 'risk' capital from abroad. Petroleum, agro-industry, and petrochemicals were the key sectors of the economy to be favoured. Menem's promises on foreign debt were also abandoned. The government now insists that foreign debt payments in accordance with the terms set by foreign creditors were 'a matter of honour'. In 1990, not only were policies congenial to the IMF and World Bank continued, but foreign debt servicing, which had been interrupted in 1988, was renewed.[22] Furthermore, debt for equity swaps, as part of a wholesale privatisation programme, became some of the best deals offered foreign banks in many years.

Rapanelli resigned in the wake of a new hyperinflationary peak in late 1989. The new Economics Minister, Erman González (an accountant of the Menem family from La Rioja dubbed by the local daily *Página 12* as 'Sup-Erman, and his programmes respectively 'Sup-Erman I', 'Sup-Erman II') imposed an even more severe 'adjustment', together with the complete liberalisation of the exchange market and price controls. This revealed the contradictions existing between different establishment interest groups. The exchange market became more liberalised than almost anywhere else in the world, thus causing great uncertainty. He also contained the 'excess liquidity' in the banking system by prohibiting the free disposal of time deposits which were exchanged for devalued public bonds, a move affecting mainly small business and the middle classes. Thereafter González continued a very dubious process of privatisation. In the meantime, unemployment reached record levels as factories closed and public offices began dismissing personnel.

Another hyperinflationary peak occurred in January–February 1991. González was replaced by Domingo Cavallo, the Minister of Foreign Affairs who in April instituted the full convertibility of the austral, pegging it to the dollar. In doing so, he stabilised the exchange rate and brought down inflation somewhat, but he also placed public finances in a strait-jacket. No currency issues could be carried out if they were not backed by foreign exchange. Cavallo expected this measure, which was approved by the legislature, to cause prices to fall and thus compensate for an overvalued austral which tended to hurt exports. Nevertheless, prices did not fall enough, and inflation, though low by Argentine standards (1–3 per cent per month), meant that inflation increased in dollar terms, something quite extraordinary in the recent monetary history of Argentina. Subsequently, real wages (because of the inevitable nominal wage freeze) and employment continued falling; the situation in mid-1991 had become desperate for the mass of the population despite the new-found 'stability'.

It is doubtful that this economic policy would have stuck were it not for the increased concentration of power the Menem administration sought, particularly in the wake of increasing opposition by the legislature, the official party itself and large segments of society at large. Menem managed to bypass Congress and govern by decree. He was able to do this because of his control over the Supreme Court of Justice. A law of Congress increased the membership of the Supreme Court from five to nine members. This permitted the President to appoint five judges (a member of the previous court resigned), all of whom were supportive of his policies.

The policy which elicited the greatest opposition, especially from human rights organisations, was the wholesale *indulto* (pardon) Menem signed in favour of more than 260 military officers. They were accused, and many condemned, for human rights violations during the *proceso* years, the Malvinas War, and the Rico and Seinheldin (fundamentalist) military uprisings during the Alfonsín administration. The *indulto* was also to affect the remnants of the totally discredited Montoneros, the guerrilla group active in the 1970s, who at present support Menem wholeheartedly. In late December 1990 Menem also pardoned and freed the condemned members of the military junta and other military officers indicted and imprisoned on charges of human rights violations. According to Menem this was to set the stage for a 'reconciliation' and 'pacification' of Argentine society. What seemed more in the making was the consolidation of a new regime of state power necessary to carry out Menem's social and economic programme which tends increasingly to restrict the confines of democracy. In this respect Menem declared: 'One can govern without the armed forces but one cannot govern *against* the armed forces.'

In many respects, the recent social and economic policies are simply extreme versions of the series of 'adjustments ' applied in Argentina since the mid 1970s. This was clearly stated by Jorge Triaca (one of the labour leaders of Menem's entourage) just prior to assuming the post of Labour Minister in July 1989:

> Nothing of what is coming in Argentina can be understood unless we realise that a *new block of social, political, economic and perhaps military power is being born*, and that [the new Menem government] is ready to take all necessary steps to cut in one swathe all the evils of the past and begin the *task of the reconstruction of Argentine capitalism.* (quoted by Smith 1989, p. 37)

Democracy under Menem

Menem's political and economic programme could, in large measure, have been that of a military regime. This does not mean that the present situation is identical with that prevailing under the *proceso*. The maintenance of constitutional legality, limited as it is, means that political and social movements can operate within a narrow 'democratic space'. Freedom of the press also prevails, although ownership and control of the media are more concentrated than ever. The lower classes, however, do not always have access to 'democracy'. Access to human and social rights and the rule of law is not always available for the underprivileged. The continuing *razzias* on the shanty towns and new police powers have resulted in arbitrary detentions and the death of a number of young people and marginalised residents.

In many respects, Menem's policies can be seen as the continuation and intensification of the policies of the Alfonsín regime. Menem's new policies have potentially disastrous consequences for Argentine democracy. Following what has been called the 'Fujimori effect', Menem has tried to govern single-handedly, 'from above', concentrating power in the hands of the executive, bypassing the legislature and disturbing the balance of powers required in a republican federal state. He has also set aside the traditional political parties and trade unions, including his own party, as important social actors of the political game. Another departure from the Alfonsín years is the greater direct power of the economic establishment. As well as the first Economics Ministers being ex-employees of Bunge and Born, several other economic policy makers are ex-employees of foreign banks, petroleum companies, or advisers and consultants of domestic or foreign establishment interests. The situation is similar on the military front. Menem managed to confront the fundamentalist military factions during the uprising of 3 December 1990 by falling in line completely with the mainstream corporate military establishment, which acquired a renewed political power.

In 1991 the political scene began changing somewhat. Despite continuing assertions that the economic programme was doing well – 'estamos mal pero vamos bien' (things are getting along badly but we are doing well) – the renewed inflationary outburst of January and February 1991 and the extreme nature of the 'adjustments' during 1991 deepened doubts about the Menem administration's economic policies. By mid-1991, the Menem administration seemed to be on a collision course with much of civil society. Menem's personal credibility has been tainted by corruption charges affecting prominent members of his government and political family, including allegations of drug laundering. It is difficult to predict what the short- and medium-term prospects are for Argentine democracy. Menem's programme is for a 'viable' democracy, one that limits democratic procedures and closes off the space for popular participation. This means that repression will be much more on the future agenda of Argentine society as popular sectors inevitably resist antipopular measures and conflicts of all sorts increase.

Conclusions and Future Prospects

According to some observers, with Menem's ascent to the presidency in 1989 the foundations of a new state were established in Argentina. For the first time in many decades, a new structure of state power that can respond fully to the interests of the corporate establishment is in place. The necessary disciplining of the subordinate classes, which was lacking under Alfonsín, has finally been established. While it is true that the concentration of power in the hands of the executive and policies favouring the corporate elites are now more prominent than before, this new structure of state power has not acquired full legitimacy. On the one hand, it has not achieved the necessary consensus among vast sectors of society. Neither has it succeeded in creating a new working model of capitalist development.

This is not due to any lack of effort in 'disciplining' the subordinate classes: trade unions and the popular opposition operate under severe constraints. What in essence was lacking – that is, from the perspective of a 'successful' capitalist strategy – was a necessary 'discipline' among the *grupos económicos* themselves. The establishment continued acting as a speculative elite, interested only in short-term gains. This lack of discipline among the different factions of the corporate economic establishment was compounded by the lack of a long-run strategy of capitalist development and modernisation. There has been a total lack of an industrial export strategy which could increase integration into the world economy. Nor is there a corresponding science and technology strategy that could make this long-run strategy viable. What prevails is a primitive form of savage capitalism, which excludes vast sectors of the population.

The ideologues of the present regime look to Chile and Bolivia as the ideal models for their incessant 'adjustments' and restructuring. These models are difficult to implement in Argentina because of the existence of heterogeneous classes – which form the previously 'articulated' segments of society: middle, working and assorted popular classes, small businesses oriented to the domestic market, much of the informal sector, and so forth. A savage capitalist strategy has so far been difficult to impose in such a conflictive society as Argentina because the exclusion and marginalisation which this strategy inevitably requires is much more widespread than in other Latin American countries. This is one of the reasons why the assorted 'adjustments' have yet to acquire the degree of legitimation necessary for stability.

It is only within the framework of what we might call this essential 'structural insufficiency' that we can understand several seemingly contradictory phenomena. Firstly, it is clear, for example, that the 'articulated alliance' hardly exists in any organised form. Trade unions can strike but do not appear to threaten the system; and under Menem they have even had trouble striking. At the same time, a tradition of democratic participation at the grass-roots level continues to provide a basic dynamism to Argentine civil society. Secondly, Menem's victory in the mid-1991 election can be interpreted as an affirmation of his policies.[23] But this victory has been accompanied by an increase in organised opposition to these policies:

a) Popular multisectoral 'uprisings' have occurred in Chubut, Salta, Jujuy, Catamarca, and the province and city of Buenos Aires against the 'adjustments' and certain *indultos* and a lack of guarantees of justice.

b) A new and revitalised trade union movement seemed to have been emerging since early 1991, despite the profound crisis in which it is immersed. This was reflected in some of the strikes carried out. For example the railway workers went on strike for 45 days in January and February 1991 in the face of opposition by the trade union bureaucracy, obliging the government finally to give in.[24]

c) Other social movements, though at present still weak, have also emerged. Since the return to democracy in 1983, a new housing and squatter movement has been organised in greater Buenos Aires. There is a growing women's movement, particularly among working-class women. Finally, mention can be made of the retired people's movement, which in the winter (June–July) of 1991 was protesting against extremely low pensions and retirement payments. While non-governmental organisations (NGOs) in Argentina have not been as widespread as they are in Brazil, Chile or Peru, here too advances have been made, in both urban and rural areas.

Within this setting there seems to be a realignment of political forces emerging as the traditional party and trade union structures are immersed in a profound crisis. The elections of 8 September 1991 partially reflect some of this realignment of forces. On the one hand there is the crisis of representation of much of the electorate as both the Peronista and Radical parties have moved substantially to the Right, constituting at present – together with the UceDe – *partidos del ajuste*, parties of the 'adjustment'. The Peronista party, by now totally dominated by Menemismo, is vying with the other two parties for the preference of the corporate establishment. The 1991 election gave it a clout which it had not expected. The Right of the Radical Party, led by Angeloz and de la Rúa, has also grown. Although Alfonsín triumphed in primaries, his stand on many issues, though much less *social democratic* than it used to be, did not prevent his being one of the losers in the election, probably because people still remember the debacle of his administration.

In any case, the Radicals, while accepting the inevitability of the *ajuste*, try to convey to public opinion the idea that their privatisations and 'adjustments' would have been much tidier and human-faced.

The new strategy of the US with regard to Argentina is 'stabilising' Argentine democracy on the basis of an alliance of Radicals and Peronistas, the two main political parties. This would imply the alternation of government within a two-party system. Given the right-wing trends which dominate both parties, this would signify the 'stabilisation' of the 'adjustments' which have so far been implemented. Apart from the difficulties both these parties have in reaching a political accord (a Moncloa Pact such as that which was concluded in Spain is usually alluded to), the problem with this is that this new *partido del ajuste* has not acquired the necessary consensus, despite the elections.

Adjustments are still being strongly resisted because of their devastating effects. Given the trend towards the Right of the main political parties, a vast sector of the population which is generally Left of centre remains on the whole unrepresented. This temporarily unoccupied political space provides for the progressive movement a unique opportunity for advance. But the assorted groups vying to occupy this political space have, up to now, failed. Nothing like the Movimiento de la Revolución Democrática of Mexico or the Partido do trablhadores of Brazil seems to be emerging. Progressive forces are splintered and highly segmented. The possibility of constructing a party based on the new social movements is far from being feasible at present. Progressive forces, coming from the Peronista movement, or the Left itself, have yet to converge on the basis of a programme which unites all the diverse splinter groups in a vast mass movement. The opportunity is there for anti-adjustment groups to unify on the basis of a common programme. If they continue to fail in this historic task, the future of authentic participatory democracy in Argentina is very much in question.

Notes

1 In the past 60 years, only a few civilian governments have escaped being overthrown by a military coup. Military interventions terminated civilian rule in 1930, 1943, 1955, 1962, 1966 and more recently in 1976. Only in 1945, 1952, 1973, 1983 and 1989 were 'free' general elections staged in the sense that no political parties were banned. In the general elections of 1958 and 1963, the Peronistas were not permitted to run for office. Prior to the recent election, the only year in which a civilian president was elected after a normal period of civilian rule was 1952 when incumbent President Peron was re-elected for another term in office. His government was interrupted by the coup d'état of 1955.

2 The date for the presidential election preceded by seven months the effective transfer of power to the newly elected President.

3 This hyperinflation was initially induced by successive devaluations beginning on 6 February, due to prior capital flight, and the subsequent run on the foreign exchange market which, in almost instantaneous fashion, resulted in increases in domestic prices. Large financial interests and creditors, as well as agricultural interests, seemed to have colluded in carrying out this de facto coup d'état (see Bleger 1989; and other issues of *Realidad Económica*).

4 These pressures were critically enhanced after members of a small left-wing group, Movimiento Todos por la Patria, carried out a freak attack on the army barracks of La Tablada in the Greater Buenos Aires, on 23 January 1989. More than 20 persons including several officers, were killed and five of the attackers disappeared, presumably shot after having surrendered. Afterwards, the government instituted a Commission on Internal Security which included as part of its functions an increase in domestic intelligence.

5 At the time of the presidential election no agreement with the IMF was in effect and the government had accumulated arrears in the payment of interest on foreign debt since April 1988 for US$3 billion. Apparently the strategy of the foreign creditors

consisted of obliging the impending administration to negotiate from a position of weakness, given that foreign reserves had been reduced to a minimum. According to one author, 'the economic aspects of this transition period implied a strong conditioning of the future government's economic policy. In this sense strong pressures from the creditors and the 'group of the eight' (a business group that had just been formed, not to be confused with the dissident Peronista political group, MT) seemed to have been successful' (Bleger 1989, pp. 9,19; my translation).

6 Peronism has a long history in Argentina. Factions within it have ranged from extreme Right to extreme Left. The Isabel Perón government (1974–6) ended in total failure precisely because it gave leeway to the more right-wing factions of the Peronista movement. This was apparently one of the reasons for Alfonsin's success in the 1983 elections: many people feared that a Peronista victory would mean that right-wing trade unionists would combine with the military to make a farce of democratic legality. After its defeat, the Justicialista (Peronista) Party underwent a process of renewal in the late 1980s. Party life was democratised and the *renovador* factions acquired control of the party apparatus. Menem, the Governor of La Rioja, together with Cafiero and Grosso, were at first the visible heads of this trend. Soon after, Menem's presidential ambitions pushed him to cut loose from the *renovadores* and ally himself with the more right-wing factions of the party. It was with this faction that Menem engineered his victory in the July 1988 primary elections. Upon reaching the presidency, Menem used his power to gain positions within the party and finally managed to control it completely by August 1990. Despite this history, it cannot be denied that the greater part of Peronista militants are profoundly democratic and participate actively in many trade union and other popular organisations.

7 Argentina in the 1980s has had one of the worse growth and development records of Latin America (see Teubal 1990).

8 The Economics Ministry was initially entrusted to officials of Bunge and Born, the large Argentine–Brazilian grain transnational, with major interests in Argentina. One of Menem's officials in charge of the presidency of the Central Bank was a consultant to foreign banks; the new president of Yacimientos Petroliferos Fiscales, the state oil company, is also a consultant to private oil companies; the Minister of Education represents the interests of private schools and private universities and has fluid relations with the Catholic Church; the former Minister of Public Works had direct interests with the *Patria contratista* (State contractors).

9 Rural elites and landowning interests of the pampas and their corporate representation, the Sociedad Rural Argentina, Confederaciones Rurales de Buenos Aires y la Pampa CARBAP, Confederaciones Rurales Argentinas CRA and so on, acquired much greater economic and political power in Argentina than the Brazilian coffee producers and exporters of São Paolo and the Sociedade Rural Brasileira did in Brazil. In Brazil the political and economic interests of the coffee exporters did not relate to the centre of political power based in Río de Janeiro in the same way that agro-export interests of the pampas did in the 1870–1943 period to the different governments of Buenos Aires. Neither was the relation between the Brazilian coffee exporters and industrialists as conflictive as that which emerged in Argentina in the post-1930 period. After the crisis of 1929 many strong coffee interest groups began diversifying their investments, orienting some of them towards industry and thus creating an interbourgeois cohesion that did not exist in the case of Argentina (see Acuña, 1991, pp. 32–3).

10 Braun has characterised the 1960s as the period in which monopoly capital became predominant (see Braun 1970).

11 Large devaluations caused substantial income transfers to agro-export interests and implied falls in real wages. Together with restrictive monetary policies they also reduced global demand, having a recessionary impact on industry. On the other hand, land taxes and controls on food prices implied the opposite: income transfers in favour of wage earners and local industry. For models which analyse some of these processes see (Braun and Joy 1968) and (Canitrot 1980, 1981).

12 In the advanced capitalist industrialised economies, the share of wages in GNP is over 60 per cent, in the US it was 72 per cent compared with the case of Argentina where it fell from 40–50 per cent in the early 1970s to no more then 20–30 per cent in recent years. A high share of wages in GNP implies a much more 'socially and sectorially articulated' accumulation regime, a factor which induced a 'fordist' mode of regulation in the post-Second World War years.

13 Several authors point out that the 'bureaucratic-authoritarian' states of the 1960s and 1970s correspond to the emerging 'difficult' stage of ISI (see O'Donnell and Hirschman in Collier 1979). The argument can be understood better in terms of Amin and de Janvry's concepts of social and sectorially articulated and disarticulated regimes of accumulation. See Amin 1974 and de Janvry 1981 and 1985.

14 During the military regime, 'the armed forces attempted to transform profoundly the behaviour of the economy. This ambitious project to be carried out by a firm authoritarian management was oriented ideologically by the principles of liberalism ... Two main courses of economic policy were followed: the *Apertura* destined to open the domestic market to external competition, and the *reforma financiera* (financial reform) which was to liberalise the capital market. Both were concieved as instruments necessary for a long-run transformation destined to substitute a closed economic system and a strong interventionist state for a free enterprise system' (Canitrot 1981, p. 5; my translation).

15 Peronism did not generally challenge bourgeois hegemony from a socialist perspective, though many of the early Peronista trade union leaders came from the Socialist Party and many of the welfare measures adopted by the first Peronista government formed part of previous Socialist demands.

16 During the first Peronista government of 1945–55 the Radicals actively conspired with the military to overthrow the government. On the other hand, during the Radical government of President Illia (1963–6) Peronist trade union leaders were active in conspiring for its overthrow in 1966.

17 The freeze was based on the idea that there was an 'inertial' inflation that had to be stopped; and this was partly proved to be true since inflation was at least temporarily and in relative terms controled. The reduction of inflation also permitted the government to reduce its public deficit, and to pay a substantial portion of the foreign debt servicing.

18 The main exports continued to be mostly agricultural and agro-industrial products and commodities such as steel or paper. But new industries incorporating new technologies which would have been employment creating, and would have dynamised technology creation, were not promoted. The *apertura* did not increase the international competitivity of domestic industry.

19 On this issue see the recent paper by Nochteff (1991).

20 The only accord with trade unionists was made with the most reactionary *grupo de los 15*, which was offered for a short period of time by the Ministry of Labour. But this was done for political reasons: to reduce the power of the mainstream unions and the *renovador* factions within the Peronista party.

21 According to recent estimates, real wages in two years of the Menem government (July 1989 to July 1991) have fallen by at

least 26 per cent in relation to the years of the Alfonsín administration (see Marcelo Zlotogwiazda, *Página 12,* 13 July 1991).

22 Initially Rapanelli told the banks that they would have to wait until the economy was reactivated before any debt servicing could be made. Evidently, this was one of the reasons for his rapid exit from office.

23 There were several factors which changed the mood of the electorate, beginning two months prior to the election. The newly acquired 'stability' with prices only rising 1–3 per cent per month and a certain 'reactivation' in certain sectors of industry and commerce were factors which induced many of the lower classes to give the government another chance. The spectre of hyperinflation and the chaos it would create if a change in policy came about were additional arguments used in favour of Menem. At the same time, much of the middle and upper classes set aside much of their previous ideological qualms concerning Peronism and voted for Menem. The UCeDe was the loser in this respect. Finally, the anti-system vote of the marginalised and underprivileged went in large measure to Rico, the ex *carapintada* military officer. The Left and Centre Left had no alternative propositions whatsoever to the propaganda of the government. Due to bickerings of all sorts it also lost a unique opportunity to consolidate an anti-adjustment front, in particular in the federal capital where the sum of the votes of all the Left of centre groupings amounted to 18 per cent.

24 For an overview of the Argentine labour movement, see Munck, Falcon and Galitelli 1987 and Godio 1991.

References

Acuña, C.H. 1991. 'La relativa ausencia de exportaciones industriales en la Argentina. Determinantes políticos y sus consecuencias sociales sobre la estabilidad y tipo de democracia esperables', *Realidad Económica,* no. 100, 3rd bimestre.

Amin, S. 1974. *Capitalismo periférico y comercio internacional,* Buenos Aires, Ediciones Periferia.

Auyero, C. 1989. *Desde la incertidumbre.* Buenos Aires, Legasa.

Azpiazu, D., Basualdo, E.M. and Khavisse, M. 1986. *El nuevo poder económico en la Argentina de los años 80.* Buenos Aires, Legasa.

Basualdo, E. 1987. *Deuda externa y poder económico en la Argentina.* Buenos Aires, Ediciones Nueva América.

Bleger, L. 1989. 'La explosión', *Realidad Económica,* no. 88, 3rd bimestre.

Borón, A. 1986. 'Democracia y reforma social en América Latina: reflexiones a propósito de la experiencia europea', in Centro de

Investigaciones Europeo-Latinoamericanas (EURAL), *Crisis y Regulación Estatal: Dilemas de Política en América Latina y Europa*. Buenos Aires, Grupo Editor Latinoamericano.

Braun, O. 1970. *Desarrollo del capital monopolista en la Argentina*, Tiempo Contemporáneo.

Braun, O. and Joy, J.L. 1968. 'A Model of Economic Stagnation. A Case Study of the Argentine Economy', *Economic Journal*, December.

Bresser Pereira, L.C. 1989. 'A Pragmatic Approach to State Intervention: The Brazilian Case'. Paper presented to the LASA XV International Congress, Miami.

Calcagno, A.E. 1985. *La perversa deuda argentina*. Buenos Aires, Legasa.

Canitrot, A. 1980. 'La disciplina como objetivo de la política económica. Un ensayo sobre el programa económico del gobierno argentino desde 1976', *Desarrollo Económico*, no. 76, vol. 19, January–March.

—— 1981. 'Teoría y práctica del liberalismo. Política antiinflacionaria y apertura económica en la Argentina, 1976–1981', *Desarrollo Económico*, no. 82, vol. 21, July–September.

—— 1991. 'Programas de ajuste y estrategias políticas: las experiencias recientes de la Argentina y Bolivia: un comentario', *Desarrollo Económico*, no. 121, vol. 31, April–June.

Cardoso, F. H. 1979. 'On the Characterization of Authoritarian Regimes in Latin America', in Collier 1979.

Cavarozzi, M. and Grossi, M. 1989. 'From Democratic Reinvention to Political Decline and Hyperinflation – The Argentina of Alfonsín'. Paper presented at the LASA XV International Congress, Miami.

Collier, D. ed. 1979. *The New Authoritarianism in Latin America*. Princeton University Press.

Cumings, B. 1989. 'The Abortive Abertura: South Korea in the Light of Latin American Experience', *New Left Review*, no. 173, January–February.

de Janvry, A. 1981. *The Agrarian Question and Reformism in Latin America*. Baltimore, Maryland, Johns Hopkins University Press.

—— 1985. 'La desarticulación social en la historia de América Latina' in *Investigación Económica* (Mexico), no. 172, April–June.

de Janvry, A. and Sadoulet, E. 1983. 'Social Articulation as a Condition for Equitable Growth', *Journal of Development Economics*, no. 13, pp. 275–303.

Ferrer, A. 1963. *La economía argentina*. Mexico, Fondo de Cultura Económica.

Godio, J. 1991. *El movimiento obrero argentino (1955–1990)*. Buenos Aires, Omnibus-Legasa.

Hirschman, A. O. 1979. 'The Turn to Authoritarianism in Latin America and the Search for its Economic Determinants', in Collier 1979.

Inter-American Dialogue 1990. *Las Américas en un Mundo Nuevo*. Informe del Diálogo Inter-Americano para 1990, Aspen Institute.

Maira, L. 1985 'La hegemonía internacional de Estados Unidos y el proceso de democratización en América Latina', in EURAL (eds), *La vulnerabilidad externa de América Latina y Europa*. Buenos Aires, Grupo Editor Latinoamericano.

McMahan, J. 1985. *Reagan and the World*. New York, Monthly Review Press.

Munck, R., Falcon, R. and Galitelli, B. 1987. *Argentina: From Anarchism to Peronism*. London, Zed Books.

Nochteff, H. 1991. 'Reestructuración industrial en la Argentina: regresión estructural e insuficiencias de los enfoques predominantes', *Desarrollo Economica*, no. 123, October–December.

Nun, J. 1987. 'La teoría política y la transición democrática', in Nun and Portantiero (eds), *Ensayos sobre la transición democrática en la Argentina*. Buenos Aires, Puntosur.

O'Donnell, G. 1979. 'Tensions in the Bureaucratic-Authoritarian State and the Question of Democracy', in Collier 1979.

Petras, J., private communication.

Portantiero, J.C. 1978. 'Economía y política en la crisis argentina, 1958–1973', *Zona Abierta*, no. 14/15 (Madrid).

—— 1987. 'La concertación que no fué: de la Ley Mucci al Plan Austral', in Nun and Portantiero (eds), *Ensayos sobre la transición democrática en la Argentina*. Buenos Aires, Puntosur.

Potash, R.A. 1989. 'Alfonsín and the Argentine Military'. Paper presented to the LASA XV International Congress, Miami.

Rouquié, A. 1982. 'Hegemonía militar, Estado y dominación social', in Rouquié, A. (ed.), *Argentina, hoy*. Mexico, Spain, Argentina, Siglo Veintiuno Editores.

—— 1983. *Poder militar y sociedad política en la Argentina*, vol. II. 1943–73, Argentina, Emecé.

Smith, H. 1989. 'Notes on the Political Economy of Alfonsinismo' paper presented to the LASA XVth International Congress, Miami.

Teubal, M. 1989. 'Hambre y alimentación en la Argentina', *Realidad Económica*, no. 89, Buenos Aires.

—— 1990. 'Impacto de las políticas de ajuste', *Realidad Económica*, no. 96, 5th bimestre.

Villarreal, J. 1985. 'Los hilos sociales del poder', in Jozami, E., Paz, P. y Villarreal, J., *Crisis de la dictadura argentina*. Mexico, Spain, Argentina, Siglo XXI.

8. Lost Opportunities, Deepening Crisis: The Philippines under Cory Aquino

JOEL ROCAMORA

On 25 February 1992, Corazon Aquino completed her six-year term as President of the Philippines. During her tenure, ex-President Aquino had faced an onerous legacy of 14 years of dictatorship, plus six coup attempts, natural disasters and assorted other economic and political crises. For Aquino, survival was achievement enough. Measured against the hopes of the dramatic popular uprising which overthrew the Marcos dictatorship in February 1986, the same six years were years of disillusionment and lost opportunities. In May 1992, a new President, National Assembly and local officials were elected.* Electoral campaigning generated a deceptive dynamism in Philippine politics. But underneath the intensifying political activity was a widely felt sense of frustration at the failure of the former Aquino government to make headway in solving massive economic and political problems and cynicism about the ability of the political system to produce better leaders.

The experience of the Aquino government illustrates the severe limitations of what has been called 'redemocratisation' in many parts of the Third World. In the Philippines, as in countries as diverse as Argentina, Guatemala and Pakistan, 'Centrist' governments have been replaced by right-wing regimes. The institutions of formal democracy have failed to broaden political participation. What can, at best, be called 'elite democracies' in effect coexist with military dictatorship. Social reform agendas which could have provided the base for broader political participation have been abandoned. Human rights violations continue unabated. Weak central governments are more easily manipulated by instruments of international capitalism such as the International Monetary Fund (IMF). Economic policies

---

* The election of former Defence Minister General Fidel Ramos, an ex-Marcos loyalist, represents a continuation of the elitist politics which have dominated Philippine politics for decades, and further consolidation of the new 'Low Intensity Democracy'.

mandate austerity for the majority without, in most cases, bringing about significant economic growth. Powerful militaries propped up by American military assistance prevent military victory even for the most powerful revolutionary groups.

The key question in assessing the Aquino presidency is whether she could have done more than she managed to do during her six-year term. The re-establishment of formal institutions of democracy is achievement enough, but could she have done more to implement social reform, to redistribute land and other economic assets and lay the basis for participatory democracy? Could she have attempted to control the right-wing military without succumbing to a coup? Questions also need to be asked about the role of international actors, especially the US government. American influence was generally used to push the Aquino government to the Right. Could the Aquino government have taken a more independent national-ist stance in relations with the US and other international actors such as the IMF and the World Bank? Finally, what responsibility does the Left have for developments since 1986? What role can it play in deter-mining the future of the Philippines?

From Centre to Right: The Aquino Regime, 1986–1990

Corazon Aquino came to power in February 1986 on the crest of a dramatic popular uprising that swept away the Marcos dictatorship. While it appears, writing seven years later, that ex-President Aquino had more limited personal goals, that is that she saw herself mainly as an instrument for rebuilding the formal institutions of elite democracy, the 'February Revolution' that brought her to power had a more substantive reform agenda. The popular organisations that served as the organisational backbone of the anti-dictatorship movement called for social reform and the building of institutions of participatory democracy. Aquino betrayed these hopes. Frustra-tion and cynicism pervade Philippine political life as a consequence. Aquino's abandonment of the anti-dictatorship movement's reform agenda – her government's steady drift from Centre to Right – was the most powerful current of change in Philippine politics.

This was not a process where powerful political interests imposed their will on a helpless but brave President. A more nuanced picture would show that the character of the Aquino regime soon after its inception was merely a reflection of the composition of the anti-dic-tatorship coalition that brought Aquino to power. One part of that coalition was made up of popular organisations with nationalist and reform agendas generated during the long years of the anti-dictatorship struggle. Aquino's role in what was then called the 'parliament of the streets' was based on her husband's imprisonment, exile and dramatic murder in August 1983. Another part of the coalition was made up of powerful institutions, families and individuals who wanted Marcos out while retaining their privileged positions. Aquino tried to balance these two parts of the anti-dictatorship movement in her appointments and early policies. During the first few months of the Aquino government, the key issues were centred on dismantling the Marcos regime. This gave prominence to the more liberal members of the new government who handled these issues and therefore appeared more powerful than they really were. As it turned out, the more powerful positions occupied by conservative members of the cabinet gave them an edge in cabinet battles. Cabinet conservatives were given added power by pressure groups outside the cabinet. Over the course of time, Aquino's own family and class interests began to push her in a direction that corresponded roughly to that demanded by power interests.

Corazon Aquino's class background placed her closer to the conservatives than to the leaders of the 'parliament of the streets'. Her family, the Cojuangcos of Tarlac province north of Manila, have a powerful economic base in a 6,000-hectare sugar plantation and sugar mill. In addition, the Cojuangcos have large stakes in real estate, banking, telecommunications and many other lines of business. Although the Aquino family that Corazon Cojuangco married into was not as powerful economically as the Cojuangcos, they have been close to the centres of national political power since before the Second World War. Her husband, Benigno Aquino Jr, was the main challenger to Marcos's political dominance in the years immediately preceding the declaration of martial law in 1972. Through her immediate family therefore, Corazon Aquino lived in the centres of economic and political power in the Philippines.

When Cory Aquino announced her cabinet soon after her inauguration on 25 February 1986, the character of her regime should have been immediately clear. The military was placed in the hands of two holdovers from the Marcos era, Generals Ramos and Enrile. Economic policy was assigned to another Marcos holdover, together with two big business leaders. Security and economic policy were then, as now, the most important centres of power in the Philippine government. At the time, this aspect of the Aquino regime was overshadowed by its first few policy decisions. Despite pressure from right-wing elements in her coalition to retain Marcos's 1973 constitution and the National Assembly elected in 1984, Aquino chose to abolish both and rule through a unilaterally imposed 'Freedom Constitution', a hastily assembled document that provided a semblance of legality to what was basically an extra-constitutional regime. Aquino followed this decision by sacking all Marcos-era local government officials. Aquino also created two government agencies, the Presidential Committee on Human Rights (PCHR) and the Presidential Commission on Good Government (PCGG). The PCHR, given the task of investigating and prosecuting human rights violations during the Marcos period, was staffed by human rights activists and headed by the respected human rights lawyer, Jose Diokno. The PCGG investigated Marcos-era corruption and took steps to recover 'illegally acquired wealth'.

These policies generated public confidence in Aquino's resolve to move decisively away from the hated policies of the Marcos dictatorship. In addition, Aquino gave the impression of being serious about negotiating with the left-wing, underground National Democratic Front (NDF) during her crucial first few months. Despite opposition from the military and the US, Aquino released top underground NDF leaders and moved towards negotiations with the NDF and, later, the secessionist Muslim organisation, the Moro National Liberation Front (MNLF). Negotiations were necessary and a political settlement possible, Aquino said, because the real roots of these rebellions were the social injustices which her government would address.

Aquino's appointment of human rights lawyer Augusto Sanchez as Minister of Labour was taken as an indication of her social reform agenda. Sanchez's first steps as minister led even the most militant labour unions to believe that for the first time in the history of the Philippines the government would not take an anti-labour stance. While the Minister of Agrarian Reform did not inspire similar confidence, Aquino's speeches at this time always gave importance to the need for comprehensive agrarian reform. Finally, her closest adviser and head of the presidential staff, Joker Arroyo, was a respected human rights lawyer and nationalist.

A few months into her presidency, Aquino looked like a leader with a serious reform agenda. Even her concessions to the military and big business in cabinet appointments seemed like pragmatic adjustments to the realities of survival. Many believed Aquino's claim that hers was a Centrist government. Though it took at least a couple more years for this image to be dispelled, the Aquino regime's drift to the Right had actually started by the autumn of her first year in office. In the course of the next two years, the more progressive members of Aquino's cabinet were slowly eased out, her reformist policies were reversed and a brutal 'total war' policy was imposed by the military. The focal points of change in the cabinet were the removals of Sanchez and Arroyo, one year apart from each other. Both of them were removed after campaigns by the US government, big business and the military; in each case, it was after *coup d'état* attempts that their removal was explicitly demanded.

Several major centres of power worked together to push Aquino to the Right. The first of these was the US government. It was no accident that Aquino's steady drift to the Right started soon after Aquino's state visit to the US in September 1986. Reagan administration officials did not believe that Aquino was strong enough to manage the transition from the Marcos regime. While the US was eventually forced to accept Marcos's removal, it did not want too many of his policies changed. In particular, the US was worried about the influence of the few liberals in the Aquino government who were pushing for the removal of US military bases in the Philippines. To put pressure on Aquino, the Reagan administration openly sided with conservative elements on key policy debates in the early months of the Aquino government. The key instrument of pressure was US financial assistance, which was crucial because Marcos had bankrupted the treasury before he went into exile. It was only in June 1986 that American assistance began to come in and only after Aquino's US visit that more substantial financial arrangements were made.

The second power bloc was the military. All factions in the military were pro-American and shared the Reagan administration's concerns, especially over the influence of supposed 'Leftists' in the cabinet. The military was particularly worried about the importance given to prosecuting human rights violators in Aquino's early pronouncements. Military concerns about this issue were heightened by the fact that key liberals in the cabinet, like Diokno, Sanchez, and especially the Executive Secretary Arroyo, had defended political prisoners during the Marcos period. Another issue was Aquino's push for negotiations with the NDF, which implicitly recognised the legitimacy of rebel demands. Although big business, foreign and local, the Catholic Church hierarchy and provincial politicians also supported these changes, the key power blocs pushing Aquino to the Right were the US and the military.

For these power centres, the overriding issue in the first few months of the Aquino regime was continuity with or, as some put it, 'reconciliation' with remnants of the Marcos dictatorship. Aquino, on the other hand, had more than enough personal reasons for striking decisively against remnants of the Marcos dictatorship. A more important reason was the then Defence Minister Juan Ponce Enrile's attempt to put together a coalition of his supporters in the military and Marcos loyalists as a base for challenging Aquino's political dominance. Two coup attempts, the July 1986 Manila Hotel takeover and the abortive 'God Save the Queen' plot in November 1986, emphasised the seriousness of the Enrile threat. To secure support for removing Enrile from the cabinet, Aquino compromised her policies and began the steady process of reversal. The first victim was Aquino's policy towards urban workers. Labour Minister Augusto Sanchez was fired as a quid pro quo for Enrile's ousting. The process of dismantling repressive labour laws from the Marcos era was decisively stopped by Sanchez's successor. In October 1987, Aquino finally outlined her policy towards workers in a speech to over 1,000 cheering local and foreign business people. Accusing militant workers of being communist dupes, Aquino said: 'We will not allow an unruly minority to use the rights of labour to achieve a communist victory instead.'

The betrayal of Aquino's land reform promises took a longer and more circuitous but no less decisive route. During Aquino's first year, when she had decree-making powers, land reform advocates pushed her to decree a land reform law because they were afraid that the Congress which would be convened in July 1987 would be dominated by landlords. Neither Aquino nor her agrarian reform minister paid any attention until 13 protesting farmers were killed in a rally near the Presidential Palace in January 1987, an event now popularly known as the 'Mendiola Massacre'. Even then, the land reform legislation that Aquino submitted to Congress six months later was heavily criticised as too limited. In its main outlines, the proposal was no different from what Congress eventually passed. It took Congress close to a year to pass a land reform law. Although the law maintained Aquino's high rhetoric and pledged 'comprehensive' agrarian reform, high retention limits for landlords, a policy of full payment at 'market rates', and a long, drawn-out implementation process, it led analysts to conclude that the law would be difficult to implement. More than two years after the law was passed, critics were proven correct. The only thing that has happened that comes closest to land reform is the continuing implementation of Marcos's land reform law affecting only rice and corn lands. This involved not much more than giving so-called 'emancipation patents' to former tenant farmers who had been in effective control of their farms for years (cf. Putzel and Cunningham 1989; Punongbayan 1990).

The last major policy area that Aquino reversed was security policy. By the time that a ceasefire was in place and negotiations had started in December 1986, it was already clear that a political settlement was not possible in the face of US and military opposition. When Aquino visited the US in September 1986, she conceded publicly that she was entering into negotiations mainly in search of moral justification for the resumption of all-out war. The military took a more active stance. They arrested an adviser of the NDF negotiating panel and many analysts believe that the brutal November 1986 murder of Rolando Olalia, head of the progressive labour centre Kilusang Mayo Uno, was the military's handiwork. Despite these provocations, the NDF went ahead with the ceasefire, but the negotiations proper quickly ground to a halt as a result of the government's insistence that negotiations had to take place within the framework of the still-to-be-ratified constitution. The NDF insisted that a political framework was precisely what had to be negotiated. It was in the midst of these disagreements that the Mendiola Massacre occurred, ending negotiations in the process.

In a speech to cadets at the Philippines Military Academy in March 1987, Aquino announced that her government had 'unsheathed the sword of war'. Although she did not announce the connection, it was also at this time that Aquino abandoned her attempt to punish human rights violators in the military. The PCHR was abolished in April 1987 without the members of the committee even being informed. A new human rights commission was created and staffed by some people who have spent more time defending the military than prosecuting human rights violators. By mid-1987 it was clear that Aquino had surrendered control over security policy to the military. The result was a steadily increasing rate of human rights violations that groups such as Amnesty International, which had sympathised with Aquino early on, came to recognise. Other branches of the Aquino government worked closely with the military. The Supreme Court, for example, made a mockery of the constitution's Bill of Rights and its own rules of due process by justifying arrests without warrant and the denial of bail to political prisoners.

Even ex-President Aquino's most ardent supporters cannot deny that many of the more progressive policies that she espoused during the early years of her government were later abandoned. Some defend the regime's inexorable drift to the Right as a result of the exigencies of regime survival and the limits on policy formation imposed by domestic and international 'realities'. But it is precisely the interpretation of those 'realities' that is at issue. From a nationalist and progressive vantage point, much more could have been done by the regime to push those limits and at least set the government on a course towards reform. Except for the first few months of her tenure, Aquino chose to interpret those limits in a way which blunted the momentum for reform and, not incidentally, served elite interests. The Aquino regime was not a politically neutral institution that merely reflected relations of power in Philippine society. Aquino's family and class interests played a major part in the regime's calculations of what reforms were possible and desirable. This can best be seen only through closer examination of key policy areas and regime relations with major centres of power such as the US government and the military (see Flamiano and Goertzen 1990).

The New Political Framework

The main achievement of her government, Aquino repeated over and over again, was the restoration of 'democracy' in the Philippines. This claim is based on the promulgation of a new constitution in February 1987, elections for Congress in May 1987 and local government officials in January 1988, and finally elections for the President, Congress and local officials in 1992. The mere fact of having re-established 'constitutional democracy' and a functioning electoral system is claimed as an achievement, irrespective of what these institutions have done.

The constitution was written by a Constitutional Commission appointed by Aquino in mid-1986. The majority of its members were traditional politicians and business people with a significant minority of people from the more progressive popular organisations. The document they produced reflected the composition of the Commission. It is a 'modern' constitution with an elaborate Bill of Rights that extends the concept of rights to economic and social issues. It includes ringing declarations about the rights of labour, women and indigenous communities. It commits the government to social reform and ecological sustainability and even includes provisions against nuclear weapons. At its core, however, the 1987 constitution is deeply conservative. It mandates a political framework that simply reconstructs the pre-1972, American-style presidential system. Its commitment to social reform is high on rhetoric but deeply compromised. Its provisions on agrarian reform, for example, empower Congress to determine the main outlines of the programme, a provision that, as it turned out, meant no reform at all. The Bill of Rights has not fared much better. The military has violated many of its provisions with the faithful approval of the Supreme Court, the supposed defender of the constitution.

The political framework established by the 1987 constitution is supposed to be headed by a powerful President who sets economic policy and is Commander-in-Chief of the armed forces. The President also exercises power over Congress and local officials through control over the disbursement of funds and patronage. In practice, the main outlines of economic policy under Aquino were set by the IMF and the World Bank and their allies in the Central Bank and the Department of Finance. Early on, Aquino effectively surrendered security policy to the military. Although the largest parties in Congress supported the Aquino administration, Aquino failed to exercise effective leadership over Congress. She never joined any political party and cultivated an image of being above the partisan political fray.

Congress is divided into two houses, a 200-member Lower House elected by district and a 24-member Senate elected by all voters. The restoration of the pre-1972 bicameral system has also restored the control of the legislature by traditional politicians and their particularistic interests. Studies on the composition of the Lower House show that most of its members came from old political clans (Coronel 1988). While the two houses are supposed to be coequal, with the Lower House's budgetary powers balanced by the Senate's treaty ratification powers, in practice the Lower House determines legislative output. The Senate tends to take more progressive positions on key issues and legislation, but during the Aquino years it capitulated to the more conservative Lower House in conference committees. Increasing public dissatisfaction with traditional politicians – the emotional force behind the derogatory term *trapo*, 'dirty dish rag' in the national language – derives from the public perception of the performance of Congress. Congress members are perceived, with justification, as being preoccupied with cornering public funds and patronage for themselves and their political allies. When they are not influence-peddling, they engage in public posturing on current issues and conduct innumerable 'investigations' that seldom go anywhere.

During the Aquino years, more than two-thirds of the members of the Lower House belonged to the *Laban nang Demokratikong Pilipino* (LDP, Struggle of Democratic Filipinos). Although the Senate was controlled by another party, the Liberal Party of Senate president Jovito Salonga, the LDP is generally considered the ruling party. The LDP was led by ex-President Aquino's brother, José Cojuangco, and other Aquino relatives. Most LDP members in Congress joined because they assumed, correctly, that access to slush funds and patronage is possible only through a party led by the President's relatives. Most of the bills submitted to Congress by Aquino were passed by Congress. Except for the small Marcos loyalist parties grouped around former Defence Secretary Juan Ponce Enrile and then Vice-President Salvador Laurel, all the parties in Congress considered themselves supporters of the Aquino government. But there was no evidence of teamwork between the executive and the legislative branches, the two institutions that are supposed to provide leadership in the country. The only instances when the two bodies worked together effectively were to stop social reform measures, such as land reform and debt relief, proposed by the few progressives in Congress.

The third branch of government, the judiciary, has not done much better. It takes five years, on the average, to decide on cases. The only way to speed up the process, and to secure favourable decisions, is to bribe prosecutors and judges. To be fair, these are problems that go back many decades and the Aquino regime should be faulted only for not having done enough to reform the system. It is in the adjudication of political cases, the implementation of the constitution's Bill of Rights, that the Aquino judiciary's faults are most stark. In a series of decisions, the Supreme Court upheld military counterinsurgency tactics that included rounding up residents of whole neighbourhoods in the middle of the night, then lining them up while hooded military informers pointed out 'subversives'. On repeated occasions, the Supreme Court upheld arrests of suspected subversives without warrant.

Is the political framework that Aquino administrated democratic? Not even Aquino herself claimed that the executive and the legislature were in any way 'representative' of the population. The members of Congress and Aquino herself represented only a tiny sliver of Philippine society. Could Aquino have done more to build institutions of participatory democracy – to go beyond the limits of elite democracy? She appointed members of the Constitutional Commission unilaterally. Through these choices and through her informal but decisive influence on the Commission's deliberations, she could easily have secured a more progressive constitution. In elections for Congress, Aquino could have actively supported more progressive candidates from popular organisations. Instead, she backed her brother José Cojuangco's campaign to build the ruling party (LDP) on the foundation of provincial political clans, many of them former Marcos allies. She could have strengthened the progressive bloc in Congress by appointing the 25 sectoral representatives that the constitution mandated her to do. Yet by 1991, with only one year left of its tenure, Aquino had appointed less than half of the sectoral representatives to Congress and those she did appoint were not representative of the sectors they came from. As a result, the formal institutions of constitutional democracy are in place, but they are not only not democratic, they have often been used for anti-democratic ends. It is against this background of failure and dissatisfaction with existing political institutions that the May 1992 elections were played out.

The 1992 Elections

The May 1992 elections selected a full complement of public officials, from the President to the town mayors. It was striking to observe that underneath the intense political activity was a sense of resignation, a grudging acceptance of the fact that the elections would not bring about much change. This is the result of widespread cynicism about the institutions put into place by the Aquino regime. There are two elements in this cynicism; first, a feeling that the elections only pitted various factions of the narrow political elite against one another, and second, a conviction that none of these factions offered agendas for resolving the country's political and economic crisis.

The fact that Aquino did not run for re-election does not mean that Aquino and her family did not participate actively in the elections. One of the constants of Philippine elite politics, going back to independence in 1946, is that elite family interests can be advanced only by maintaining strong influence, if not control over the levers of government power. Control over these levers before the election provided the Aquino–Cojuangco families with tremendous advantages:

1. Presidential discretion in the disbursement of government funds provided tremendous leverage for gaining the support of local government officials who were heavily dependent on the national government for these funds.
2. President Aquino manoeuvred to gain greater control over the Commission on Elections through her appointment of a close ally to head the Commission.
3. In the run-up to the election Aquino had greater control over the military and its leadership than any of the contending factions, including that of ex-Defence Secretary Fidel Ramos. She achieved this by removing the Philippine Constabulary from military command and incorporating it into a national police command with carefully selected civilian leaders. The new national police structure was particularly useful for electoral purposes because it placed the only truly nationwide quasi-military structure under executive command.
4. Government TV and radio stations and Aquino family allies among families who control other broadcast media facilities

provided a powerful electoral tool. While print media is more broadly based, it has less reach than broadcast media.

The ruling party, LDP, provided the Aquino family with a powerful electoral tool. Its members include two-thirds of the members of Congress and a majority of local government officials. LDP factions, led by Aquino's brother and LDP General Secretary Congressman, José Cojuangco, and Aquino's uncle, Congressman Francisco Sumulong, provided a party electoral base for the family. To strengthen this base, Aquino slowly built up a quasi-party 'movement' called *Kabisig* (Arm-in-arm) which targeted local government officials. By setting up a structure for directly reaching local government officials and providing them with national government funds without the intercession of members of Congress, Aquino undercut the position of Congress Speaker and presidential aspirant Ramon Mitra.

These levers of power placed the Aquino–Cojuangco families in the strongest position to determine the outcome of the 1992 elections, especially the presidential race. The family supported candidate ex-Defence Secretary General (retired) Fidel Ramos, who had developed a 'presidential' image and who was not so well established that he would be unwilling to serve Aquino family interests once elected. Ramos joined the LDP, and obtained Aquino family endorsement on the basis of his having stopped six coup attempts and that he enjoyed alleged American support. Ramos obtained less than 25 per cent of the votes cast and stands for a continuation of Aquino policies, including a stagnant social and agrarian reform agenda, a gridlocked and corrupt judiciary, anti-labour repression and bloody counterin-surgency operations. None of the other would-be presidential candidates had the network of political clan allies and financial resources to mount a credible challenge. This is unfortunate because it is precisely the other candidates who had developed policy alter-natives on issues such as land reform, the US military bases and the Philippine foreign debt. Candidates such as Senators Jovito Salonga, Aquilino Pimentel and Joseph Estrada had taken progressive positions on these and other policy issues. With the exception of Estrada, however, these candidates began to backtrack and develop what they perceived to be 'safer' positions. This meant that the presiden-tial election was devoid of issues and was determined almost completely by the dynamic of elite factional infighting.

No one suggested that the 1992 elections should not be held at all, not even the underground NDF. At the same time, there was a pervasive sense of unreality about these elections. The new President and Congress will certainly play key political roles in the course of their six-year terms. At the same time, it is clear that several political players who have and will play even more important roles in the next few years are not part of the electoral process. Present patterns of political interaction are determined more by these unelected actors than by elected ones. The Philippines economy is in crisis, but the most important economic decisions are being made by IMF and World Bank bureaucrats. Relations with the US are at a crucial turning point. The military is continuing to accumulate political power and threatens to turn into a Latin American-style military. The Left is in the throes of debating the form an alternative society would take and the strategy and tactics for achieving victory. To understand Philippine politics today and define the parameters of change in the future, these actors have to be carefully examined.

The Military

The military significantly expanded its power as an institution under Aquino. The regular armed forces grew from about 160,000 to more than 200,000; its share of the national budget increased as US military assistance multiplied. More importantly, its political clout expanded steadily. The presidency of retired General Fidel Ramos is only a symbol of this political power. The six coup attempts in six years and the continued existence of a military rebel underground represents a sea change in military role perceptions. Organising a coup is premised on the imposition of political decisions at the point of a gun. While none of the coup attempts succeeded, each attempt was followed by Aquino government concessions which strengthened the military as an institution. Increases in the military budget and in aid requests were less important in the long run than pressure to remove members of the cabinet, the abandonment of government attempts to punish human rights violators and negotiate with the NDF, and a free hand in determining counterinsurgency strategy and tactics. As a result, the military has become the main institution determining the exercise of constitutionally mandated political rights, a vital aspect of democratic practice.

The current political role of the military has its roots in the period of the Marcos dictatorship. Prior to the declaration of martial law in 1972, the military was a small, ill-trained and ill-equipped force with no discernible institutional political power. The Armed Forces of the Philippines (AFP) was organised into four services totalling only 60,000 regulars. The small air force and navy were equipped mostly with dilapidated Second World War American equipment. The infantry was divided into an army which served as a strategic reserve, and a larger Philippine Constabulary (PC) which was garrisoned in all the provinces and major cities. The PC was often used by local politicians during election campaigns and to intimidate opponents between elections. During annual budget discussions in Congress, generals had to inflate 'battle reports' and coax and cajole Congress members into raising military appropriations. The AFP had no external defence capability, and through most of the 1950s and 1960s had no significant internal insurgency to fight.

For almost two decades, the military had no independent political role in national politics. All this changed after the declaration of martial law in 1972. By abolishing electoral and representative institutions that had been in place since independence in 1946, Marcos suddenly changed the nexus of power between the government and the governed from representation to repression. In the process, he moved the military from the periphery to the centre of the new political framework. The military became not only the enforcers of Marcos' political will, but also increasingly the implementors of government policy. At a time when 'normal' political processes had been suspended and remaining laws reinterpreted and revised to suit the dictatorship's requirements, the military not only arrested people, it also judged them in military tribunals. Military censors determined what could and could not be covered by the media. Military officers were posted to key positions in the bureaucracy and a new system for 'prodding' line agencies was created and run mainly by the military.

This new power was reflected in the military's financial circumstances. Generals no longer had to beg for funds from Congress members. The military budget increased from 0.77 per cent of the national budget in 1972 to 8.66 per cent in 1986 (Miranda and Giron 1987). The proportion would be much larger if one includes the 'intelligence' funds that were hidden in many parts of the budget. Officers at all levels were quick to translate their new power into profit. The economic clout of the military as an institution was greatly increased with military management of sequestered corporations, the formation of development corporations, banks and massive pension funds.

The military's repressive capability was also greatly expanded. From 60,000 in 1972, it grew to approximately 160,000 regulars by 1980. Service intelligence units were expanded and a large, new intelligence body, the National Intelligence and Security Authority (NISA) was formed. In addition, a large paramilitary force called the Civilian Home Defence Force (CHDF) was created. Control over police forces was transferred from local governments to the PC. By

1980, analysts estimated the total number of personnel controlled by the military as approaching 250,000. This rapid increase in military personnel was justified as necessary to fight the rebels of the MNLF and, increasingly after 1976, the New People's Army (NPA) and the underground NDF. But it was not the mere fact of combat against the MNLF and the NPA that shaped the political character of the AFP during the Marcos years as much as the character of that combat. Both the MNLF and the NPA are guerrilla armies, fighting only hit-and-run battles in areas where they have significant popular support. Combined with the military's ineptitude in combat, this meant that the preferred military strategy soon settled into illegal arrests, torture of prisoners, assassinations, indiscriminate bombing of villages and other 'unconventional' tactics. These tactics shaped the military's relationship with the population – a relationship that continues to this day.

Even as the political power of the military outside Manila grew, Marcos maintained effective control over the AFP and the military continued to see itself as subservient to the national civilian leadership. It was not until the very end of Marcos's rule that sections of the military leadership began to think of a *coup d'état*, that is, of the military as an arbiter of national leadership if not the leadership itself. This fateful shift in institutional self-perception in the military was the result of developments in the military in the last few years of Marcos's rule. As Marcos's control over the situation steadily deteriorated, he turned the military more and more into a palace guard. The build-up of resentment among officers who were not in the narrow inner circle combined with the fast-growing anti-dictatorship movement to create the Reform the Armed Forces Movement (RAM). Built around the security force of then Defence Minister Juan Ponce Enrile, the RAM became a focal point of anti-Marcos activity within the military. The rest is well-known history. After a RAM coup plot was uncovered by Marcos, Enrile and General Ramos gathered their supporters in a Manila military camp, precipitating those fateful three days which led to Marcos's departure for exile in the United States in February 1986. RAM officers were lauded as heroes who took down Marcos and brought the popular Cory Aquino to power. But this storybook ending unravelled thereafter in a series of anti-Aquino coup attempts led by the very same RAM. Having played key roles in a regime change, RAM officers and an increasing number of other officers came to believe that they had the right to use their military power for political purposes.

When Aquino took over in 1986, she had a chance to change the military radically and halt its politicisation. The military was thoroughly discredited as an instrument of Marcos repression and she had broad support for reversing its accumulation of political power. The key to this process was her policy of negotiating a political settlement with the underground NDF and punishing human rights violators in the military. Successful negotiations would have moved contention with the Left from the military to the political realm. Punishing human rights violators would not only have removed brutal officers, it would have denied the military a whole range of tactics with which it imposed its political will on the population. Aquino abandoned these two planks in her political platform precisely because of resistance from the military. In the process, Aquino left herself with only one tactic for controlling the military, that of manoeuvring within its highly factionalised power structure. The result was not only six coup attempts but growing military political power.

To control the military, Aquino turned to General Fidel Ramos and his clique of officers from the Philippine Constabulary. Aquino appointed Ramos Chief of Staff, and when he was later promoted to Defence Secretary, another PC general, General Renato de Villa, took over as Chief of Staff. General Ramos was crucial because the other key leader of the military establishment in 1986 was the then Defence Secretary Enrile, who used the RAM and his influence over the military and remaining pro-Marcos factions to challenge Aquino. While Ramos's support was crucial in blocking Enrile, it also fed festering resentments in the officer corps over corruption and lack of professionalism within the military. The PC was the most corrupt and unprofessional service in the armed forces; its officers were generally looked down upon by officers from other services, in particular the army. This worked in favour of the RAM because its leadership was mainly from the army and the elite of the officer corps, graduates from the Philippine Military Academy.

The six coup attempts failed less because of the military prowess of loyalist forces under Ramos than because of the tactical ineptitude of military rebels. The rebels also operated under severe political disadvantages. One faction, later called Soldiers of the Filipino People (SFP), could not get away from the shadow of being Marcos loyalists. The RAM started out with the political capital of its role in the overthrow of Marcos but over time, became identified with the political ambitions of Juan Ponce Enrile. Only the Young Officers' Union (YOU) is not tied to politicians and has developed a nationalist reform programme.

The decline of the military rebel threat enabled the Aquino regime to make changes in the military leadership. In April 1991, Aquino appointed General Lisandro Abadia as armed forces Chief of Staff and

General Arturo Enrile as army commander. At the same time, the PC was removed from the armed forces command and integrated into the Philippine National Police under a new Department of Interior and Local Governments. By picking a relatively junior general to become the new Chief of Staff of the armed forces of the Philippines, Aquino undercut existing power relations within the military and, for the first time, had someone running the military who was beholden to her and not to military power structures. Not incidentally, it also undercut the influence of then Defence Secretary Fidel Ramos, whose candidates to head the national police and later the armed forces were passed over in favour of junior officers personally selected by Aquino and her family.

The appointment of younger and more professional generals to key commands in the armed forces and the separation of the PC should help to resolve some issues that have provided strong support for military rebels. These do not change the essentially repressive character of the military. The appointment of General Abadia, the main figure behind the military's counterinsurgency operations as AFP operations chief, has meant even more intensified counterinsurgency. The separation of the PC from the armed forces command strengthens civilian control over one large segment of the military, but the new Philippine National Police will continue to be involved in counterinsurgency operations. The plan to phase out the army in counterinsurgency operations is unlikely to be fulfilled. As long as counterinsurgency operations continue, the main rationale for the continuing growth of the military and its political power will also continue. Large doses of American military assistance intensify this process.

The US Government

In the middle of June 1991, in a perverse Filipino irony, the Mount Pinatubo volcano eruption became a net gain for the Philippines because it resulted in the expulsion of the Americans from Clark Airbase. The difficult and often acrimonious negotiations on the extension of the US military bases lease provide a good illustration of the current state of US–Philippines relations. Everyone knew that the Aquino regime's dependence on American money and the influence of her official development assistance (ODA) donors would secure an extension of the bases' lease. What was surprising was the Bush administration's arrogance and insensitivity to Filipino nationalist sentiments and, on the Philippines end, the Aquino regime's nationalist posturing – even as it knew that it would eventually have to capitulate to American demands.

The agreement that was finally concluded in mid-July 1991 cannot be seen as anything other than the Aquino regime's abject surrender to US demands. The regime had asked for the withdrawal of the bases over a period of five to seven years from September 1991, the end of the current 25-year lease. The agreement provides that American military facilities, most importantly the sprawling Subic Naval Base, would remain for 10 or more years. An 'orderly and expeditious US withdrawal' would begin at the end of the tenth year, but the length of time it would take to withdraw is not spelled out. The turnover of Clark Airbase in September 1992 was not the result of negotiations. The base had been ravaged by the Mount Pinatubo eruption and the Bush administration's decision to abandon the base was nothing more than the acceptance of a disaster-imposed *fait accompli*. The financial components of the agreement are equally one-sided. The Aquino regime had asked for a US$825 million per year compensation package, including $500 million in cash and the rest in debt and trade concessions. The original US offer was for $360 million per year in cash. One would have expected that negotiations would result in 'splitting the difference'. Instead, the final agreement is that the US would provide its original offer of $360 million only in the first year of the agreement and a considerably smaller $203 million in subsequent years.

The Aquino administration tried to justify its capitulation to American demands on the length of the extension by saying that the cost of restoring Subic Naval Base to operational effectiveness required a longer stay. The administration also claimed that trade concessions in the compensation package would raise the total value to at least US$773 million a year. Bush administration officials refused to participate in the charade. One unidentified official was quoted as saying that the Philippine side engaged in 'hyperbole' to make the agreement more palatable to its constituents *(International Herald Tribune*, 18 July 1991).

The negotiations over the US bases highlighted changes in the nature of US–Philippines relations. The stance indicates an American failure to appreciate changes in the Filipino elite's perception of its long-time ally. These changes can be traced to Filipino resentment of American support of the Marcos dictatorship especially during the Reagan years. Many people remember then Vice-President Bush's toast to Marcos's 'adherence to democratic principles' during Marcos's 1981 re-election inauguration. At the end of the Marcos era, a large part of the political public had become cynical about the US role in the

Philippines. Even elite politicians stopped waxing sentimental about the supposed 'special relationship' between the US and the Philippines. A limited change, perhaps, but distinct enough to affect relations during the subsequent Aquino period.

Despite these changes in public perceptions of the US role, the US government continues to wield considerable economic, political and military influence in the Philippines. This influence is greater than in any other country in Asia and is analogous only to that wielded in some Central American and Caribbean countries. The Aquino regime, in fact, was more dependent economically on the US than Marcos was. Whereas Marcos had billions of dollars of commercial bank loans to play with, Aquino was almost totally dependent on IMF, World Bank and Japanese loans, which are heavily influenced by the US government. American military resources in the bases near Manila, combined with the Philippine military's dependence on US military assistance, provide the US with tremendous military clout. Even if the Filipino colonial mentality is slowly eroding, the mere fact of US economic and military power in the country translates into considerable political influence.

Given the reality of American power in the Philippines, it is difficult to understand why the Bush administration refused to make even cosmetic concessions to nationalist sentiment and instead took an arrogant negotiating stance. The demand for a 10-year extension of the bases' lease comes across as political conspicuous consumption since the security situation in the region is likely to result in substantial reductions in US military forces anyway. The Bush administration's refusal to meet the Aquino regime halfway in financial negotiations was resented even by pro-American politicians, who do not understand why billions of dollars in debt relief is provided to Egypt and Poland and not to the Philippines. Manila analysts have concluded from all this that the Bush administration took advantage of the Aquino regime's dependence to secure concessions out of proportion to America's actual needs.

The protracted and acrimonious negotiations for the extension of the US military bases lease does not in fact provide an accurate picture of the character of US government relations with the Aquino government in the last few years (see Bello 1986). The euphoric success of the Aquino state visit to the US in September 1986 was followed by several years of bipartisan support for the Aquino government – through large increases in economic and military assistance and unstinting political support. US government pressure for changes in the Aquino cabinet, in its security policy and in many aspects of its economic policy were, by and large, followed by the

Aquino government. By 1990, however, enthusiasm had given way to scepticism in Washington. Declining levels of assistance were accompanied by thinly veiled criticism. Preoccupied by other issues, the Bush administration chose to use its power to secure concessions without concern for the longer term implications of its actions.

The US government will continue to use this power to influence the course of events in the Philippines. Further into the future, regional trends indicate an erosion of American influence. The end of the Cold War and the demise of the old Soviet military position in Asia, combined with continuing US budgetary problems, will inevitably result in decreasing American military involvement in the region, though at a pace much slower than in Europe. Japanese economic dominance in Asia will also, just as surely, spill over into the Philippines. In the last decade or so, Japanese economic expansion into the Philippines has been hindered not just by economic mis-management by the Marcos and Aquino regimes but also by Japanese perception of the Philippines as an American economic preserve. Despite this, Japanese aid and investment is considerably bigger than that of the US, and trade with Japan is about equal to that with the US. Regional economic realities, including the steady evolution of Asia as a trading bloc competing with a North and South American bloc, will draw the Philippines closer to Japan and further away from the US economically.

Japanese economic power in the region will inevitably translate into political influence. For the first time since 1945, the Japanese government has taken slow and careful steps to increase its political influence in the region in recent years. In the 1980s, the assertion of Japanese political influence in the region was hindered by lingering memories of the Second World War and by Japanese willingness to play second fiddle to the United States. These factors have been particularly strong in the Philippines, given American dominance and the fact that the Philippines suffered more destruction and Japanese brutality than any other South-East Asian country in the Second World War. More and more Philippine politicians, however, are noting the contribution of Japanese trade and investment to the buoyant economies of neighbouring Malaysia, Indonesia and Thailand. The conclusion that Japan is the only possible source of funds for a Philippine economic takeoff is inescapable. Securing these funds will require establishing closer political links with the Japanese. As Japanese–American economic contradictions intensify, Japanese aid and investment will be secured less through American intermedia-tion. Politicians in the region could even find themselves increasingly forced to take sides with the Japanese in Japanese–American conflicts.

Economic Levers of Power

The most important levers of American power in the Philippines today are economic. This power is exercised less through private trade and investment than through direct US aid and influence on the IMF, the World Bank, the Paris Club and the Philippine Aid Plan. The way this power has been exercised is illustrated by the most recent round of Philippine government negotiations with these institutions. In the last quarter of 1990, the Aquino government suffered the worst economic crisis of its then four and a half years in office. At the end of September 1990, the balance of trade deficit was already US$2.85 billion, almost a billion more than the deficit for the same period in 1989. Instead of the projected surplus of $400 million for 1990, the government faced a $1 billion balance of payments deficit.

It was under these circumstances that the IMF decided to crack the whip. Disbursement of the next instalment of the IMF US$900 million 1989–91 Extended Fund Facility loan was cancelled. In quick succession, commercial bank creditors and other lenders also held back other 1990 loans, altogether totalling more than US$700 million. Official development assistance donors postponed negotiations for 1991 loans and grants. Prior to the arrival of an IMF team to conduct negotiations for a new standby agreement, IMF team head Ulrich Baumgartner sent a memo to the Aquino government laying out IMF demands. The memo, which was quickly leaked to the press, demanded a massive cut in the projected 1991 public sector deficit and a devaluation of the Philippine peso. Hidden among the jumble of technocratese was a severe austerity programme that would hold GNP growth for 1991 and 1992 to 0–2 per cent.

After only the mildest form of resistance, the Aquino government quickly capitulated to IMF demands. On 1 November the government devalued the Philippine peso from P25 to P28 to the US dollar. A month later, the government raised oil prices and announced the deregulation of the oil industry. In fact there were good technical reasons for taking these two specific steps. Supporting the Oil Price Stabilisation Fund was adding to the government's budget deficit and what had started out as a programme to keep oil prices low had ended up becoming a subsidy for oil companies. The overvalued peso had also, in effect, become a subsidy for imports. What made these steps objectionable was that they formed part of an overall policy framework imposed by the IMF that mandated austerity for the majority of the population while providing other hidden subsidies for big business. The main reason for the IMF demand for keeping GNP growth down to a 0–2 per cent rate was to keep the country's financial requirements low while enabling it to continue making debt service payments.

The disastrous economic performance of 1990 marks a severe downturn from substantial growth in the period from 1987 to 1989. After the contraction of the economy during the last couple of years of the Marcos period, the Aquino regime benefited from rapid recovery, cresting in the impressive 6.9 per cent GNP growth of 1988. The government blamed natural and foreign disasters as the source of the Philippine economy's ills. While factors beyond the government's control such as earthquakes and oil price increases undoubtedly made matters worse, the real reason for the 1990 crisis can be traced to the Aquino administration's economic policies. The Aquino regime started with substantial economic advantages. The very fact of contraction during the last two years of the Marcos period meant that there was substantial underutilised capacity. Combined with increases in world prices of Philippine commodity exports, low oil prices and the return of flight capital, business was buoyant during the first few years of the Aquino period. A large amount of official development assistance and IMF permission to run up larger government budget deficits than those allowed under Marcos enabled the government to pump-prime the economy, leading to consumption-led growth.

This easy growth could have been sustained only by changing the basic policy framework. Instead, the Aquino regime intensified the implementation of IMF–World Bank policies. The main requirement of the IMF was full payment of the Philippines' US$28 billion foreign debt. In 1987, when the IMF Extended Fund Facility agreement concluded by the Marcos regime in 1984 was being renegotiated, Economic Planning Secretary Solita Monsod argued for selective debt repudiation and pegging debt service payments to a small percentage of export receipts as a way to assure high levels of growth. Aquino instead supported the late Finance Secretary Jaime Ongpin's position that the financial requirements of Monsod's 6.5 per cent annual GNP growth target could be achieved through debt rescheduling and ODA. As it turned out, Monsod, who later was forced to resign from the cabinet, was proved right. While other analysts believe that debt repudiation would have been difficult to pull off given the economy's weaknesses and dependence on Western aid, the same analysts also believe that the government could have pushed harder for better terms in negotiations with commercial bank creditors and for forgiveness of at least part of the official debt.

The decision to pay the country's foreign debt fully affected other important aspects of economic policy. Debt service payments, which averaged 35 per cent of foreign currency receipts during the Aquino years, have led to restrictive government monetary policies. Pressure on the country's dollar reserves translated into speculative pressure on the Philippine peso. To maintain the peso–dollar exchange rate, the government periodically bought pesos in circulation and kept tight control on bank liquidity. In the process, interest rates averaged 30 per cent in the last four years of the Aquino administration. High interest rates depressed investment, since business people could make more money by buying treasury notes. Speculative real estate investments gave Manila and a few other urban centres such as Cebu the look of booming business centres but contributed little to the country's productive capacity. Debt service payments have also been the main source of the country's balance of payments problems. In addition, the overvalued peso in effect provides a subsidy to importers. High rates of growth in the country's manufactured exports, mainly garments and electronic components, pushed up imports because an average of 70 per cent of the export value of these exports are imported. Finally, these factors, plus the Aquino regime's IMF-imposed policy of accelerated import liberalisation, assured rates of import growth running at more than twice export growth. For a couple of years, inflows of ODA and favourable terms of trade kept the balance of payments in surplus. When the terms of trade reversed in 1989, the balance of payments deficit of 1990 became inevitable.

Finally, the Aquino government's budgetary problems could be traced to debt service payments which averaged 45 per cent of the budget. Some 70 per cent of the additional public sector deficit for 1990 derived from increased foreign and domestic interest rates. While a large chunk of debt service payments is for the domestic debt, this debt has been built up as a result of pressure from the foreign debt. The government's characteristic response to these budgetary constraints was to place the burden on the people. The December 1990 increase in oil prices was accompanied by a new 10 per cent levy on oil imports. By deregulating the oil industry, the government divested itself of subsidies to the oil companies while getting more revenue from the import levy. The oil companies benefited from increased prices. Combined with the devaluation of the peso, the net result was upwards of 15 per cent inflation in 1991, a burden that was borne mainly by the poorest sectors of the population.

Aquino's economic managers insisted that inflows of foreign funds after the conclusion of the agreement with the IMF in February 1991 would enable them to return the economy to 1988 levels of growth in a few years. There was little basis for this official optimism. The world economy has moved into a period of slow growth, starting with the Philippines' main trading partner, the United States. This has been reflected in the steep decline in Philippine export growth. Never significant during the Aquino period, foreign investment became a source of net outflow of funds in 1990. Combined with continued heavy debt payments, reduced inflow of migrant worker earnings and yet another natural disaster, the Mount Pinatubo eruption in mid-June 1991, the Philippines is likely to suffer many more years of balance of payments deficits.

During the Aquino period, official development assistance was a major source of funds for covering balance of payments deficits. ODA increased from US$705 million in 1984–5, Marcos's last year in office, to $1.5 billion in 1986–7 and $2.2 billion in 1987–8. One study estimates that ODA covered as much as 50 per cent of the balance of trade deficit between 1986 and 1988 (Alburo, n.d.). ODA was also used slowly to change the composition of the Philippine foreign debt from one owed largely to commercial banks to debt owed to multilateral and bilateral ODA creditors. In the coming years, this pattern is likely to continue, but with the Philippines receiving much less than it received in the last few years. The IMF insistence on 0–2 per cent GNP growth means, among other things, that inflows of ODA are going to be severely cut back. This aspect of the political economy of the Aquino years has strengthened American leverage. While Japan has provided more than twice the amount of ODA from the US, the Japanese have followed the American lead on most political issues, including its recent insistence on the retention of US military bases.

The Left

More than anything else, deteriorating living conditions among the country's poor have made it possible for Left groups to remain politically viable, an experience unique in the Association of South-East Asian Nations (ASEAN) region. Despite innumerable obituaries in the past few years, the main Left formation, the National Democratic Front, remains very much alive. NDF's organising among urban workers is moving at a fast clip, with rapid growth especially among government employees and public school teachers. In the countryside, brutal military tactics have shrunk the national democratic base among peasants by some 10 per cent, according to some reports. But the NPA has upgraded its fighting capacity with improvements in officer training, communications and home-made weapons. The most serious problem of the guerrillas is how to fine tune the balance between military operations and organising work among the peasantry. Another difficulty is how to protect its leadership from the military's greatly improved intelligence capability.

The NPA dilemma of balancing military and organising work is a microcosm of the national democratic movement's problem of finding a balance between armed struggle and political settlement. While the NDF's military and organisational capability remains intact, it has not managed to regain the political momentum it lost when it boycotted the 1986 electoral battle between Aquino and Marcos. This has led to big debates within NDF ranks about strategy, with an increasing number of cadres arguing for a more imaginative combination of military and political tactics. Debates have spilled over into disagreement about the nature of the national democratic alternative offered by the NDF in the aftermath of the collapse of socialist regimes in Eastern Europe and the former Soviet Union. Many top- and middle-level cadres believe that the NDF cannot regain political momentum without a thoroughgoing repudiation of Stalinist economic and political tenets. Of more immediate relevance, there is debate about how much importance to give to coalition work with progressive groups such as BISIG, an independent socialist organisation, and the less anti-communist among the social democratic groups, such as Pandayan (see *Marxism in the Philippines* series and Petitjean 1991).

BISIG and social democratic groups such as Pandayan have small but growing bases among workers and peasants compared to the national democrats. But their strength among urban middle-class groups, especially in the media and among academics, gives them the kind of political clout that is out of proportion to their organisational strength. They have also built whole networks of development non-governmental organisations (NGOs) as a base for rapid organising work in urban and rural areas. Some national democrats argue that it is only by working more closely with these groups in developing a viable political alternative to the Aquino regime that the national democrats can advance their political agenda in the short term.

There have in fact been major advances in coalition work among these groups in the last couple of years. The broadest, most firmly established and most influential are the Congress for People's Agrarian Reform (CPAR) and the Freedom from Debt Coalition (FDC). While the CPAR's legislative agenda continues to be stymied by a pro-landlord Congress, it has successfully kept land reform at the centre of national political discourse. More importantly, CPAR member organisations have steadily built up their capacity for what they call 'people's initiatives' in agrarian reform, such as land occupations, cooperatives and other socioeconomic projects in the countryside. These activities are being supported by another coalition, the Caucus of Development NGO Networks. The FDC achieved the unprecedented feat of getting the majority of members of both houses of Congress plus the conservative Cardinal Jaime Sin to support its position of selective debt repudiation. Other coalitions exist among urban poor, civil rights, military bases and other groups. It is only among workers that coalition work is facing difficulty. The Labor Advisory and Consultative Council (LACC), a coalition of major labour centres, has been under attack by a coalition of the right-wing Trade Union Congress of the Philippines (TUCP) and the Philippine Democratic Socialist Party (PDSP).

The careful approach to coalition work adopted by its leaders has gone a considerable way towards eroding the mistrust and bad feeling created by the failure of similar efforts in the past, especially in the last year of the Marcos era. It has also had some impact on the two main political tendencies within the coalition, the social democrats and the national democrats. While the PDSP appears to be consolidating its right-wing, anti-communist contacts with the Aquino regime and the TUCP, the Pandayan is at the active core of most coalitions. The experience of working within coalitions such as CPAR has pushed the national democrats' some distance away from its tendency to shy away from coalitions it does not control. At the same time, as more and more popular organisations became disillusioned with the Aquino regime, the national democrats early oppositionist position became less problematical in coalition efforts.

These coalitions, called the 'cause-oriented groups', exercise considerable political influence over a number of other more powerful actors. The right-wing of the Catholic Church has been pushed to take more progressive positions on issues such as land reform and foreign debt. Cardinal Sin's pronouncements on debt are a good example. The Aquino regime's abortive *Kabisig* project was an attempt to bring the government closer to the cause-oriented groups and their issues. Even the military has not been immune. The most recently organised military rebel faction, the Young Officers' Union, takes a nationalist, pro-reform position on relations with the US, debt and agrarian reform that is unprecedented in Philippine military history.

These coalitions and the key organisations within them have been steadily increasing their organisational capacity in the last couple of years. They do not yet have the political clout to match their influence on issues. They are not in a position to determine the direction of political events in the short term. But the cause-oriented groups will play a more important role in the medium term. In the event of a successful coup, the cause-oriented groups will become the centres of opposition activity, whether in the open or underground. There is consolidated opinion within their ranks that elections constitute a significant arena of political struggle. Careful research on what it takes to participate actively in this arena, on how to translate their organised strength into votes is being undertaken. The perspective is one of slowly building up their capability to intervene effectively in the electoral arena in the future.

The Future of Democracy in the Philippines

The Cory Aquino regime was a perfect example of the problems attendant on the transition from authoritarian regimes to elite democracy in the Third World. No one argues that the shift from the Marcos dictatorship to the Aquino regime was anything but a positive step. Everyone agrees that the restoration of the institutions of formal democracy constitute a significant reform. At the same time, it is also clear that the Philippine political system today is not, in any substantive sense, a democracy. The level of political participation under Ramos and Aquino has not advanced beyond limited elite circles. Obstacles to the organisation of workers and peasants, the majority of the population and the proper subject of democracy, continue to be imposed by President Ramos in the name of counterinsurgency. Violations of constitutionally mandated civil rights continue. By failing to implement social reform, in particular land reform, the Aquino government failed to advance the economic conditions for effective political participation by the lower-class majority.

It is tempting to focus responsibility for the failure to extend the limits of democratic reform on ex-President Aquino. In her first year in office, Aquino had more domestic and international support than any Philippine president since Magsaysay in the 1950s. She had decree-making powers for a whole year. During that time, she had the power and the opportunity to take steps that could have radically advanced democracy in the Philippines. First, she could have used her tremendous political authority and decree-making powers to secure a constitution and a political framework that facilitated movement away from elite domination to more participatory democracy. Second, she could have negotiated more favourable terms for the country's heavy debt burden. In the process, she could have established a precedent for an independent negotiating stance with international capitalist institutions. Third, she could have decreed a real land reform programme instead of the landlord-devised charade that now passes for a land reform programme. Fourth, by taking her promise to punish human rights violations seriously, she could have altered the military and stopped its inexorable advance as an independent political force. Finally, by doing all these things, she would have laid the groundwork for a negotiated political settlement with the NDF. These are only a few of the more important steps she could have taken.

Ex-President Aquino and her supporters argue that if she had taken all or even only a few of these steps, she would not have survived. Aquino's failure to control the military, for example, is usually excused as being a simple exercise of survival skills. In fact, Aquino had a chance in her first few months in office to make substantial changes in the nature of the military. But by backtracking on her promise to punish human rights violators in the military and by abandoning negotiations with the NDF, Aquino created the very conditions for an independent political role for the military and, not incidentally, the many coup attempts that plagued her regime. Aquino's second argument for her failure to extend the limits of reform was her adherence to democracy. Her supporters say that while they may have wanted genuine land reform, the limited programme was all that is achievable under a democracy. This interpretation of democracy would limit it to a set of formal institutions for sustaining existing power relations. An alternative interpretation of democracy goes beyond formal political institutions to relations of power in the society as a whole. If existing relations of power are grossly unequal and therefore undemocratic, as they are in the Philippines and in much of the Third World, leadership requires the use of all available formal political authority to reform existing power relations. Without substantive redistribution of economic assets, representative institutions, no matter how democratic in form, will only mirror undemocratic power relations in the society.

Predicting the future, especially that of large social formations such as the Philippines, is a hazardous exercise. But the political and economic paralysis that has turned the Philippines into the 'sick man' of Asia is surely going to result in major changes in the not too distant future. Whatever the particular political shape of that future, it is, again just as certainly, going to include the repudiation of the anti-democratic and economically inept elite. The Philippine elite has historically been dominated by landlords and by business interests dependent on foreign connections, what the Left calls the *compradors*. New manufacturing and commercial business groups have long been chafing under the limits to economic growth imposed by the policies of landlord- and *comprador*-dominated governments. The temptation to return to Marcos's strategy of building up central government economic power to support national capitalists, a Philippine version of South Korea's *chaebol*, will be great.

Such a strategy will not promote democracy if it serves the interests of business groups at the expense of small farmers, workers and the environment. The experiences of South Korea and Taiwan provide ample illustration of the human and environmental costs of the Asian Tiger model of development (see Bello and Rosenfeld 1990). Such a strategy can only be imposed by repressing organisations of workers and other popular sectors and establishing a new form of authoritarianism. The new business classes will be better served by working out a social pact with labour and other popular sectors. This will, of course, be difficult to achieve. There is no precedent for such a social pact in Philippine history. But the new business classes should remember that they face powerful enemies in the old landlord and *comprador* classes. Without the support of popular sectors, it is doubtful that the dominance of these old ruling classes can be overcome.

At the same time, the Left has to undergo important changes. What happens in ongoing debates within national democratic ranks will be crucial because national democrats continue to have the largest organisations of workers, peasants and most other popular sectors. To live up to its historic potential as a force for democracy, the national democratic movement will have to repudiate Stalinist elements in its theoretical legacy. Old conceptions of socialism cannot be sustained in the face of momentous changes in the former Soviet Union and Eastern Europe. Other Left groups have to begin seriously to develop their strategic conceptions in order to break out of their tendency towards pragmatism. As Alex Magno once put it, without developing strategy, groups such as BISIG will continue to be 'compelled to interpret their positions *vis-à-vis* the main formation – ... to engage the revolutionary paradigm and praxis of the CPP' (Magno 1988).

Internal conditions for achieving a historic shift in the class composition of the Philippine elite are favourable. Public disgust with their rulers, the *trapos*, is at an all-time high. The Philippine economic crisis continues to deepen. But external opposition to these changes will be great, not least because one of the first changes will have to be a return of economic sovereignty to Filipinos. Specific changes in fiscal and monetary policy, including, most importantly, a change in policy on foreign debt service payments, will be strongly opposed. To prevent these changes, the US government and other foreign entities will support landlords and *compradors* and, if necessary, mobilise the military. The second major change therefore will have to be to stop the growth of the military's political power. This will require the imposition of a strong policy in support of human rights. To deny the military's rationale for greater power and the violation of human rights, the peace process has to be brought to its conclusion in a political settlement based on a consensus on solutions to fundamental economic and political problems.

For now, the international situation is not conducive to these kinds of changes in the Philippines or in any other Third World country. The collapse of the socialist bloc and the resulting disarray in the international anti-imperialist movement has removed sources of political and material support for these kinds of changes. There seem to be no further ideological or material obstacles to the further advance of international capitalism. The US seems prepared to intervene, militarily if necessary, anywhere in the world. But if socialism is in crisis, so is capitalism. Without the political glue of the Cold War, economic competition between major capitalist powers is likely to spill over into political disagreements. The hegemonic role of the US cannot forever be sustained on military might without economic and social renewal. Nationalist governments in the Third World can manoeuvre more effectively in the spaces created by these fissures in the capitalist camp. People power brought down dictatorship in the Philippines, other Third World countries and Eastern Europe. For the people, the results everywhere have been meagre. It is time that people power is mobilised for the people's own ends.

References

Alburo, Florian (n.d.). 'Aid and the Growth Process – Its Role and Institutional Setting in the Philippines', unpublished manuscript.

Bello, Walden 1986. 'Edging toward the Quagmire: The United States and the Philippine Crisis', *World Policy Journal*, winter.

Bello, Walden and Rosenfeld, Stephanie 1990. *Dragons in Distress*. San Francisco, Institute for Food and Development Policy.

Coronel, Sheila 1988. 'Dynasties Hang on to Power', *Manila Chronicle*, 24 January.

Flamiano, Dolores and Goertzen, Donald (eds) 1990. *Critical Decade: Prospects for Democracy in the Philippines in the 1990's*. Berkeley, Calif., Philippine Resource Center.

International Herald Tribune, 18 July 1991.

Magno, A. R. 1988. 'The Filipino Left at the Crossroads: Current Debates on Strategy and Revolution', in Third World Studies Center, *Marxism in the Philippines*. Manila, p. 77.

Marxism in the Philippines, vols. I and II, series published by the University of the Philippines' Third World Studies Center.

Miranda, Felipe and Giron, Ruben 1987. 'Development and the Military in the Philippines: Military Perceptions in a Time of Continuing Crisis'. Paper presented at the Workshop on Defence and Development in South-East Asia, 20–2 August 1987, p. 22.

Petitjean, Paul 1991. 'New Debates on the Philippine Left', *International Viewpoint* no. 211, 22 July.

Punongbayan, Grace Arcilla (ed.) 1990. *Lupa at Buhay – Agrarian Reform in the Philippines*. Amsterdam, Philippine Development Forum.

Putzel, James and Cunningham, John 1989. *Gaining Ground: Agrarian Reform in the Philippines*. London, War on Want.

9. Korean Capitalism and Democracy

BARRY GILLS*

Since the popular uprising of June 1987, democracy has been developed in South Korea on a formal basis, though essentially the same political and economic elite remains in power. While a more open and competitive political system has replaced the former military dictatorships, the extent of socioeconomic change has been quite limited. The development of formal democratic institutions is not unique, since South Korea has previously experienced formal democracy in 1948–61, and 1963–71. Nevertheless, there is a widely held assumption that this time the transition to democracy is fundamentally different. In fact, it is only an 'adjustment' of the pre-existing state.

The main political changes that have occurred should be viewed as adjustments to the *existing* system that reflect underlying structural trends. This includes the increasing autonomy of capital *vis à vis* the state and expansion of the ruling coalition by the incorporation of the middle class. Therefore, the most substantive political change has been in the relations of power *within* the governing coalition. The political power of the business class has increased. Democratic pluralism in the political system increases the importance of financial contributions by business to the political parties. The previously well-insulated state is more vulnerable to interest group pressures. Yet democratisation did not bring in its wake a breakthrough to a fundamentally new society. On the contrary, with the emergence of a new ruling party early in 1990, a full conservative restoration took place. The primary aim of this restoration is the achievement of permanent conservative hegemony, not through military seizure of power but through formal democratic processes. The legacy and trajectory of the Korean economic system are the critical factors in the development of this form of Low Intensity Democracy.

At all times since the seizure of power in 1961, the military regimes have presented themselves as 'democratic'. Despite appearances, the

*The author would like to thank the Transnational Institute and the Research Grants Committee of the University of Newcastle-upon-Tyne for grants that made possible the research for this article.

denial of democracy for some three decades was a systematic policy. Authoritarianism was a vehicle to preserve a capitalist state in the South, against the opposition of the Left in the South and the communist regime in the North, which were virtually synonymous in the view of the southern conservative elite. At the time of the southern military *coup d'état* in 1961, North Korea was far more industrialised than South Korea. Therefore, rapid national economic growth became a regime obsession, as a means to achieve national security and, eventually, national reunification under southern dominance. In pursuit of this political goal the state subordinated all – even and especially the business class. Authoritarianism reached its greatest intensity in the 1970s. However, state domination of the business class became economically distorting and produced gross inefficiencies, leading to an economic catastrophe in 1978–80. Thereafter, the underlying structural trend was towards a very gradual decrease in direct state controls over capital in favour of market mechanisms.

The restoration of formal democracy in 1987 should be viewed in the light of this structural trend. Korea's economic structure was moving away from dependence on light, labour-intensive manufactures towards high-tech, capital-, skill- and research-intensive production. This upward adjustment was partly compelled by increasing competitive pressure from economies in the structural tier below Korea, particularly those in South-East Asia. Capital needed more autonomy in order to compete effectively under new conditions in the world market. In order to increase its autonomy, the business class needed to reduce state authority. This could be achieved through restoration of electoral competition for power. The business class would benefit from an electoral alliance with the middle class. Political democracy was necessary in order to consolidate this alliance's influence *vis à vis* the traditional military elite. Democratisation was viewed by both business and pragmatists in the military elite as instrumental to a successful transition to a more competitive economy. Thus the liberal-reformist wing of the ruling party accepted the agenda of sharing state power with the rising bourgeois bloc.

The democratisation of 1987 succeeded because it was viewed as instrumental to stabilisation of the existing socioeconomic system and due to a convergence of interests. The Korean military elite bowed to mounting popular demonstrations in order to diffuse tension and preserve its prospects of holding power in the future. The business elite supported democratisation as a means of enhancing its autonomy from state tutelage and gaining a share of state power. The United States supported democratisation in order to nip revolutionary change in the bud, stabilise a tottering regime and thereby protect its own strategic and economic interests.

While preserving the status quo and blocking the prospect of radical change, democratisation inevitably facilitated an expansion of the political space in which popular forces could organise and challenge the regime. The 'abortive abertura' (Cumings 1989), that is, limited and merely formal democratisation, brought about a far-reaching realignment of sociopolitical forces in South Korea. Yet the opposition remains impotent in the formal democratic institutions of the restructured state. Therefore, rather than perpetuate the assumption that the achievement of electoral competition and some enhanced individual liberties and less press censorship is in itself a great historic breakthrough, we should focus our attention on *the inherent limitations of democratisation* in Korea. These limitations are embedded in the structure of Korea's economic model and its position in the global political economy.

Korean Capitalism: The Anatomy of a 'Model'

The Korean development model has attracted a great amount of attention, both academic and political, due to its record of sustained economic growth and industrial deepening. Today, as the post-communist states search for a model of economic success, the debate on the Korean experience becomes of even greater political relevance. The Korean experience is being used to buttress contending arguments in this new debate. For instance, a former Soviet Finance Minister, Boris Fyodorov, argued that the Korean case illustrates that an authoritarian government is the prerequisite for economic recovery in the former states of the Soviet Union. On the other hand, Alice Amsden's (1989) views on the relevance and applicability of the Korean experience to Eastern Europe and elsewhere imply that the key economic policies can be disarticulated from authoritarianism and still bring similar results. Given the political direction of Eastern Europe this is an argument many are eager to accept. Yet the hard realities of economic transition imply that Fyodorov's observation on authoritarianism cannot be ruled out, not as prescription, but as a distinctly possible outcome of the transition to a market economy.

The debate on Korean economic development has so far been dominated by economistic assumptions, which downplay the social dimension of political authoritarianism. The central analytical task has been defined as the need to explain the political factors contributing to rapid economic growth or which account for the 'success' of the Korean economy (Cole and Lyman 1971; Kuznets 1977; Jones and Sakong 1980; Kim and Roemer 1979; Wade and Kim 1978;

Woronoff 1983; Amsden 1989, 1990). The statist approach explained South Korea's economic success in terms of the 'strong' state's capacity for efficient macroeconomic intervention (Haggard and Moon 1983; Johnson 1987; Wade and White 1988). This efficacy is explained as a consequence of the policymakers' insulation from contending societal and political pressures, and the organisational capacity and autonomy of the state. What they do not explain is precisely how a state achieves such insulation and capacity without some form of authoritarianism. The neoclassical analysts (Krueger 1979; Balassa 1981) explain economic success on the basis of state regulation of the economy according to liberal, market-conforming principles. However, this view has been undermined by the greater credibility of the general theses of the statist approach.

Outside this literature, only a few critical studies of the Korean economic development experience directly challenge the legitimacy of authoritarianism, whatever its putative economic success (McCormack and Gittings 1977; Hamilton 1986; Harts-Landsberg 1984, 1987; Bello and Rosenfeld 1990; Ogle 1990). Such studies prioritise social goals other than rapid economic growth and capital accumulation. These include economic and social justice, human rights, political democracy, and human health and environmental safety. Many critical analyses on the nature and structure of Korean capitalism have appeared in the Korean language in recent years. (Park 1986; Lee D.K. 1987; Lee J.K. 1986; Choi 1985; Kim *et al*. 1987; Cho *et al*. 1988; Park *et al*. 1987; Cho *et al*. 1984) Often informed by neo-Marxism, these studies generally interpret Korean capitalism as a peripheral formation dominated by monopoly capital and in which the authoritarian state played the dominant role in an alliance with domestic and foreign capital.

The domestic political content of the model of Korean capitalism, as outlined below, originated in the military *coup d'état* of 1961. The model consists schematically of the following essential elements:

1. Authoritarian government (military regime)
2. State dominance over capital (state-dependent bourgeoisie)
3. Extreme concentration of capital (monopoly capital: *chaebol*)
4. Export oriented industrialisation (neo-mercantilism)
5. Political subordination of labour (repression/corporatism)

The Authoritarian Government
The Korean state enjoyed relative autonomy; it was raised above the classes. Nevertheless, the state supported the interests of capital over labour. The authoritarian regime defended capitalist relations of

production and facilitated the emergence of an industrial bourgeoisie (Kim K.D. 1976). Its ideology combined anti-communism, which in practice was both anti-labour and anti-democratic, with developmentalism, which appealed to nationalism to mobilise support for state-led economic expansion, while simultaneously extolling the virtues of 'free enterprise'.

The structure of administration was never entirely monolithic. There was some intra-bureaucratic conflict within the regime over the policy making process, which increased over time as the assertiveness of institutional interests and their constituents increased (Haggard and Moon 1990). Nevertheless, government was characterised by executive dominance and the weakness of the legislative and judiciary branches. Extreme centralisation of power and the absence of elective local government enhanced state capacity and domination over civil society. The President could personally appoint over 100,000 posts, ranging from generals to heads of the local Chambers of Commerce.

The ultimate centre of power in the military regimes was the so-called 'T–K Clique'. This clique is composed of officers sharing a background in Kyongsang province, especially Taegu city (thus 'T–K'), and close personal ties cemented through similar career tracks, such as a common graduating class of the Korean Military Academy. However, the military government 'civilianised' itself, that is, it was led by retired military officers, as opposed to active duty ones. This was undertaken as a legitimising device.

At the juridical core of the authoritarian state were the national security and anti-communist laws, the so-called 'bad laws' which effectively banned any political activity outside the consensus of the establishment. Organised labour was forbidden to have any political or financial ties to political parties. State power was held indefinitely by a ruling party which was the vehicle of the dominant military clique and its paramount leader. The KCIA (Korean Central Intelligence Agency) was founded at the outset by the original coup-makers as a mechanism of domestic political control. It became the strongest political institution in the country during the 1970s.

State Dominance over Capital

The apparent contradiction between state-led industrialisation and 'free' (i.e. private) enterprise is not what it may seem. On the contrary, free enterprise in Korea positively flourished within the parameters set by authoritarian regimes. However, it would be mistaken to regard the Korean model as based purely on the interface of the state and private enterprise. There has always been a substantial public sector, though particularly during the 1980s many state-owned firms were privatised. State intervention in the private sphere of the economy was most successful when implemented according to market-conforming principles, in the sense implied in Chalmers Johnson's model of the capitalist developmental state (Johnson 1982, 1987, 1989). However, state intervention in the economy could also be distorting and damaging, such as during the heavy and chemical industrialisation programme in the 1970s.

This planning mechanism was particularly relevant to state-directed sequential development of targeted industrial sectors. Product cycle theory is therefore especially useful to understanding the logic of economic planning in Korea (Cumings 1989). According to Johnson's theory of the capitalist developmental state, one of the key tasks of the elite economic bureaucracy is correctly to identify industrial sectors for development in conformity with the requirements of maintaining competitiveness in the world market (Johnson 1982, 1987).

Historically, the bourgeoisie was very late to develop in Korea and then emerged in an extremely weak position. There was never any real bourgeois revolution in Korea, and this should be recognised as a highly important aspect of Korean capitalism. Instead, the state first established the capitalist class, facilitated its growth and then very slowly allowed it more autonomy. However, business was restrained from articulating its own interests in the political arena, despite the existence of impressive business associations and the dependence of the ruling party on financial contributions from business sources.

Through control of the banking system, the state controlled the allocation of investment capital. Therefore, it could direct available financial resources to sectors and firms it deemed most promising and internationally competitive. The business groups of Korea were not permitted to own banks or to make independent alliances with banks as was the case in Japan. This lack of control over their own sources of credit, particularly for firms with such a generally high debt-to-equity ratio, made Korean firms very dependent on state approval of investment plans. However, big business gradually increased its financial leverage through the equities market and insurance companies.

The form of economic planning used by the authoritarian regimes in Korea should not be confused with communist-style central planning. Privately owned firms implemented the mainly indicative five-year plans, but these firms were closely tied to the state through inter-elite communication networks and direct instruments of control such as credit allocation. The role of the Economic Planning Board was essential to the state's coordination of economic development. The Economic Planning Board (EPB) was established to act as a kind of 'economic Tsar' among the other ministries of the Korean government concerned in any way with the economy. The head of the Economic Planning Board was also concurrently Deputy Prime Minister and directly responsible to the President. The secret of the power of the Deputy Prime Minister, and of the EPB, was the personal political backing of the President. Without such executive support, and executive dominance in government, the coordination of the economic ministries by the EPB would have become very difficult, due to the usual problems of intra-bureaucratic politics.

Without the discipline that the EPB, the banks, and industrial policy guidelines imposed upon private enterprise, Korean capitalists would have broken free of state-imposed investment restrictions. Chun Doo Hwan's liberalisation policies in the 1980s loosened the restrictions of industrial policy. Therefore business increasingly made investment decisions on profit criteria and market conditions, rather than on the interests of overall long-term national economic development as defined by the state. However, this trend to state retreat from direct economic management in favour of market principles entailed the political consequence of increased business influence within the ruling coalition.

Concentration of Capital

The military government actively facilitated the emergence and growth of big business via the giant conglomerates known as the *chaebol*. Credit was disproportionately allocated to firms which excelled in exports and to those which cooperated best with central economic directives in general. Exports were not always directly profitable, but the foreign exchange generated by export was used to finance necessary imports to promote economic development (Hamilton 1986). The overall regulatory framework and incentive structure had the systemic effect of producing greater concentration of capital. This turned out to be an advantage in the world market. For an economy based on export of manufactures, this strategy was an efficient way to achieve economies of scale, price competitiveness and market access, and it reduced overproduction by reducing competition between firms operating in the same sectors.

The result was one of the highest concentrations of capital in the world, whereby the national economy was overwhelmingly dominated by a handful of giant company groups. According to Korean economist Lee Kyu-uk, in 1985 the top 10 *chaebol* accounted for one-third of total exports and one-third of total GNP (Cho 1990). *Chaebol* dominance in the economy has resulted in serious structural and regional imbalances. Small and medium businesses are at a distinct disadvantage, whilst industry has concentrated physically in the south-east and the area around Seoul.

One of the most distinctive features of these *chaebol* is their ownership structure. They are family owned and usually family managed, thereby violating the modern norm of separation between capital ownership and management. This means that the big business elite is clearly identifiable socially, both as individuals and by family. This all too visible gulf between the super rich and 'the rest' sharpens the sense of social alienation and moral outrage felt by the have-nots in Korea, especially when confronted with conspicuous consumption and arrogance on the part of the upper class. In recent years, the government has even harnessed this popular resentment in order to conduct a campaign against foreign luxury goods consumption.

The Export Orientation

The military junta in 1961 inherited a policy of import substitution. This policy was in crisis, since it depended upon large inflows of US economic assistance, which was being significantly reduced in the late 1950s. The interim democratic regime of 1960–1, under US guidance, had already prepared the ground for a shift in policy toward economic planning, export promotion and re-establishing economic links with Japan. The military government did not so much invent the export-oriented strategy as become the willing accomplice of the United States and Japan in a regional industrial restructuring (Gills 1993 forthcoming). That is, there was not a *national* model, apart from the role assigned to South Korea by the US and Japan in the new international division of labour.

The military government executed the national export drive as if it were a military campaign, and demanded efficiency from all actors involved in the process, whether public or private sector. Developmentalist ideology was employed to maximise the mobilisation of national human resources. The strategy called for a high degree of trade-dependence, and South Korea became one of the most trade-dependent economies in the world, and eventually one of the world's top trading nations. Being a resource-poor country, Korea's strategy was to import, assemble and export, thereby adding value during the production process. The state established a credit and regulatory system that encouraged export and facilitated the concentration of capital in groups that in effect were groomed as national champions, Korean gladiators in the world market arena. This set in motion a spiral of more and more export and concentration in tandem, through which the national economy became increasingly identified with and dependent upon the export performance of a small number of firms. The domestic market was relatively protected from encroachment by foreign firms, and import liberalisation was slow and very selective. Nevertheless, Korea ran a chronic trade deficit, primarily due to its structural negative trade balance with Japan, the source of so much vital technology and other imports. Just when Korea finally achieved a trade surplus in 1986 it came under increasingly heavy bilateral pressure from the US to liberalise its domestic market and reduce its trade surplus.

The Political Subordination of Labour

The low cost of labour underpinned rapid accumulation by the business class via export-oriented industrialisation. This strategy required political control over labour by the state and employers, but it was always the state that ultimately guaranteed the repression of labour and low costs of production (Launius 1984; Park 1987; Deyo 1989; Ogle 1990). The low cost of production via low labour costs was a necessary, though not sufficient, means of achieving international competitiveness.

Nevertheless, the authoritarian regime could not entirely ignore the political interests of labour. The military government could not legitimise itself through the pretence of 'guided democracy'. It had to rely primarily on economic performance for this purpose. Therefore, the state allowed real wages to rise slowly and steadily behind increases in productivity and spurts of economic growth. The general rise in real wages over time had little or nothing to do with an increase in organised labour's bargaining power. Rather, it was a controlled process that kept social tension contained, while allowing the national economy to approach the goal of a more skill- and capital-intensive production system.

The most exploited and politically vulnerable section of the working class was and still is unmarried female labour in light industry, such as textiles. These workers were largely responsible for the economic miracle of the 1960s and, despite repression, were capable of politically destabilising strikes, as illustrated in the pivotal YH strike in 1979, which contributed to the fall of the Park regime (YH Labour Union 1984). Increased industrialisation during the 1970s produced a unionised, skilled and predominantly male working class, with the potential to cripple industrial production through militant strike action. Changes in the composition of the working class, in parallel with changes in industrial structure, were responded to by the state with adjustment in the labour laws under the Chun dictatorship. In particular, the banning of industrial unions, of third party mediation in industrial disputes and of financial ties to political parties crippled the national organisational potential of the industrial working class (Deyo 1989; Ogle 1990).

Above all, in contrast to the Latin American experience, the Korean elite never established a populist alliance with the working class. Perhaps the most convincing explanation for the absence of populism in South Korea is to be found in an analysis of the domestic political effects of national division into rival communist and capitalist regimes. The labour movement in the South was always suspected of subversion, and regarded as a natural ally of the workers' party in North Korea. The great fear of the Right in the South has always been, and remains, that the southern working class and other oppressed and deprived sectors of the population will form a Fifth Column. Therefore, repression of labour in South Korea is not only caused by direct economic factors, that is, capital–labour relations, but also by political circumstances resulting directly from national division; the national security state cannot take the political risks associated with an independent labour movement.

Maintenance of the Model

The model of Korean capitalism did not emerge perfectly formed out of the mind of Zeus. It evolved dynamically in a unique conjunctural situation, dependent on specificities of Korean historical development and American and Japanese hegemonic influences. (Cumings 1987; Gills 1993). The maintenance of this model required frequent periodic adjustment in both the economic and political sphere. In fact, one of the keys to South Korea's success was its ability to make very difficult adjustments at the right moment, rather than remaining a static model. Despite its air of stability, South Korea has been one of the most crisis-ridden states in the modern Third World. If crisis means a period of severe tensions producing a significant regime adjustment, then the periods of regime crisis in South Korea might be outlined as follows: 1945(8)–52; 1958–62(3); 1969–72; 1978–82; and 1987–90. The years of relative 'stability' sandwiched between the years of crisis constitute less than half of the total period.

The crisis of 1945(8)–52 was different from those which followed because it was a crisis of origins rather than of adjustment, being essentially about establishing and preserving a capitalist state on Korean soil. The crisis of 1958–62(3) was a crisis of aid-dependent import substitution industrialisation (Kim S.J. 1988). The crisis of 1969–72 was a crisis of the limits of growth in the labour-intensive industrialisation phase. The crisis of 1978–82 was a crisis of heavy and chemical industrialisation. The crisis of 1987–90 was a crisis of economic liberalisation. All of these economic crises endangered the 'legitimacy' and above all the stability of authoritarianism. Though popular resistance to authoritarianism is a constant in Korean politics, the economic cycle affected the intensity and efficacy of popular protests. In the cycle of Korean politics a regime crisis usually occurs at the intersection of two curves:

1. growing dissent (paralleled by growing repression), and
2. economic recession/and or restructuring.

Bruce Cumings has identified a cycle between more or less coercive regimes in Korea, which in his view corresponds with the logic of economic development (Cumings 1989). The political adjustments in the three crises until 1987–90 all involved use of extra-constitutional means. Prior to 1987, each period of 'guided-democracy' ended in a reversion to overt authoritarianism rather than in a further flowering of democracy. Han Sung-Joo likewise identifies a general cycle of democratisation followed by renewed authoritarianism (Han 1989).

The demands of the democratisation movements have always been at odds with this model of Korean capitalism. Elite reaction to the threat of reform has been restoration of authoritarianism. The rationale for this has usually been couched in expressions of concern for preserving economic growth. The upshot is that the only type of political system acceptable to the elite is one which prevents the unravelling of the economic model developed over 30 years of authoritarian government. Democracy has never been compatible with Korean capitalism.

The 1987 Uprising and the 'Democratic Opening'

Economic Conditions

Just as the opposition succeeded in combining its forces for a national campaign against the Chun dictatorship in 1986, inspired by the recent example of the overthrow of Marcos in the Philippines by 'people's power', the Korean economy scored a substantial trade surplus and a very high rate of growth. The abrupt shift from a structural trade deficit to a surplus can be explained primarily in terms of favourable external economic conditions. The so-called 'three lows' that facilitated the boom were: the low cost of imported oil, the low dollar (high yen) and low international interest rates. Chun's success in forcing industrial and corporate restructuring in the early 1980s consolidated the prerequisites for growth in 1986. Overcapacity in heavy industry had been reduced, while the new leading industrial sectors such as automobiles, shipbuilding, iron and steel and electronics, were poised to capture new market shares for Korea.

Therefore, the impression of finally having arrived at the promised land of economic success, after decades of tight discipline and national sacrifice, was very difficult to resist. Workers and middle class alike wanted to share more fully in the gains of 30 years of development and relax somewhat to enjoy the fruits of their labour. It became increasingly difficult in these economic circumstances to justify the military government's continued existence. In short, the military was a 'victim' of its own economic success.

Political Conditions

Four factors account for the ripeness of political conditions for a transition to formal democracy in 1987–88:

1. Chun had promised both the Americans and the Korean people that his would be a single presidential term with a 'peaceful transfer of power'.
2. The Seoul Olympics were due in the late summer of 1988. The Olympics were a historic opportunity to win a new and positive international image, and popular protests would seriously embarrass the regime.
3. It became clear during the uprising in June 1987 that people's power was overwhelming, since it included the middle class. Therefore, the pragmatists in the elite understood the futility of using military force to repress this uprising. It was far better to make timely concessions to popular demands.
4. The United States firmly ruled out the use of military force either in the form of martial law to repress the uprising or a military *coup d'état* to overthrow a prevaricating Chun Doo Hwan. These political conditions determined that the regime could not resort immediately to familiar authoritarian methods, but was compelled to find an alternative way out.

In the National Assembly elections of 1985, the opposition New Korea Democratic Party, led by Kim Dae-Jung and Kim Young-Sam, made such impressive gains as to become a real threat to the ruling

Democratic Justice Party (DJP). By 1986 a national opposition movement had been constructed around the issue of constitutional reform, particularly the direct popular election of the President. In the months following the bizarre and bogus 'death of Kim Il Sung' incident in November 1986 (when it was falsely announced in the South that Kim Il Sung, President of North Korea, was dead), it became clear that the Chun regime was in a succession crisis (Gills 1987). On 8 April 1987, Chun unilaterally abandoned the 'Grand Politics' dialogue with the opposition. This announcement was tantamount to declaring seven more years of military government. The announcement on 10 June by the ruling party that former General Noh Tae Woo would be its presidential candidate sparked off massive demonstrations which persisted for 18 days. Thousands were arrested and hundreds injured in non-stop clashes between protesters and 120,000 National Combat Police.

In a series of emergency meetings of Chun's inner circle, the option of a short sharp dose of martial law was abandoned as Noh Tae Woo seized the initiative to offer a 'programme of democratisation'. The key political condition of democratisation was the regime's realisation that it could not apply old tactics of repression in this situation. Concessions were the best hope the regime had of retaining power. Therefore, on 29 June 1987, Noh announced his Eight Point Plan, including a direct presidential election, freedom for political prisoners, amnesty for Kim Dae Jung, an end to press censorship, local government autonomy and guarantees on human rights. However, there was no concession or promise on economic reform.

The United States and the transition
US interests in South Korea had been primarily strategic rather than economic. When US economic interests began to take precedence over strategic interests in North-East Asia in the mid-1980s, there was a shift in US policy towards authoritarian rule in Korea. Democratisation in the major newly industrialising countries (NICs) would have the effect of allowing wages and production costs to rise. Asian exports would thus become less competitive in US markets, while US goods would become more competitive in Asian markets, thereby reducing the US trade deficit. This shift was reflected after democratisation by intensified bilateral conflict over trade, particularly pressure to open Korea's markets, and the opening of a debate in the US on the financial benefits of military withdrawal from South Korea.

In addition, the US believed that political stability could best be assured by eliminating overt authoritarianism, thus pre-empting radical or revolutionary change. The US certainly had a clear idea of who was politically acceptable to it and who was unacceptable. The US used its considerable political and military influence in Korea to rule out any resort to military force. Ambassador James Lilley delivered a letter from President Reagan to President Chun on 19 June, urging a resumption of 'Grand Politics' and advising against repression. On 21 June, Gaston Sigur, US Assistant Secretary of State, publically expressed the US veto on a military crackdown. The US Eighth Army commander in Seoul, General Livsey, is believed to have told South Korean generals the US would oppose a coup against Chun. US Secretary of State George Schultz said it was necessary to continue talks on the 'transfer of power in a democratic manner'. The US Congress passed a non-binding resolution, with White House endorsement, calling for resumption of the constitutional talks. Senator Edward Kennedy and others introduced legislation for economic sanctions against South Korea until 'free and fair elections' were held.

The Superficiality of the Democratic Transition

The democratic reforms in late 1987 occurred within the context of a system essentially unchanged from the past. Therefore, these reforms could not go further than the limits set by the existing socioeconomic system. During the administration of President Noh (1988–93), the main elements of the model of Korean capitalism discussed above underwent only limited adjustment. There was certainly no breakthrough to a fundamentally new system. The putative elimination of the military from politics was belied by the fact that the government was still essentially a civilianised military regime. The T–K clique still formed the core leadership group in the government and the ruling party. President Noh Tae Woo was a former general, and many officials in the Noh administration were carryovers from previous authoritarian governments. In other words, the same people remained in control beneath the surface appearance of democratic change. The essential goals of the leadership remained virtually the same as ever, and therefore the structure in which they operate remained the same.

In the renovated political system, the presidency remained the real power, exercised through executive dominance over the bureaucracy. What should be the most democratic aspect of government, the National Assembly and the newly created local authorities, remained very weak. Political parties remained vehicles for leadership cliques and bastions of regionalism rather than true modern parties based on platform, principle and accountability to constituency.

The ruling party still sought a secure permanent majority in the National Assembly, practising the old politics of ignoring the opposition, railroading legislation and exploiting the power to revise the constitution at will. The popular and dissident movements which were the prime movers of the 1987 democratisation remained 'out' of power, while state repression continued to be used against radicals and critics much as before. The 'bad laws' of the national security state remained in force after minor revision. The conservative elite continued to fear and veto independent political activity by organised labour.

No social and economic reform beyond limited cosmetic change has been possible, such as the reform programme of former Deputy Prime Minister Cho Soon discussed below. This is because democratisation is a very limited sphere of action, constricted within the pre-set boundaries of the pre-existing socioeconomic structure. Therefore, the *chaebol's* dominance in the economy remains essentially unchanged. The essentials of the relationship between government, business and labour remain the same. It is still defined by the demand of business to have unequivocal government support in export promotion. Growth and national economic competitiveness still override considerations of social justice, welfare and environmental health and safety. As the editor of one of South Korea's leading weekly news magazines put it (interview August 1990): 'The System may be changed but the essence remains the same.'

Political Realignment and Permanent Conservative Hegemony

The logic of the political system after democratisation is the same as before democratisation: the reproduction of conservative hegemony. The democratisation from June 1987 set in motion a re-alignment of political forces which continues to the present. However, it would be an error to mistake these ceaseless and Byzantine political intrigues among leaders and factions as the genuine substance of democracy, as much of the Korean news media seems to do. On the contrary, these political machinations are about power and attest to the continued *poverty* of democracy. Even debate concerning the very serious issue of what form of government the republic should have – whether presidential or parliamentary – has been an expression of the elites' competition for power, rather than a sincere exploration of the best forms of democratic practice for Korea.

In the immediate aftermath of June 1987, the anti-dictatorship movement quickly fragmented. This division changed the character of popular mobilisation; disempowering the people while empowering the politicians. From the outset of democratisation, this fragmentation facilitated a realignment that led to reconstructed conservative hegemony. Kim Dae Jung and Kim Young Sam split and formed separate parties. This split the national opposition vote, facilitating Noh Tae Woo's victory in the presidential election with one-third of the national vote. The result was that the old regime survived intact, given executive dominance in the political system. Their split also prepared the ground for future realignments among the conservatives. Popular disillusion with the ambition of politicians, and thus with the electoral process, intensified from that point onward. This produced a familiar paradox of Low Intensity Democracy, that democratisation increases alienation and political apathy rather than participation.

During the first year of the 'Noh democracy', the government was preoccupied with regaining domestic legitimacy. Much emphasis was placed on promised reforms and rectification of past misconduct. It was only during this brief period that the government was temporarily constrained by public mood and specifically by the new opposition majority in the National Assembly, resulting from elections in April 1988. The government was obliged to tolerate a critical atmosphere as the nation's attention was riveted on televised National Assembly proceedings investigating the corruption of Chun's Fifth Republic.

However, this preoccupation with punishing Chun and his cronies distracted both the nation and the politicians from the real issue of democratic reform. It also served Noh and his faction in the purpose of further distancing themselves from Chun and thus enhancing their own popular legitimacy. Noh pointedly styled himself an 'ordinary man'. This period was likewise influenced by the impending 1988 Olympic Games in Seoul, during which the government was particularly keen to present the best image possible to the world's television cameras. The 'Olympic Honeymoon' ended in late 1988, and thereafter the tone of the regime shifted sharply back to conservatism.

During the period of four-party cohabitation up to January 1990, the DJP remained the single largest party in the National Assembly. The DJP held 130 seats, whereas the Party for Peace and Democracy (PPD) led by Kim Dae Jung secured second place with 70 seats. Kim Young Sam's Reunification Democratic Party (RDP) was placed third with 60 seats, followed by Kim Jong Pil's New Democratic Republican Party (NDRP) with 35 seats. Though the PPD, RDP and NDRP combined forces in a loose congressional coalition to form an anti-DJP bloc on some issues, the extent to which they ever constituted a united opposition has been greatly exaggerated. Suggestions that this loose informal coalition should be formalised were rejected, even by Kim Dae Jung. As a result the opposition lost the opportunity to control a majority of congressional committees – the real key to wielding political influence in the National Assembly. A formal coalition among the 'three Kims' was impossible because the three had substantial ideological differences, their personal political ambitions were mutually exclusive and they had separate regional support bases.

In the short term all three Kims stood to gain something by putting the ruling DJP on the defensive. Yet they could not cooperate effectively even around a narrow set of possible issues: including punishment of members of the Chun regime and exposure of the crimes and abuses of power of the Fifth Republic; electoral reform to reduce election-rigging by the ruling DJP; rectification of the 'bad laws' such as the national security law; the political neutralisation of the police force; and compensation for victims of the Kwangju Massacre of 1980. The three Kims were, as an old Korean saying puts it, 'In the same bed, but dreaming different dreams.'

The first year of the Sixth Republic was actually an exercise in letting the steam escape from the kettle to prevent an explosion. This is why it was characterised by relative liberalism on the part of the government. Some political prisoners were released, press censorship was relaxed and unions were given greater leeway to organise independently of government and management, while strikes were tolerated as never before. All of this enhanced the general impression that democratisation was bringing about real changes. However, no fundamental challenge to the model of Korean capitalism was tolerated. The conservative forces regrouped in 1989 and unleashed a wave of repression.

Economic Crisis and Restoration

Some of the worst fears of conservatives concerning democratisation (for example, that it would bring economic 'chaos' and decline, unleash the political power of labour and allow unification policy and thus national politics to escape the control of the government) all seemed to be coming home to roost in 1989. This nightmare spectre of spiralling disintegration of the socioeconomic model built during the past 30 years of authoritarianism was summed up in the phrase 'Argentine Syndrome', invoked by the conservative leadership with increasing urgency. Business and government circles were obsessed by the loss of international competitiveness, which they blamed almost exclusively on high wages and the militancy, unruliness or sloth of the workforce since democratisation. Less favourable external economic conditions and the increasing internationalisation of the economy (with unrelenting US bilateral pressure to open Korea's markets) were conveniently downplayed as factors contributing to a sharp decline in economic growth, the evaporation of the trade surplus and sluggish exports.

Though the number of strikes and the size of wage settlements were at their highest in 1987–8, the severity of key strikes in heavy industries in 1989 caused record damage in production and export loss. Some of the principal *chaebol*, such as Hyundai, were particularly hard hit by militant strikes. Business demanded a stern government response. The administration had taken a softly-softly approach to labour disputes during the Olympic Honeymoon. Meanwhile the employers defended their own interests by unleashing private armies of mercenary thugs, called 'save the company corps' (*Kusadae*), physically to beat recalcitrant trade unionists into line. Business was much more anti-labour than government was in this period. The industrial relations crisis went far beyond the usual implications of collective bargaining disputes. It went right to the political heart of the democratisation process. Business interests were incompatible with the rational extension of the democratisation process into industrial relations. The politicisation of labour's strike demands infuriated business, yet reflected a much wider popular mood of moral outrage over the social and economic inequality in Korea, and the conspicuous consumption of the *chaebol* elite.

The perceived necessity for the political defeat of organised labour was at the heart of the agenda of conservative restoration. Democratisation immediately resulted in a huge increase in unionisation and an increase in the autonomy of the FKTU (Federation of Korean Trade Unions), which had formerly been merely a corporatist expression of government and business domination of labour. As in all past regime crises in South Korea since liberation in 1945, the mobilisation of labour coincided with a general political mobilisation of dissident and left-wing movements. Given the division of Korea into rival communist and capitalist regimes, the simultaneous mobilisation of labour, the Left and the radical reunification movement conjured up the traditional spectre of a Fifth Column which threatened to sweep the conservatives out of power and usher in a social revolution. While organised labour directly challenged the power of the *chaebol* on the production site, its political allies on the Left directly challenged the authority of the state and the legitimacy of Korean capitalism. In each previous regime crisis force was used to crush the political power of labour and the Left.

Business rounded on the government with bitter accusations of ineffectiveness, indecision and incompetence. Weak executive leadership and a sense of confusion over the aims and goals of economic policy seemed to infect the bureaucracy. Even the EPB temporarily suffered in purgatory while trying to comprehend whether the nature of its authority had undergone fundamental change. The administration was condemned as 'anti-big business', which really meant that it was not following a strong pro-big business line as in the past.

The *chaebol* were caught on the horns of a dilemma. On the one hand, they were enjoying increased autonomy from state tutelage. This was reflected in financial liberalisation that allowed business more flexibility and control over its own investment and credit decisions. On the other hand, business felt itself to be suffering from a decline in overt government support, both in the promotion of exports and in the subordination of labour. Business wanted to have its cake and eat it too. It wanted to be autonomous from the state when it came to key economic decisions, but it wanted the state's unflinching support for its interest in finding markets and 'disciplining' the workforce.

This is precisely why the period was one of confusion and indecision. It was in fact the business elite which was wavering between two potential directions: either to return to the traditional alliance with the military regime, or to abandon it in favour of a modernised relationship with a business-funded conservative party backed by the middle class. However, the ambiguity and contradiction in this transitional period was so acute that no simple solution was possible. In the end, therefore, business supported a compromise solution which incorporated both alternatives.

The interim solution came in the spring of 1989 with an abrupt change in government policy. The Noh administration capitulated to intense pressure from leading *chaebol* and decisively shifted to support business against labour. One example of this was the renewed use of huge phalanxes of national combat police to storm union barricades at key strike locations. Another was the enforcement of the ban on public sector unions, nowhere more harshly implemented than in the break-up of the newly formed National Teachers Union and the sacking of over 1,500 teachers for their participation in the outlawed union. This was the beginning of an active policy of strike-breaking and arrest of union leaders. On the other side of the same coin, the government sharply stepped up repression against the dissident reunification movement. The signal event was the arrest and imprisonment of long time Southern dissident leader Reverend Moon Ik-Hwan, upon his return from visiting North Korea. Thereafter, government repression of left-wing and dissident activists and intellectuals intensified. The national security situation was again invoked, as in the past, to justify increased repression.

The Liberal Phase and the Economic Policies of Cho Soon

The rise and fall of Cho Soon is a parable of the transition period. It reflects the growing political influence of business over the state during the transition period. During the initial liberal phase, President Noh promised the people that higher priority would be given to social justice and welfare. He also promised to take action to redress the imbalances in the economy between sectors and between regions. Noh's public pronouncements on reform encouraged liberals to cooperate with his administration. Noh approached a professor of economics and well-known liberal, Cho Soon, to head the Economic Planning Board as his new Deputy Prime Minister.

Cho Soon's economic policies were not in fact designed to achieve specific welfarist goals. His message to the establishment was that in order for the Korean economy to continue to develop successfully, social development must not be neglected, but rather brought into harmony with economic development. The essence of his approach was to construct a regulatory framework that facilitated an open competitive domestic economic environment. The key goal was to reduce the stranglehold on the domestic market long enjoyed by the *chaebol*, and to end the strangulation of investment funds for small and medium-sized business and farmers resulting from past discrimination in favour of *chaebol*. This approach to a modernised version of capitalism cut directly against the grain of the existing model which relied on and served *chaebol* concentration.

The loosening of the control over business by government produced an orgy of speculative investment activities. Productive investment seriously declined while non-productive speculative investment raced out of control. Rampant private speculation, especially in real estate and securities, threatened to accelerate the gradual deindustrialisation of Korea, as services overtook manufacturing at an alarming rate. The short-term profit perspective threatened to stifle the tight investment discipline of the authoritarian era, and thus to kill the goose that laid the golden eggs – Korea's manufacturing base. This situation highlighted the urgency, widely perceived in government circles, for effective action, and public support for such measures was running high.

Among Cho Soon's main policy proposals was the 'Real Name System' (which would require registration of the actual name of the owner of assets or depositor of sums) in financial transactions, contained in Noh Tae Woo's presidential campaign platform. This simple reform would have curtailed secret movements of capital, including hitherto undetected capital flight, and undermined both speculation and tax evasion. The 'Public Concept of Land' legislation proposed by Cho Soon would have placed social responsibility above the private rights of landowners, and thus curtailed rampant land speculation and irresponsible developers. These two regulatory policies were the flagships of Cho Soon's wider reform programme. However, both policies were abandoned after heated internal debate in the late summer of 1989.

Cho Soon's attempt to implement even limited reforms, though objectively in the national economic self-interest, encountered fierce resistance from the *chaebol* and their political allies. The right wing of the DJP attacked him on the basis that he spoke too much and too often about reform of the *chaebol*. As a direct result, he was first isolated within the administration, and then abandoned completely by President Noh. The lack of presidential support for Cho directly undermined his authority as Deputy Prime Minister and contributed to a sense of drift at the EPB. Cho's successor at the EPB, Lee Soon Yun, rose to prominence by frontally attacking the Real Name System and the Public Concept of Land on behalf of vested interests. Lee's pro-*chaebol* attitude contrasted sharply with Cho's supposedly anti-*chaebol* position. The sacking of Cho Soon signified a shift back towards the traditional role of the state in supporting export promotion through the *chaebol*.

The Restoration Completed

The final solution to the contradictions of the transitional period was to combine the two fundamental options available to the business elite. This was achieved in such a way as to retain the strong state while simultaneously creating an expanded conservative hegemonic bloc which could use the electoral system to stay in power indefinitely. In this sense, we might conclude that the ultimate outcome of the democratisation process from 1987 to 1990 was to consolidate a type of bourgeois revolution, but with a bourgeoisie which is inherently authoritarian.

The middle class was easily and speedily demobilised after the transition to a formal electoral political system. The key point to note is that the middle class formed no lasting political alliance with workers and in fact supported the conservative backlash against organised labour. The middle class was most susceptible to renewed appeals by business and the political elite to national developmentalist ideology, anti-communism, and law and order.

During 1989, the conservative parties, which together formed a real majority in the National Assembly, came to a mutual understanding that ultimately produced a new ruling party, the Democratic Liberal Party (DLP), in early 1990. The DJP, the RDP and the NDRP merged, while retaining factional identities around prominent leaders on the model of Japan's ruling Liberal Democratic Party (LDP). It is no coincidence that just when the conservative parties combined to form the DLP,the government simultaneously banned the new breakaway national federation of democratic unions (Chun No Hyup) and arrested most of its leaders.

The political logic underlying the merger was the perceived benefit of unifying several parties' regional support bases in order to produce a secure parliamentary majority and permanent electoral dominance. That ideological affinity was *not* the sole determining factor in the creation of the new ruling party is illustrated by the fact that a similar offer to join a new ruling party coalition is believed to have been made by President Noh Tae Woo to both Kim Young Sam and to Kim Dae Jung.

Such a dominant conservative party was bound to be more attractive to business, since it provided a single focus for political funding, and thus more efficient use of political funds, than supporting several rival conservative parties. As in Japan, its success depended on the realisation of some formula for sharing power among the faction leaderships, and this consideration fuelled a subsequent debate on a proposed shift to a parliamentary form of government. The fact that the model for this new party was the LDP of Japan was openly acknowledged. It is interesting to note in this regard that Chalmers Johnson maintains that 'capitalism in the Japanese form does not produce or even seem to need political democracy in order to function' (Johnson 1989 p. 2).

The upshot of forming such a new majority ruling party was that the conservative restoration of 1989 was completed, but business was in a strengthened position in the ruling coalition. If Japan is truly the model of Korean democracy, then we can expect the influence of business to increase as that of individual politicians decreases and the ruling party becomes entirely dependent on finance provided by business. Whereas business becomes more autonomous from the state, it never entirely breaks from the model of a state-dependent bourgeoisie. This is a relationship primarily between the business elite and the technocracy, in which politicians function more as brokers. As business concentrates its political funding on one party it overwhelms any party denied access to these political funds. So long as organised labour, the other major social institutional source of political funds available, is forbidden by law to support political activity, then conservatives have built-in electoral advantages over their poverty-ridden opponents.

Therefore, although formal electoral practices have been re-established, the logic of the political system is now perpetually to reproduce conservative hegemony via these formal practices. Within such hegemony, economic policy will be set by some consultative mechanism between business, politicians and the bureaucracy, insulating policy from popular democratic pressures. Thus there is very little scope for popular democratic alternatives.

The Impotence of the Opposition and Radicalism
The overwhelming majority created by the formation of the new ruling party gave conservatives a monopoly over legislation in the National Assembly. The abuse of parliamentary procedure in the National Assembly reached a peak on 14 July 1990, when the new ruling DLP railroaded the passage of 26 new bills in only 33 seconds. This was a clear return to tactics of the ruling party familiar under authoritarianism. The PPD thereafter boycotted the National Assembly and months of stalemate ensued. The imbalance between the government and opposition was so great that it threatened to delegitimise both the DLP and the new electoral democracy. The problem was one of finding an opposition willing to go along with the rules of the game, that is, to remain impotent. Such was the power of the DLP that it could write legislation and even rewrite the constitution with impunity. However, this style alienated the electorate to such a degree that the DLP realised it had to moderate the exercise of its power. If it continued to reign without an opposition it would be exposed to public view as an emperor with no clothes.

The ruling party was not initially supported in opinion polls. The effect of its formation was in fact a deeper alienation by the popular majority. Kim Young Sam lost popularity, because he had suddenly changed his colours from the opposition to the government party. The DLP was preoccupied for some time with internal factional rivalry and struggles over how to share power. This rivalry threatened the stability of the new hegemonic bloc. To redress these problems of voter alienation, the boycott of the opposition and excessive internal leadership rivalry, the ruling party softened its approach by

dropping the issue of constitutional revision and making some concessions to the opposition.

Kim Dae Jung seized upon Noh's campaign promise of granting
local autonomy (local councils and magistrates). He made local
autonomy the key concession demanded from the ruling party in
order for the PPD to resume participation in the National Assembly.
The PPD, the largest opposition party, viewed local autonomy as the
best hope for increasing its chances of winning a majority in future
National Assembly elections. If the opposition could win local power,
particularly in the largest cities, it could both reduce the DLP's ability
to manipulate election returns and gain popular support through dis-
pensation of local government resources. It would also decentralise
state power. As remarked earlier, with the extreme centralisation of
government in Korea, the President could personally appoint some
100,000 government officials. In 1990, there were still only 300
elected officials in the entire government apparatus – the President
and the National Assembly members. Compare this to the some
500,000 elected regional and local government officials in France.

However, disarray among opposition parties was reflected in the
failure to form a national party that effectively transcended regionalism and mustered an electoral weight commensurate with the
DLP. From the onset of democratisation, the radical wing of the
democratisation movement also fragmented, preoccupying itself
with internal debate and conflict among contending factions. Much
of this debate revolved around the question of whether to participate in the electoral arena or remain underground. Among those
supporting electoral participation there was a further split between
those favouring support for one mainstream opposition party and
those wanting to form a separate left-wing party. The lack of coherent
national organisation that resulted from this fragmentation of progressive opposition forces was a primary cause of the relative ease
with which the ruling coalition defeated radical and dissident forces
from the spring of 1989 onward.

Though the PPD succeeded in early 1991 in forming a coalition
with some dissidents, this was of primarily symbolic importance, since
these dissident forces were not electorally significant. Although the
PPD had expected local autonomy to break the mould of the Korean
political system, the ruling party swept the local elections in the spring
of 1991 against a divided opposition. The PPD easily carried its
regional base of Cholla, in south-west Korea. Elsewhere the combined
opposition vote usually represented a majority, but the ruling party's
candidates most often won the largest single share of votes and thus
the seat. Voter turnout was low, reflecting a general mood of apathy

and alienation towards politicians. The debacle of the divided opposition exposed its weakness. In September 1991, Kim Dae Jung merged his reorganised party, the Shin Min Dang, with the Minju Dang (Democratic Party) led by Lee Ki-taek, whose main base is in the south-east. This merger signalled a revival of the potential for the mainstream opposition successfully to contest the upcoming National Assembly elections.

The only substantial political party on the Left (Min Jung Dang) won only one seat in the local elections. The Min Jung Dang includes some of the organisers of the previous 'Party of the Masses' and the 'Hankyoreh Party', which unsuccessfully contested National Assembly elections in 1988. The party programme included the nationalisation of basic industries, a national health service and reunification with North Korea. Under first-past-the-post single-member district rules, applying in the National Assembly elections, the Left has very little chance of winning seats. Min Jung Dang was therefore in favour of multiple member districts, which could enable the party to win seats in second or third place in large urban areas. Its active support base was in the democratic workers' and farmers' movements.

The Left remains divided between those supporting the parliamentary path, and those still operating in an extra-parliamentary or underground mode. However, both the parliamentary Left and the mainstream opposition remained hampered by the ban on direct political links with organised labour. The emergence of even a reformist labour party, though it might actually stabilise the new political system, has met with continual conservative obstruction.

In the absence of a labour party, the most genuine social democratisation is taking place in civil society, outside the sphere of formal electoral politics. This democratisation is expressed in the proliferation of new popular organisations, including new independent unions, farmers' groups, women's organisations, 'citizens' groups, urban poor, and environmental activists. The emergence of a more autonomous civil society undermines the vulnerable corporatist framework inherited from authoritarianism. However, these new popular organisations are even more impotent in the formal electoral system than are the conventional opposition parties. Nevertheless, their energetic activity represents an important period of conscientisation which could have important long-term effects on the political culture. The increased freedom of expression and relatively more open political space in the Sixth Republic is being exploited very effectively by many of these organisations. More and more sectors of Korean society have increased their organisational autonomy in a struggle to break free of the limitations imposed by corporatism. The new farmers' movement is one case in point. Formerly, farmers were mobilised by the government through the New Village Movement and official cooperatives. They are increasingly breaking away from such controls and independently articulating their cumulative grievances against the government, including vociferous protest against the threat to Korean agriculture in the Uruguay Round of the General Agreement on Tariffs and Trade (GATT).

The one area in which the government appears to be politically vulnerable is the environment. This issue cuts across all class lines and affects all citizens in all regions. Popular demonstrations against corporate polluters have occurred even in the most conservative bastions, such as Taegu. Environmentalism is fast attracting a host of veteran dissident activists. This in itself is symptomatic of the wider impotence of the opposition, since this appears to be the only avenue of dissidence remaining that is not subject to overt repression. However, it is difficult to imagine how environmentalism could ever be the vehicle for the overthrow of conservative hegemony. Environmentalism's social strength and political weakness are the same: it is inherently decentralised and its ability to cut across social divisions does not extend to other fundamental political and economic issues. In any event, the limited 'greening' of the ruling party is the obvious systemic response to defuse this challenge.

With the electoral road to reform a dead letter, the Left attempted to use street politics to gather momentum for radical change. Chun Dae Hyup, the principal radical national student organisation, and Chun Min Ryun, a national coalition of dissident groups, gambled their political capital in an all-out offensive against the ruling party in the spring of 1991. However, both the aims and the tactics of the extra-parliamentary Left were ineffective. The aims were direct removal of the Noh Tae Woo administration, withdrawal of US forces from Korea, including its nuclear arsenal, and direct popular negotiations on reunification with North Korea. These demands did not inspire the middle class to join mass protests as it had done in 1987. The tactics employed, mainly street demonstrations, direct confrontation with police and, most drastically, numerous self-immolations, proved to be futile in the face of overwhelming government power and a lack of broad public support. So long as the National Security Law and other repressive laws carried over from authoritarianism remain in force, left-wing dissident forces will continue to operate in a context of frustration and even desperation, which so often contributes to the adoption of direct confrontational tactics, however ineffective or self-defeating such tactics may be.

Neither the local elections, nor the formation of new popular organisations, nor the all-out spring campaign by radicals against the DLP regime in 1991 had much impact in mounting an effective political challenge to conservative hegemony. On the contrary, the upheavals of spring 1991 reinforced the government's determination to suppress radical dissent. Indeed, illegal underground reunification activists, socialist cells and militant unionists continued to be the object of systematic surveillance and arrests.

Not only had the middle class not heeded the radical call, but even most organised labour was cool towards this manifestation of radicalism. The mainstream unions in the FKTU, which continue to represent the vast majority of unionised workers, reached an accommodation with business and government that included restraint in wage demands. Strikes and production losses dramatically decreased in 1990. Likewise, the share of the workforce represented by the breakaway radical union federation Chun No Hyup decreased. Steady repression used against Chun No Hyup succeeded in stemming its expansion, but the fundamental political potential of militant unionism was not so easily staunched. Even the mainstream union movement remains uneasily within the continuing political constraints imposed upon it by government and big business.

The struggle between radical militants, reformists and corporatists for control of the union movement continues. The question of whether South Korea's political system will yet undergo a progressive stage of democratisation rests to a large extent upon the outcome of this struggle to determine the political role of labour. The emergence of a genuine labour party would alter the fundamental character of electoral politics in Korea. It would pose a serious challenge to the prevailing regionalism and clientelism of the present political parties of the opposition and their leading personalities.

In the National Assembly election of spring 1991, conservative hegemony was stabilised despite increasing signs of factionalism. The ruling DLP remained the largest single party. However, its working majority was reduced by about 60 votes. The unified opposition represented by the Democratic Party made some gains but the new player on the scene, the Kukmin Dang Party established by the *chaebol* magnate Jung Ju-Yong, made the most important gains at the DLP's expense. The 31 seats won by Jung's party put it into a power-brokering position. A competition to win over an additional 21 'independents' ensued. The government needed the votes of Kukmin Dang and the independents to ensure a two-thirds majority. Jung's 'rebellion' against the ruling DLP highlighted the volatility of the political system, but did not fundamentally threaten it.

The presidential campaign of late 1992 indicated a stabilisation of the new political system rather than a crisis. Both the DLP and Jung Ju-Yong essentially agreed that government policy must serve the interests of business first and foremost and that the county's export orientation should not be undermined.

The inauguration in February 1993 of Kim Young Sam as President of Korea was the first succession of a true civilian in over 30 years. Kim Young Sam has publicly declared his intent to reform the power of the military and the *chaebol*. As this book goes to press, it is too early to assess the fundamental impact of Kim Young Sam's presidency on the state and economy. However, his succession does seem to be a step towards the institutionalisation of formal democracy in Korea.

Conclusion

The democratisation process in Korea came full circle. Authoritarianism was challenged by a mass movement for democratisation in 1987. This produced a period of rapid change in which corporatism was weakened and civil society gained more autonomy from the state. However, elites adjusted by forming a broad coalition of the military, business and the middle class in order to restore conservative hegemony. Therefore, the fundamental nature of the system remained unchanged. Despite several years of 'democracy', the main opposition forces continued to represent themselves as the legitimate democratic alternative to reigning authoritarianism.

There has been very limited change in the model of Korean capitalism, and what little there has been was designed to adjust to underlying structural trends and international conditions. The authoritarian government, despite the electoral competition, remains essentially intact, especially in so far as economic policy is concerned. The state remains predominant, but the trend to increasing autonomy of capital continues to gather gradual momentum. The extreme concentration of capital remains basically as before, as does the export orientation, while the pressure to internationalise the economy also continues to increase. The political subordination of labour continues, but has been somewhat weakened. It is perhaps the deterioration of corporatism that represents the most significant change brought about by formal democratisation. The independence of the judiciary is yet to be fully established, and thus human and civil rights remain subject to abuse by the state.

The recent democratisation of Korea should be analysed as a two-stage historical process. The first stage was the popular struggle to overthrow overt military authoritarianism. This struggle made some gains in terms of formal constitutional and human rights, freedom of the press and the rule of law. The restoration of conservative hegemony constitutes a second stage. During this period a coalition of the military, business and the middle class remained hegemonic, utilising the formal democracy to stay in power indefinitely and thus preserve the economic status quo.

Though this permanent conservative hegemony is challenged by a coalition of popular forces, including the labour movement, students, the Left, and other popular organisations, the radical opposition is in a weak position.

Likewise, the mainstream opposition political party remains marginal to the exercise of power and unable effectively to challenge the ruling party. Conservative hegemony is intact, despite the 'defection' of the Hyundai chairman Jung Ju-Yong. Under the prevailing conditions of conservative hegemony, the utmost to be expected from the democratisation process, in terms of reform, is perhaps a new social pact with labour. The liberal wing of the ruling coalition may support a social pact whereby workers will restrain their wage demands and suspend damaging strike activity in exchange for capital's commitment to the material welfare of workers and a concomitant welfarist commitment on the part of the state, including anti-inflationary measures. Such a class compromise is intended to avoid open conflict and the increasing politicisation of the demands of the labour movement, while nevertheless preserving conservative hegemony.

Even if such a social pact emerges, no breakthrough can be expected on significantly reducing the enormous power of the *chaebol* in the economy. Even liberal proposals for diffusing the ownership pattern of the *chaebol* groups to a wider shareholder circle or to financial institutions; for separating ownership of the *chaebol* from professional management; and for limited deconcentration of business groups, are unlikely to overcome entrenched conservative opposition. Basic reforms such as the Real Name System or overhaul of the financial system remain as elusive as ever. The establishment's fear of economic decline, the so-called Argentine Syndrome, remains a real limitation on reform. This fear reflects the elite's attitude that there are strict limitations on how far the democratisation process can be permitted to go, lest it threaten to unravel the 'economic miracle' established during 30 years of overt authoritarianism. The recent adjustment in the South Korean political system since 1987 occurred in the context of an economic boom, but was stabilised in the context of growing economic difficulties and worldwide recession. In this situation its limits are even more strict than they might have been had the South Korean economy continued its previous levels of expansion. For the ruling elite, the overriding preoccupation remains competitiveness in the world economy. Further democratisation therefore, will face these formidable economic constraints.

References

Amsden, Alice 1989. *Asia's Next Giant: South Korea and Late Industrialisation*. Oxford, Oxford University Press.

—— 1990. 'Third World Industrialisation: "Global Fordism" or a New Model?', *New Left Review*, July–August.

Balassa, B. 1981. *The Newly Industrialising Countries in the World Economy*. New York, Pergamon.

Bello, Walden and Rosenfeld, Stephanie 1990. *Dragons in Distress*. San Francisco, Institute for Food and Development Policy.

Cho, Dong Sung 1990. *Hankuk Jaebol Yongu* (A Study of Korean Chaebol). Seoul, Maeil Kyongje Shinmun Sa.

Cho, Y.B., *et al.* 1984. *Hankuk Dokjom Jabon Kwa Jaebol* (Korean Monopoly Capital and Chaebol). Seoul, Pul-bit.

—— 1988. *Hankuk Jabon-ju-ui Song-kyuk Nonjaeng* (The Debate on the Characteristics of Korean Capitalism). Seoul, Dae-wang Sa.

Choi, J.J. (ed.) 1985. *Hankuk Jabon-ju-ui wa Kuk-ka* (Korean Capitalism and the State). Seoul, Han-uhl.

Cole, D.C. and Lyman, P.N. 1971. *Korean Development: The Interplay of Politics and Economics*. Cambridge, Mass., Harvard University Press.

Cumings, Bruce 1987. 'The Origins and Development of the Northeast Asian Political Economy: Industrial Sectors, Product Cycles, and Political Consequences', in Frederick Deyo (ed.), *The Political Economy of the New East Asian Industrialism*. Ithaca, NY, Cornell University Press.

—— 1989. 'The Abortive Abertura: South Korea in the Light of Latin American Experience', *New Left Review* no. 173, January–February, pp. 5–32.

Deyo, Frederick, 1989. *Beneath the Miracle: Labour Subordination in the New East Asian Industrialism*. Berkeley, University of California Press.

Gills, Barry 1987. 'The Coup that Never Happened: The Anatomy of the "Death" of Kim Il Sung', *Bulletin of Concerned Asian Scholars*, vol. 19, no. 3/July–September, pp. 2–19.

—— 1991. 'North Korea and the Crisis of Socialism: The Historical Ironies of Reunification', *Third World Quarterly*, vol. 13, no. 1.

—— 1993. 'The International Origins of South Korea's Export Orientation', in Palan and Gills (eds), *Transcending the State/Global*

Divide: The Neo-Structuralist Agenda in International Relations, Boulder, Colo., Lynne Rienner.

Haggard, S. and Moon, C.I. 1983. 'Liberal, Dependent or Mercantile? The South Korean State in the International Economy', in J.G. Ruggie, (ed.) *The Antinomies of Interdependence*. New York, Columbia University Press, pp. 131–89.

—— 1990. 'Institutions and Economic Policy: Theory and a Korean Case Study', *World Politics* vol.42, no.2 (January) pp. 210–37.

Hamilton, C. 1986. *Capitalist Industrialization in Korea*, Boulder, Colo., Westview Press.

Han, Sung-Joo 1989. 'South Korea: Politics in Transition', in Diamond Linz and Lipset, (eds), *Democracy in Developing Countries: Asia*, vol. III. Boulder, Colo., Lynne Reinner.

Harts-Landsberg, M. 1984. 'Capitalism and Third World Economic Development: A Critical Look at the South Korean "Miracle"', *Review of Radical Political Economics*, 16 (2/3), pp. 181–93.

—— 1987. 'South Korea: The Fradulent Miracle', *Monthly Review*, 39.

Johnson, Chalmers 1982. *MITI and the Japanese Miracle: The Growth of Industrial Policy, 1925–1975*. Stanford, Calif., Stanford University Press.

—— 1987. 'Political Institutions and Economic Performance: The Government–Business Relationship in Japan, South Korea, and Taiwan', in Frederick Deyo (ed.), *The Political Economy of the New East Asian Industrialism*. Ithaca, NY, Cornell University Press.

—— 1989. 'South Korean Democratisation: The Role of Economic Development', *The Pacific Review*, vol. 2, no. 1, pp. 1–10.

Jones, Leroy and Il Sakong 1980. *Government, Business and Entrepreneurship in Economic Development: The Korean Case*, Cambridge, Mass., Harvard University Press.

Kim, Kwang Suk and Roemer, Michael 1979. *Growth and Structural Transformation*. Cambridge, Mass., Harvard University Press.

Kim, Kyong-Dong 1976. 'Political Factors in the Formation of the Entrepreneurial Elite in South Korea', *Asian Survey*, vol. XVI, no. 5 (May).

Kim, Suk Joon 1988. *The State, Public Policy, and NIC Development*. Seoul, Dae Young Moon Hwa Sa.

Kim, S.M. *et al.* 1987. *Hankuk Jabon-ju-ui wa Nong-ob Munje* (Korean Capitalism and the Agricultural Question). Seoul, Ah-chim.

Krueger, Anne O. 1979. *The Development of the Foreign Sector and Aid*, Cambridge, Mass., Harvard University Press.

Kuznets, Paul 1977. *Economic Growth and Structure in the Republic of Korea*. New Haven, Conn., Yale University Press.

Launius, Michael A. 1984. 'The State and Industrial Labor in South Korea', *Bulletin of Concerned Asian Scholars*, vol. 16, no. 4, October–December, pp. 2–10.

Lee, D.K. 1987. *Hankuk Kyongje ui Kujo wa Jon-gae* (The Structure and Development of the Korean Economy). Seoul, Chang Jak Kwa Bipyong Sa.

Lee, J.K. 1986. *Sahoe Kusongche Ron kwa Sahoe Kwahak Bangbop Ron* (Theory of Social Formation and Social Science Methodology). Seoul, Ah-chim.

McCormack, Gavan 1977. 'The South Korean Economy: GNP versus the People', in Gavan McCormack and John Gittings (eds), *Crisis in Korea*. London, Korea Committee, Spokesman Books.

Ogle, George 1990. *South Korea: Dissent within the Economic Miracle*. London, Zed Books.

Park, H.C. 1986. *Hankuk Kyongje Kujo Ron* (On the Structure of the Korean Economy). Seoul, Il Wol Suh Gak.

Park, H.C. *et al.* 1987. *Hankuk Kyongje Ron* (On the Korean Economy). Seoul, Kka-chi.

Park, Moon Kyu 1987. 'Interest Representation in South Korea: The Limits of Corporatist Control', *Asian Survey*, vol. XXVII, no. 8, August, pp. 903–17.

Wade, L.L. and Kim, B.S. 1978. *The Political Economy of Success: Public Policy and Economic Development in the Republic of Korea*. New York, Praeger.

Wade, R. and White, G. 1988. *Developmental States in East Asia*. Basingstoke, Macmillan.

Woronoff, J. 1983. *Korea's Economy: Man-Made Miracle*. Seoul, Si-Sa-Yong-O-Sa.

YH Labour Union 1984. *YH Nodong Johap Sa*. Seoul, Hyungsung Sa.

Index